W32

Legal Aspects of Medicines

Other titles in the Legal Aspects in Healthcare series by Quay Books include:

Legal Aspects of Consent 2nd edition
Legal Aspects of Death
Legal Aspects of Patient Confidentiality 2nd edition
Legal Aspects of Pain Management 2nd edition
Legal Aspects of Health and Safety 2nd edition

Note

Healthcare practice and knowledge are constantly changing and developing as new research and treatments, changes in procedures, drugs and equipment become available.

The author and publishers have, as far as is possible, taken care to confirm that the information complies with the latest standards of practice and legislation.

Legal Aspects of Medicines

2nd Edition

by

Bridgit Dimond

QUAY
BOOKS

A division of MA Healthcare Ltd

Quay Books Division, MA Healthcare Ltd, St Jude's Church, Dulwich Road, London
SE24 0PB

British Library Cataloguing-in-Publication Data
A catalogue record is available for this book

ISBN-10: 1-85642-416-2
ISBN-13: 978-1-85642-416-5

Cover design by Louise Cowburn, Fonthill Creative
Associate Publisher: Thu Nguyen

Printed by CLE, Huntingdon, Cambridgeshire

Table of Contents

Foreword to the first edition
Preface to the first edition
Acknowledgements
Glossary
Abbreviations
Table of useful websites

Foreword to the first edition

There are several reasons why the law on medicines has become increasingly complicated over the last few years. The creation of a European drug regulatory system (the European Medicines Agency) and the extension of prescribing privileges (and responsibilities) to wider groups of health professionals are only part of the story. Public and professional revulsion over the activities of the late Dr Shipman (who was responsible for poisoning over 200 of his patients), concerns about the increasing use of drugs for recreational purposes, and worries about the extent to which avoidable errors in prescribing lead to serious harm, have all played a role in the way our laws have been – and continue to be–shaped. Professor Dimond's easy and accessible synthesis of the UK's current legal framework for medicines is both appropriate and timely. It will be an essential work of reference for all of us who work in healthcare.

Professor Sir Michael Rawlins
National Institute for Health and Clinical Excellence, London WC1
August 2005

Preface to the first edition

Like the other books in this series, this monograph follows the publication of a series of articles in the *British Journal of Nursing* on the law relating to medicines. Those articles, revised and updated, form the basis of a concise publication covering the main concerns which arise in the law relating to medicines in the NHS and private sector.

This book is intended for all health professionals who are likely to be involved in the dispensing, administration, prescribing or supply of medication, whether in hospitals or in the community. It may also be of assistance to others, such as health service managers, patient groups and their representatives, lecturers and clinical supervisors.

Each chapter uses a situation to illustrate the relevant laws so that the law can be explained in a practical jargon-free way. The basic facts of the legal system are briefly set out in the first chapter. The book does not pretend to be encyclopaedic in its coverage; rather, it is intended to introduce readers to the basic principles which apply and the sources of law, so that they can, by following up the further reading and web sites provided, add to their knowledge. Changes in the statutory provisions and new cases will require some amendments over time. The NHS Plan (Department of Health 2000) envisaged that the old demarcations will be shattered and nurses, midwives and therapists would be able to take on a wider range of clinical tasks, including running clinics and discharging patients and pharmacists will be able to take on a new role as they shift away from being paid mainly for dispensing of individual prescriptions towards rewarding overall service. As a consequence, roles in relation to the supply and prescribing of medications and in the role of the hospital and the community pharmacist have changed ever more rapidly over recent years, and this will ultimately have a profound influence on the care of the patient and the organisation of healthcare. This book will provide a baseline on which readers can develop their knowledge and understanding of the law relating to medicines.

Preface to the second edition

Six years have now elapsed since this book was first published and many changes have taken place in the context of medicines supply administration and prescription; many a consequence of the 4th Shipman Inquiry Report. This new edition tracks these developments and also notes the changing legal context: The Mental Capacity Act 2005 implemented in 2007 has filled the gap on decision making on behalf of the mentally incapacitated adult; the Equality Act 2010 has brought the anti-discrimination legislation into one statute; new regulations cover herbal and homeopathic medicines. Within the NHS a revolution is taking place: the Health and Social Care Bill making its way through Parliament will, if enacted, fundamentally change the relationships of GPs and their consortia with the NHS Trusts and private sector providers. Pharmacists are finding that their advisory role is increasing It is hoped that this book will continue to provide a foundation upon which all those health professions involved in the supply, administration or prescribing of medicines can build their knowledge.

Acknowledgements

Once again I am extremely grateful for the thoroughness and care with which Bette Griffiths prepared the indexes and read the proofs for the first edition and thank her for her help. I would also like to pay tribute to the support and help provided to me by Helen Scott during her years as editor of the *British Journal of Nursing* in which publication this book took root. Her high standards, awareness, sensitivity and compassion served the journal, its contributors and readers superbly over many years and will be invaluable in her return to nursing. It is to Helen that I dedicate this book.

Glossary

Accusatorial	A system of court proceedings where the two sides contest the issue (contrast with *inquisitorial*)
Act	Of Parliament, *statute*
Action	Legal proceedings
Actionable *per se*	A court action where the claimant does not have to show loss, *damage* or harm to obtain compensation eg an action for *trespass to the person*
Actus reus	The essential element of a crime which must be proved to secure a conviction, as opposed to the mental state of the accused (*mens rea*)
Adversaria	The approach adopted in an accusatorial system
Advocate	A person who pleads for another: the person could be paid and professional, such as a *barrister* or *solicitor*, or might be a lay advocate either paid or unpaid; a witness is not an advocate
Affidavit	A statement given under oath
Alternative dispute resolution	Methods to resolve a dispute without going to court, such as mediation
Appellate court	A court which hears appeals from lower courts, e.g. Court of Appeal and House of Lords
Approved social worker	A social worker qualified for the purposes of the Mental Health Act
Arrestable offence	An offence defined in section 24 of the Police and Criminal Evidence Act 1984 which gives to the citizen the power of arrest in certain circumstances without a warrant
Assault	A threat of unlawful contact (see *Trespass to the person*)
Barrister	A lawyer qualified to take a case in court
Battery	An unlawful touching (see *Trespass to the person*)
Bench	The *magistrates*, Justice of the Peace
Bolam Test	The test laid down by Judge McNair in the case of Bolam v. Friern HMC on the standard of care expected of a professional in cases of alleged *negligence*

Bona fide	In good faith
Breach	Breaking, usually of a legal duty
Burden of proof	The duty of a party to litigation to establish the facts, or in criminal proceedings the duty of the prosecution to establish both the *actus reus* and the *mens rea*
Case citation	The reference to an earlier reported case made possible because of the reference system, e.g. 1981 1 All ER 267 means the first volume of the All England Reports for 1981 at page 267, which is the refer ence for the case of Whitehouse v.Jordan, where Whitehouse is the plaintiff, Jordan the defendant and 'v' stands for versus, i.e. against. Other law reports include: AC Appeals Court QB Queens Bench Division WLR Weekly Law Reports
Cause of action	The facts that entitle a person to sue
Certiorari	An action taken to challenge an administrative or judicial decision (literally: to make more certain)
Civil action	Proceedings brought in the civil courts
Civil wrong	An act or omission which can be pursued in the civil courts by the person who has suffered the wrong (see *Torts*)
Claimant	The person bringing a civil action (originally *plaintiff*)
Committal proceedings	Hearings before the magistrates to decide if a person should be sent for *trial* in the crown court
Common law	Law derived from the decisions of judges, case law, judge made law
Conditional fees	A system whereby client and lawyer can agree that payment of fees is dependent upon the outcome of the court action; also known as 'no win, no fee'
Criminal courts	Courts such as magistrates' and crown courts hearing criminal pros- ecutions
Constructive knowledge	Knowledge which can be obtained from the circumstances know- ledge
Continuous service	The length of service which an employee must have served to be entitled to receive certain statutory or contractual rights

Contract	An agreement enforceable in law
Contract for services	An agreement, enforceable in law, whereby one party provides serv ices, not being employment, in return for payment or other consider ation from the other
Contract of service	A contract for employment
Coroner	A person appointed to hold an inquiry (inquest) into a death in unexpected or unusual circumstances
Cross examination	Questions asked of a witness by the lawyer for the opposing side: leading questions can be asked
Criminal wrong	An act or omission which can be pursued in the criminal courts
Damage	Harm which has occurred
Damages	A sum of money awarded by a court as compensation for a tort or breach of contract
Declaration	A ruling by the court, setting out the legal situation
Disclosure	Documents made available to the other party
Dissenting judgment	A judge who disagrees with the decision of the majority of judges
Distinguished	The rules of precedent require judges to follow decisions (of cases) of judges in previous cases, where these are binding upon them.
	However in some circumstances it is possible to come to a different decision because the facts of the earlier case are not comparable to the case now being heard, and therefore the earlier decision can be 'distinguished'
Domiciliary	At the home
Ethics	The science of morals, moral principles and rules of conduct
Euthanasia	Bringing about gentle and easy death, mercy killing
Examination in chief	The witness is asked questions in court by the lawyer of the party who has asked the witness to attend; leading questions cannot be asked
Ex gratia	As a matter of favour, e.g. without admission of *liability*, of payment offered to a claimant
Ex parte	On one side only, where the other side is not a party to the action

xii

Expert witness	Evidence given by a person whose general opinion based on training or experience is relevant to some of the issues in dispute (contrast with *witness of fact*)
Re F ruling	A professional who acts in the best interests of an incompetent person who is incapable of giving consent does not act unlawfully if he follows the accepted standard of care according to the *Bolam Test*
Guardian *ad litem*	A person with a social work and child care background who is appointed to ensure that the court is fully informed of the relevant facts which relate to a child and that the wishes and feelings of the child are clearly established. The appointment is made from a panel set up by the local authority
Guilty	A finding in a criminal court of responsibility for a criminal offence
Gynaecology	The branch of medicine which devotes itself to the care and prevention of genital tract disorders in women and which for the most part is not concerned with pregnancy
Hearsay	Evidence which has been learnt from another person
Hierarchy	The recognised status of courts which results in lower courts following the decisions of higher courts (see *Precedent*). Thus decisions of the House of Lords must be followed by all lower courts unless they can be *distinguished* (see above)
HSC	Health Service Circular issued by Department of Health Security
Indemnity	against loss or damage, compensation for loss occurred
Indictable	Can be tried on an indictment (i.e. before the Crown Court – some crimes are triable either way, i.e. before the Crown Court or summarily before magistrates)
Indictment	Written accusation against a person, charging him with a serious crime, triable by jury
Informal	Of a patient who has entered hospital without any statutory requirements
Injunction	An order of the court restraining a person
Inquisitorial	A system of justice whereby the truth is revealed by an inquiry into the facts conducted by the judge, e.g. Coroner's Court
Invitation to treat	The early stages in negotiating a contract, e.g. an advertisement, or letter expressing interest. An invitation to treat will often precede

	an offer which, when accepted, leads to the formation of an agreement which, if there is consideration and an intention to create legal relations, will be binding
Judicial review	An application to the High Court for a judicial or administrative decision to be reviewed and an appropriate order made, e.g. declaration
Judiciary	Judges
Justice of the Peace (JP)	A lay *magistrate*, i.e. not legally qualified, who hears summary (minor) offences and sometimes indictable (serious) offences in the magistrates court in a group of three *(bench)*
Liable/liability	Responsible for the wrong doing or harm in civil proceedings
Litigation	Civil proceedings
Magistrate	A person (see *Justice of the Peace* and *Stipendiary magistrate*) who hears summary (minor) offences or indictable offences which can be heard in the Magistrates' Court
Mens rea	The mental element in a crime (contrasted with *actus reus*)
Negligence (1)	A breach by the defendant of a legal duty to take reasonable care not to injure the plaintiff or cause him loss
Negligence (2)	The attitude of mind of a person committing a civil wrong as opposed to intentionally
Next friend	A person who brings a court action on behalf of a minor
Non-executive	A person who does not hold office, used in relation to NHS board members who are directors but who do not hold office within the authority
Notifiable	A disease which must be notified to the authorities by law
Nuisance	A wrong which interferes with the use and enjoyment of a person's land
Obstetrics	The field of medicine dealing with the care of women during pregnancy
Offer	A proposal made by a party which if accepted can lead to a contract. It often follows an *invitation to treat*
Ombudsman	A Commissioner (e.g. health, Local Government) appointed by the Government to hear complaints
Payment into	An offer to settle a dispute at a particular sum, which is paid into court. The claimant's failure to accept the offer means that the claim

	ant is liable to pay costs if the final award is the same or less than the payment made
Plaintiff	Term formerly used to describe one who brings an action in the civil courts. Now the term *claimant* is used
Plea in mitigation	A formal statement to the court aimed at reducing the sentence to be pronounced by the judge
Practice direction	Guidance issued by the head of the court to which they relate on the procedure to be followed
Pre-action protocol	Rules of the Supreme Court provide guidance on action to be taken before legal proceedings commence
Precedent	A decision which may have to be followed in a subsequent court hearing (see *Hierarchy*)
Prima facie	at first sight, or sufficient evidence brought by one party to require the other party to provide a defence
Privilege	In relation to evidence, being able to refuse to disclose it to the court
Privity	The relationship which exists between parties as the result of a legal agreement
Proof	Evidence which secures the establishment of a claimant's or prosecution's or defendant's case
Prosecution	The pursuing of criminal offences in court
Quantum	The amount of compensation, or the monetary value of a claim
Queen's Counsel (QC)	A senior barrister, also known as a 'silk'
Ratio	The reasoning behind the decision in a court case
Reasonable doubt	To secure a conviction in criminal proceedings the prosecution must establish 'beyond reasonable doubt' the guilt of the accused
Res ipsa loquitur	The thing speaks for itself
Sanctions	Penalties, remedies following civil or criminal wrong
Solicitor	A lawyer who is qualified on the register held by the Law Society
Standard of proof	The level that the party who has the burden of proof must satisfy, e.g. on a balance of probabilities (civil courts); beyond all reasonable doubt (criminal courts)

Statute law (statutory)	Law made by Acts of Parliament
Statutory instrument	Orders and regulations having binding force. They must usually be laid before Parliament and will usually become law if they are confirmed by a simple resolution of both Houses (affirmative resolution). Some become law after they have been laid for a prescribed period unless they are annulled by resolution of either House (negative resolution)
Stipendiary magistrate	A legally qualified magistrate who is paid (i.e. has a stipend)
Strict liability	Liability for a criminal act where the mental element does not have to be proved; in civil proceedings liability without establishing *negligence*
Subpoena	An order of the court requiring a person to appear as a witness (*subpoena ad testifi candum*) or to bring records/documents (*subpoena duces tecum*)
Summary offence	A lesser offence which can only be heard by *magistrates*
Summary	A procedure whereby the claimant can obtain judgment judgment without the defendant being permitted to defend the action
Tort	A civil wrong excluding breach of contract. It includes: *negligence, trespass (to the person*, goods or land), nuisance, breach of statutory duty and defamation
Trespass to the person	A wrongful direct interference with another person. Harm does not have to be proved
Trial	A court hearing before a judge
Ultra vires	Outside the powers given by law (e.g. of a statutory body or company)
Vicarious	The liability of an employer for the wrongful acts of an liability employee committed whilst in the course of employment
Void	Invalid or not legally binding
Voidable	Can be made void
Volenti non fit injuria	To the willing there is no wrong; the voluntary assumption of risk

Ward of court	A minor placed under the protection of the High Court, which assumes responsibility for him or her; all decisions relating to his or her care must be made in accordance with the directions of the court
Wednesbury	The court will intervene to prevent or remedy abuses of principle power by public authorities if there is evidence of unreasonableness or perversity. Principle laid down by the Court of Appeal in the case of Associated Provincial Picture House Ltd v. Wednesbury Corporation [1948] 1 KB 233
Without prejudice	Without detracting from or without disadvantage to. The use of the phrase prevents the other party using the information to the prejudice of the one providing it
Witness of fact	A person who gives evidence of what they saw, heard, did or failed to do (contrast with *expert witness*)
Writ	A form of written command, e.g. the document which used to commence civil proceedings. Now a claim form is served

Abbreviations

ABPC   Association of the British Pharmaceutical Industry

ACPC   Area Child Protection Committee

ACAS   Advisory, Conciliation and Arbitration Service

ADR   Adverse Drug Reaction

BNF   *British National Formulary*

CD   Controlled Drugs (comes under the Misuse of Drugs Act 1971 and its regulations

CHC   Community Health Council

CHI   Commission for Health Improvement

CPD   Continuous Professional Development

CPS   Crown Prosecution Service

CQC   Care Quality Commission

CRHP   Council for the Regulation of Healthcare Professionals(now the CHRE)

CHRE   Council for Healthcare Regulatory Excellence

CSM   Committee on the Safety of Medicines

DHSS   Department of Health and Social Security (divided in 1989into DH and DSS)

DH   Department of Health

DHA   District Health Authority

DMD   Drug Misuse Database

DN   Deoxyribonucleic Acid

DSS   Department of Social Security

EC   European Community

ECR   Extra-Contractual Referral

EEC   European Economic Community

ETP   Electronic Transfer of Prescriptions

EU   European Union

GMC   General Medical Council

GP   General Practitioner

GSL   General Sales List

IV   Intravenous(ly) or Intravenous infusion

IVF	In Vitro Fertilisation
JP	Justice of the Peace
LREC	Local Research Ethics Committee
MCA	Medicines Control Agency (now absorbed into the MHRA)
MHRA	Medicines and Healthcare Products Regulatory Agency
NPF	*Nurse Prescribers' Formulary*
NPEF	*Nurse Prescribers' Extended Formulary*
NHS	National Health Service
NICE	National Institute for Health and Clinical Excellence
NMC	Nursing and Midwifery Council
NPF	*Nurse Prescribers' Formulary*
NPEF	*Nurse Prescribers' Extended Formulary*
NPSA	National Patient Safety Agency
NSF	National Service Framework
PCC	Professional Conduct Committee
PGD	Patient Group Direction
POM	Prescription Only Medicine
PPC	Preliminary Proceedings Committee
PPP	Personal Professional Profile
PREP	Post-Registration Education and Practice
REC	Research Ethics Committee
RPSGB	Royal Pharmaceutical Society of Great Britain
RPS	Royal Pharmaceutical Society
SI	Statutory Instrument
UKCC	United Kingdom Central Council for Nursing, Midwifery and Health Visiting
WHO	World Health Organisation

Table of useful web sites

Audit Commission http://www.audit-commission.gov.uk/

British National Formulary http://www.bnf.org/

Bristol Inquiry (Kennedy Report) http://www.bristol-inquiry.org.uk/

Civil Procedure Rules http://www.open.gov.uk/lcd/civil/procrules_fin/crules.htm

Commission for Racial Equality http://www.cre.gov.uk/

Department of Constitutional Affairs http://www.dca.gov.uk/

Department of Health http://www.dh.gov.uk/

Department of Health (research) http://www.dh.gov.uk/research/rd1/researchgovernance/

Department of Trade and Industry http://www.dti.gov.uk/

Domestic Violence http://www.domesticviolence.gov.uk/

Health and Safety Commission http://www.hsc.gov.uk/

Health and Safety Executive http://www.hse.gov.uk/

Health Professions Council http://www.hpc-uk.org/

Human Fertilisation and Embryology Authority http://www.hfea.gov.uk/

Human Rights http://www.humanrights.gov.uk/

Medicines and Healthcare Products Regulatory Agency http://www.mhra.gov.uk/

MIDIRS http://www.midirs.gov.uk/

National Audit Office http://www.nao.gov.uk/

National Patient Safety Agency http://www.npsa.org.uk/

National Service Framework (older people) http://www.doh.gov.uk/NSF/olderpeople/

National Treatment Agency http://www.nta.nhs.uk/

NHS http://www.nhs.uk/

NHS Direct http://www.nhsdirect.nhs.uk/

NHS Professionals http://www.nhsprofessionals.nhs.uk/

NICE http://www.nice.org.uk/

Nursing and Midwifery Council http://www.nmc-uk.org/

Open Government http://www.open.gov.uk/

Pain website http://www.pain-talk.co.uk/

Royal College of Midwives http://www.rcm.org.uk/

Royal College of Nursing http://www.rcn.org.uk/

Royal Pharmaceutical Society http://www.rpharms.com/

Shipman Inquiry http://www.the-shipman-inquiry.org.uk/reports.asp

Stationery Office http://www.hmso.gov.uk/

UK Parliament http://www.parliament.uk/

Victoria Climbie Inquiry http://www.victoria-climbie.org.uk/

CHAPTER I

The statutory framework for medicines

Box 1.1 Situation of ignorance

Jane has just started her training to become a registered nurse at the Roger Park Higher Education College, which is affiliated to Roger Park University. On her first week of clinical experience at Roger Park District General Hospital, she was asked by a staff nurse to give a patient her dose of painkillers. Jane is totally ignorant of the laws which apply to medicines and asks her tutor whether she was right to obey those instructions from the staff nurse. She would also like to know how she can find out about what makes a law and how she can know whether or not she is acting lawfully.

Introduction

Our laws derive from two main sources: statute law (including statutory instruments) and case law (judge-made law, also known as the common law). Increasingly, Directives and Regulations from the European Community relating to medicinal products, with which we as a member state must comply, are forming a large part of our laws on medicines.

Legislative framework for medicines

The two main sources of law on medicinal products are the Medicines Act 1968 and the Misuse of Drugs Act 1971. The Medicines Act 1968 (and its subsequent Statutory Instruments (SI)) provide a statutory framework for the manufacture, export and import and supply and control of medicines. Box 1.2 shows the basic contents of the Act and Box 1.3 sets out the classification of drugs recognised in the Act. The Misuse of Drugs Act 1971 and subsequent legislation regulates the supply of specified Controlled Drugs (CD) which are discussed in the next chapter.

These statutes have been supplemented by Statutory Instrument providing more detailed regulation.

> ## Box 1.2 Framework set up by the Medicines Act1968
> 1. An administrative system
> 2. A licensing system
> 3. Controls over the sale and supply of drugs to the public
> 4. Retail pharmacies
> 5. Packing and labelling of medicinal products
> 6. British Pharmacopoeia

Definition of a medicinal product

In the Medicines Act 1968 section 130, 'medical product' means: any substance or article (not being an instrument, apparatus or appliance) which is manufactured, sold, supplied, imported or exported for use wholly or mainly in either or both of the following ways, that is to say:

a. use by being administered to one or more human beings or animals for a medicinal purpose;

b. use, in circumstances to which this paragraph applies, as an ingredient in the preparation of a substance or article which is to be administered to one or more human beings or animals for a medicinal purpose.

'Medicinal purpose' means one or more of the following purposes:

a. treating or preventing disease

b. diagnosing disease or ascertaining the existence, degree or extent of a physiological condition

c. contraception

d. inducing anaesthesia

e. otherwise preventing or interfering with the normal operation of a physiological function, whether permanently or temporarily, and whether by way of terminating, reducing or postponing, or increasing or accelerating the operation of that function or in any other way.

Certain products, such as surgical ligatures and sutures, dental fillings, contact lenses and intra-uterine contraceptive devices have since 1994 been defined as medical devices and come under the Medical Devices Regulations 1994 SI 1994 No 3017 (as amended) (Dimond 2011). The term 'medicinal product' is also to be distinguished from food and from poisons.

Licensing

Part II of the Medicines Act 1968 and the EC Council Directives require licences to:
- Sell, supply or export any medicinal product or
- Procure the sale, supply or exportation of any medicinal product or
- Procure the manufacture or assembly or any medicinal product (S.7(2)).

Licences are also required for manufacture and wholesale dealers and clinical trials (subject to extensive exemptions which will be considered in Chapter 26 on research into medicinal products).

Section 11 of the Medicines Act 1968 exempts a registered nurse or registered midwife from having a manufacturer's licence in order to assemble medicinal products in the course of her profession. 'Assemble' means (section 132):

The enclosing of the products (with or without other medicinal products of the same description) in a container which is labelled before the product is sold or supplied or, where the product (with or without medicinal products of the same description) is already enclosed in a container in which it is to be sold or supplied, labelling the contained before the product is sold or supplied in it.

Manufacturing units within hospitals

Since the abolition of Crown immunity under the provisions of the NHS and Community Care Act 1990, manufacturing units in hospitals come under the licensing provisions of the Medicines Act 1968 and are subject to the Medicines Control Agency (MCA) (which has been the Medicines and Healthcare Products Regulatory Agency (MHRA) since 1 April 2003) and its inspectorate.

Section 10 provides certain exemptions where an activity takes place under the supervision of a pharmacist in a hospital. The pharmacy in a hospital can seek registration with the General Pharmaceutical Council (GPC) as a registered pharmacy, thus enabling it to provide over-the-counter medicines and a limited amount of wholesale dealing. The MCA (1992) has published guidance for NHS on the licensing requirements under the Medicines Act 1968.

Classification of medicinal products

The classification of medical products is presented in Box 1.3.

Box 1.3 Classification of medicinal products

1. Pharmacy Only Medicines

2. General Sales Medicines (GSM)

3. Prescription Only Medicines (POM)

Any procedure for dealing with medicines in hospitals or in a community home, whether residential care, nursing or mental nursing, should ensure that the specific requirements for these different classes of drugs are met, unless specified exemptions apply (e.g. Patient Group Directions (PGD), which are considered in Chapter 8).

Pharmacy Only Medicines refers to those medicinal products which can only be purchased under the supervision of a registered pharmacist or given out by a dispensing doctor (i.e. one who is authorised to dispense medicines). See below for exceptions to this rule in hospitals and health centres.

General Sales Medicine (GSM) covers drugs which are sold through a variety of outlets, for which a registered pharmacist does not have to be present. Under section 51 of the Medicines Act they are medicinal products which in the opinion of the Minister can with reasonable safety be sold or supplied otherwise than by or under the supervision of a pharmacist. There are two Schedules to the SI 1984 No 769 (as amended) which list the classes of medicinal products coming under GSM. The regulations also list the pack sizes. If these limitations are not observed, then the medicinal product comes under the classification of Pharmacy Medicine or Perscription Only Medicines (POM).

For example, medicines for human use containing aspirin or paracetamol may only be presented for sale in separate and individual containers or packages containing not more than:

- 16 capsules or tablets (non-effervescent)
- 10 sachets (powder or granule)
- 30 tablets containing not more than 325 mg (effervescent tablets)
- 20 tablets where the amount of aspiring exceeds 325 mg but does not exceed 500 mg (effervescent tablets).

Those medicinal products which are listed under the GSM list can be sold from automatic machines provided that these machines are located in premises which the occupier is able to close so as to exclude the public (see sections 54 and 66 Medicines Act 1968 and SI 1980 No 1923.

Certain medicinal products are excluded from GSM, including eye drops or eye ointments, medicines for administration by parenteral injection, most anthelmintics, medicines promoted as enemas or irrigations and aspirin for administration to children.

Additional provisions on the sale or supply of medicinal products

Part III of the Medicines Act 1968 covers further provisions relating to the General Sales List (GSL). Section 52 places restrictions on the sale or supply of medicinal products not on the GSL and section 53 places restrictions on the sale or supply of medicinal products on GSL. Under section 55 these restrictions do not apply to the sale, offer for sale, or supply of a medicinal product:

a. by a doctor or dentist to a patient of his or a person under whose care such a patient is (this enables doctors in recognised rural areas to dispense medicine to their patients, i.e. dispensing doctors and non-dispensing doctors can administer medicine personally to their patients).

b. in the course of the business or a health centre, where the product is sold, offered for sale or supplied for the purpose of being administered (whether in the hospital or health centre or elsewhere) in accordance with the directions of a doctor or dentist.

Nor do the restrictions apply:

a. to the sale or supply of a medicinal product of a description, or falling into a class, specified in an order made by Health Ministers for the purpose of this paragraph, where the product is sold or supplied by a registered nurse in the course of her professional practice, or

b. to the sale of a medicinal product of a description, or falling within a class, specified in an order made by the Health Ministers for the purpose of this paragraph, where the product either is sold or supplied by a registered midwife in the course of her professional practice or is delivered or administered by such a midwife on being supplied in pursuance of arrangements made by the Secretary of State.

POMs can in general only be obtained from a registered pharmacist on a prescription written by an appropriate health professional. Section 58 of the Medicines Act 1968 empowers the appropriate Minister to specify the descriptions or classes of medicinal products which can only be supplied on prescription only and also define the appropriate practitioner who can prescribe.

The definition of appropriate health profession has widened in recent years with the introduction and extension of nurse prescribing. These developments are considered in more detail in Chapters 9 and 10.

The SI 1997 No 1830 (as amended) is known as the POM order and provides exceptions to the rule that POMs can only be sold or supplied by a pharmacist against a lawful prescription or administered under the directions of an appropriate practitioner. These include:

- Specified drugs for parenteral administration to be administered by anyone for the purpose of saving life in an emergency.
- The administration of all POMs except those which are administered parenterally.
- A POM to be sold or supplied in the course of the business of a hospital provided the POM is sold or supplied in accordance with the written directions of a doctor or dentist, even though those directions do not fulfil the usual conditions which apply to the writing of prescriptions.
- The sale or supply only or parenteral administration by specified categories of persons of specified products under certain conditions such as registered chiropodists who hold a certificate in the use of analgesic, registered midwives and ambulance paramedics.
- Certain drugs to be supplied in an emergency by community pharmacists.

In 2002 the Department of Health (DH) announced that it intended to reclassify some POM to enable them to be supplied without a prescription (DH 2002). The aim was to ensure wider availability of medicines and ensure better use of resources, including freeing up time for GPs and enabling pharmacists to use their expertise to help patients manage their health conditions. Diphenoxylate hydrochloride (with atropine sulphate), Flurbiprofen and Terbinafine were to be available from pharmacists without a prescription and cetirizine hydrochloride and loratadine tablets were to be removed from the POM (Human Use) Order. There are regular checks over the suitability of the classification of a medicine as a POM.

Nursing and Midwifery Council

The United Kingdom Central Council for Nursing, Midwifery and Health Visiting (UKCC) published guidelines for the administration of medicines in 2000. These were amended by the Nursing and Midwifery Council (NMC) in 2004. While the guidelines have no legal force in themselves, they establish principles for safe practice in the management and administration of medicines by registered nurses, midwives and health visitors. In 2007 the NMC published the Standards for medicines management which replaced the guidelines published in 2004. The 24 standards are set within the following 10 sections:

- Methods of supplying and/or administration of medicines
- Dispensing
- Storage and transportation
- Standards for practice of administration of medicines
- Delegation
- Disposal
- Unlicensed medicines
- Complementary and alternative therapies
- Management of adverse events
- Controlled drugs.

These standards will be referred to throughout this book.

Unlicensed medicines

Under the Medicines Act 1968 medicines must only be put on sale, or supplied, with the appropriate marketing authorisation. An unlicensed medicine is so called because it does not have a product licence. There are, however, exemptions to the requirement of market authorisation and unlicensed medicines can in exceptional circumstances be prescribed and administered. They should only be prescribed on a patient specific prescription and cannot usually be the subject of patient group directions (see Chapter 8). The RPSGB has provided a fact sheet on the use of unlicensed medicines in pharmacy and discusses the exemptions from the formal licensing requirements in three situations:

- Where an unlicensed drug is prepared or dispensed in accordance with a prescription given by a practitioner, or preparing a stock of medicinal products for this purpose.
- Preparing or dispensing a medicinal product by or under the supervision of a pharmacist in accordance with a specification furnished by the person to whom the product is to be sold, where the product is prepared or dispensed for administration to that person or person under his care.
- Preparing or dispensing a medicinal product for administration to a person when the pharmacist is requested by or on behalf of that person to do so in accordance with the pharmacist's own judgment as to the treatment required and that person is present in the pharmacy at the time of the request (RPSGB 2004).

7

Clearly, in the event of any harm befalling the patient the practitioner prescribing the medicine and the pharmacist dispensing it would have to show that they followed a reasonable standard of care in recommending that particular medicine to the patient (although the burden of proof on a balance of probability is upon the claimant in civil proceedings). It would also be essential that the patient was informed that the product was not licensed. (See Chapter 13 on giving information to the patient.)

Answering the situation in Box 1.1

Jane should be aware that there are laws which relate to her conduct. The Medicines Act 1968 and the Misuse of Drugs Act 1971 and the subsequent regulations made under both those acts provide the statutory framework for the supply of medicines. The type of painkiller is not given in the scenario and it might be one which, if the patient were in the community, could be available on general sale; or one sold only under the supervision of a pharmacist; or one only available on a doctor's prescription. Whilst the staff nurse can delegate the administration of medicines, she should do so only to someone who is trained and competent to perform that activity. It is clear that Jane should not have been asked to administer painkillers to a patient when she had no knowledge about the medicines or the patient, and it was outside her competence. The staff nurse was at fault in giving her those instructions. It does not appear that the patient has suffered any harm, but clearly if there had been harm, both Jane and the staff nurse would have had to face an inquiry into their conduct, leading possibly to criminal (see Chapter 19) and civil proceedings (see Chapter 20). In addition, as an employee and a registered practitioner the staff nurse could also face disciplinary proceedings from her employee (see Chapter 21) and professional conduct investigations from the NMC (see Chapter 22), whether or not the patient had suffered harm.

Conclusions

This first chapter has endeavoured to explain the statutory framework of the control of medicines. In 2010 the MHSA began a review of medicines legislation and consulted on how exemptions to the Medicines Act 1968 relating to the sale, supply and administration of prescription only medicines should be determined. This is considered in Chapter 31. The next chapter looks in more detail at the Misuse of Drugs Act 1971 and CD.

Key points

■ Laws derive from statute and common (i.e. judge-made or case) law.

■ As a member of the European Community, European Directives and Regulations become part of UK law.

■ The Medicine Act 1968 and the Misuse of Drugs Act 1971 provide the statutory framework for the control of medicinal products and CD and have been supplemented by statutory instruments.

■ Professional guidelines issued by the NMC, though not part of law, should be followed by registered practitioners.

References

Department of Health (2002) press release 2002/0205 *Wider access to medicines*. London

Dimond B (2011) *Legal Aspects of Health and Safety* 2nd edn. Quay Publications, Dinton, Salisbury

Medicines Control Agency (1992) *Guidance to the NHS on the Licensing Requirements of the Medicines Act 1968*. London

NMC (2004) *Guidelines for the administration of medicines*, amending earlier publication of 2002 which was a reprint of the UKCC 2000 Guidelines. London

Royal Pharmaceutical Society of Great Britain (2004)*Fact Sheet 5: The use of unlicensed medicines in pharmacy* (November 2004).

UKCC (2000) *Guidelines for the administration of medicines* October 2000. London

Further readings

Appelbe G, Wingfield J (2005) *Dale and Appelbe's Pharmacy Law and Ethics* 8th edn, The Pharmaceutical Press, London

Merrills J, Fisher J (1995) *Pharmacy Law and Practice*. Blackwell Science, Oxford.

CHAPTER 2

Controlled drugs

Box 2.1 Situation

Mary, a newly qualified staff nurse, was asked by the night sister to draw up a syringe of morphine for a patient who was in severe pain. She had understood that she should not be doing this on her own, but the night sister said that they were too short of staff to provide another person. What is the law?

Introduction

It was stated in the first chapter that the Misuse of Drugs Act 1971, together with the Medicines Act 1968 and the many regulations made under both Acts, provides the statutory basis for the control of medicinal products in this country.

The contents of the Misuse of Drugs Act 1971 are shown in Box 2.2.

Controlled drugs

Schedule 2 of the Misuse of Drugs Act 1971 lists drugs which are subject to special controls, and the term Controlled Drugs (CD) means any substance or product so listed. Schedule 2 drugs are divided into three parts according to their degree of harmfulness, and the penalties for offences differ according to the Class of the drug:

- Class A includes morphine, mescaline, pethidine and phenazocine
- Class B includes codeine and amphetamine
- Class C includes diazepam and temazepam.

The laws relating to addicts and the use of illegal substances are considered in Chapter 28.

Under section 3 of the Misuse of Drugs Act 1971 the importation or exportation of CD is prohibited, except in accordance with a license issued by the Secretary of State or when permitted by the regulations.

Box 2.2 Misuse of Drugs Act 1971

1. Lists and classifies CD.
2. Creates criminal offences in relation to the manufacture, supply and possession of CD.
3. Gives the Secretary of State power to make regulations and directions to prevent misuse of CD.
4. Creates Advisory Council on the misuse of drugs.
5. Gives powers of search, arrest and forfeiture.

The following activities are unlawful:
- Producing a CD (section 4)
- Supplying or offering to supply a CD to another person (section 4)
- Possessing a CD (section 5)
- Cultivating any plant of the genus cannabis (section 6).

The Secretary of State has the power under section 7 of the Misuse of Drugs Act 1971 to draft regulations providing exemptions from these controls and under section 10 to draw up regulations necessary or expedient to prevent the misuse of CD.

Misuse of drugs regulations

Under the Misuse of Drugs Regulations 2001 (reenacting and amending the 1985 Regulations), drugs are divided into five schedules, each specifying the requirements governing their import, export, production, supply, possession, prescribing and record-keeping. These Schedules are shown in Box 2.3.

Subsequent statutory instruments (SI) have added more drugs to the original Schedules of the Misuse of Drugs Act.

The Misuse of Drugs Regulations makes provision for:
1. Certain exemptions from the Misuse of Drugs Act 1971 in relation to the production, importation, exportation, possession and supply of CD.
2. Prescriptions, records and furnishing of information concerning CD and for the supervision of the destruction of such drugs.

The Misuse of Drugs Regulations cover the following activities:
- Administration
- Production and supply
- Possession

Box 2.3 Schedules under the Misuse of Drugs Regulations 2001

Schedule 1 e.g. cannabis and lysergide.
Possession and supply of these is prohibited except in accordance with Home Office authority given in a licence. They cannot be used for medicinal purposes and their production and possession is limited to research or other specified purposes. Rules cover the documentation, keeping of records, preservation of records, supply on prescription, marking of containers and procedure for destruction.

Schedule 2 e.g. diamorphine, morphine, pethidine, glutethimide, and amphetamine.
These are subject to full CD requirements relating to prescriptions, safe custody and the need to keep registers. These drugs may only be administered to a patient by a doctor or dentist or any person acting in accordance with the directions of a doctor or dentist.

Schedule 3 e.g. barbiturates, diethylpropion and mazindol.
These are subject to controls similar to Schedule 2, such as the special prescription requirements, but they may be manufactured by persons authorised in writing by the Secretary of State. There is a difference in the classes of person who may possess and supply them.

Entries in the register of CD need not be made in respect of these drugs, but invoices or similar records must be kept for at least two years.

Schedule 4 Part 1 includes lorazepam and diazepam.

Schedule 4 Part 2 drugs are subject to less control. In particular, CD prescription requirements do not apply and they are not subject to safe custody requirements.

Schedule 5 includes preparations which because of their strength are exempt from most CD requirements other than retention of invoices for two years.

- Exemption for midwives
- Emergency supply
- Production
- Prescription requirements
- Record-keeping requirements
- Registers
- Labelling requirements
- Destruction requirements.

The requirements under the above activities vary according to what schedule the drug comes under. Thus for Schedule 1 drugs, administration, export and import, possession and supply can be performed only by licence.

These are some of the provisions of the Regulations relevant to hospitals and nursing homes:

1. *Possession*

   Persons entitled to have CD in their possession include under Paragraph 6(7) (f): a person engaged in conveying the drug to a person who may lawfully have that drug in his possession. (This would cover hospital porters and any other person bringing the drug to an authorised person.)

2. *Administration of drugs*

   Para. 7(2) a doctor or dentist may administer to a patient any drug specified in Schedule 2, 3 or 4.

   Para 7(3) Any person other than a doctor or dentist may administer to a patient, in accordance with the direction of a doctor or dentist, any drug specified in Schedule 2, 3 and 4.

   (Under Section 130(9) of the Medicines Act 1968 administer means 'administer to a human being or animal, whether orally, by injection or by introduction into the body in any other way, or by external application, whether by direct contact with the body or not'.)

3. *Production and supply of drugs Paragraph 8(2)(e)*

   In the case of Schedule 2 and 5 drugs supplied to her, by a person responsible for the dispensing and supply of medicines at the hospital or nursing home, the sister or acting sister for the time being in charge of a ward, theatre or other department in such a hospital or nursing home as aforesaid... may, when acting in her capacity as such, supply, or offer to supply any drug specified in Schedule 2 or 5 to any person who may lawfully have that drug in his possession.

This paragraph does not authorise:

a) the person in charge or acting person in charge of a hospital or nursing home, having a pharmacist responsible for the dispensing and supply of medicines, to supply or offer to supply any drug

b) a sister or acting sister for the time being in charge of a ward, theatre, or other department to supply any drug otherwise than for the administration to a patient in that ward, theatre or department in accordance with the directions of a doctor or dentist.

Changing classification of cannabis

In 2004 cannabis was changed from a Class B to a Class C drug as a result of pressures to change the approach to the misuse of drugs (Misuse of Dug Acts 1971 (Modification) (No 2) Order 2003 SI 2003 No 3201). However the change only lasted a short while and in 2008 cannabis was reclassified from Class C to Class B (SI 2008 No 3130). (See Chapter 28 for further details).

Prescriptions for controlled drugs

The Misuse of Drugs Regulations 2001 does not specify any prescription requirements for CD listed in Schedules 4 and 5 but specifies requirements for those listed in Schedules 2 and 3. The prescription requirements for Schedule 2 and 3 CD are shown in Box 2.4.

A prescription issued for the treatment of a patient in a hospital or nursing home and written on the patient's bed card or case sheet need not specify the address of the patient (Reg.15(3)).

The rule that the prescription must be retained on the premises from which the drug was supplied and kept for two years does not apply to NHS or local health authority prescriptions (Regs. 16(2) and 23(3)).

These prescription requirements do not apply to the drug Temazepam (SI 1995 No 3244). In the case of Temazepam computer-generated dates are acceptable and the prescription does not need to be in the handwriting of the prescriber.

The rule that the prescription is only valid for 13 weeks from the date specified by the prescriber does, however, apply to prescriptions for Temazepam.

Box 2.4 Prescription requirements for Schedule 2 and 3 controlled drugs

a) must be in ink or otherwise indelible and be signed by the person issuing it with their usual signature and dated by them

b) be written by the person in his own handwriting in respect of information in e and f below

c) except in the case of a health prescription, it must specify the address of the person issuing it

d) it must have written thereon, if issued by a dentist, the words for dental treatment only

e) it must specify, in the handwriting of the person issuing it, the name and address of the person for whose treatment it is issued

f) it must specify, in the handwriting of the person issuing it, the dose to be taken, and:

– in the case of a prescription containing a CD which is a preparation, it must specify the form and, where appropriate, the strength of the preparation, and either the total quantity (in both words and figures) of the preparation or the number (in both words and figures) of dosage units, as appropriate to be supplied;

– in any other case, it must specify the total quantity (in both words and figures) of the CD to be supplied.

g) in the case of a prescription for a total quantity intended to be supplied by instalments, it must contain a direction specifying the amount of the instalments of the total amount which may be supplied and the intervals to be observed when supplying (Reg. 15(1)).

Registers and records of controlled drugs

The Regulations specify rules which must be followed in relation to the registers and records which must be kept in relation to CD (Misuse of Drugs Regulations SI 2001 No 3998 amending and re-enacting the Misuse of Drugs Regulations SI 1985 2066). These are considered in Chapter 25 on documentation and medicinal products.

Advisory Council on Misuse of Drugs

This was established in February 1972 under the Misuse of Drugs Act 1971 (SI 1971 No 2120.). Its role is to advise Ministers on the misuse of drugs and to keep under review the situation with respect to drugs which are being or likely to be misused. Its role is considered in Chapter 28.

Safe custody of controlled drugs

The 1973 Regulations on safe custody apply to all CD except drugs listed in Schedule 4 and 5; liquid preparations, apart from injections which contain specified products; and other specified products such as cathine (SI 1971 No 2120). The 1973 regulations do not apply to the storage of CD in NHS hospitals (except for those hospital pharmacies which are designated by the General Pharmaceutical Council (GPC) as retail pharmacies) apart from the rule that the CD should be kept in a locked receptacle that can only be opened by a person who can lawfully be in possession. The 1973 Regulations are considered in Chapter 18.

Nursing and Midwifery Council's *Standards for medicines management*

The NMC in Section 10 of its *Standards for medicines management* (2007) states:

Standard 26

Registrants should ensure that patients prescribed Controlled Drugs are administered these in a timely fashion in line with the standards for administering medication to patients. Registrants should comply with and follow the legal requirements and approved local Standard Operating Procedures for Controlled Drugs that are appropriate for their area of work.

The Department of Health (DH) has provided guidance on nurse independent prescribing and CD which is considered in Chapter 10 (DH 2006a).

The Shipman Inquiry Fourth Report

On 31 January 2000, Dr Shipman, a general practitioner, was found guilty of the murder of 15 patients. An inquiry set up by the Secretary of State published five reports on the case. The first considered how many patients Shipman killed, the means employed and the period over which the killings took place (DH 2002). The second report examined the conduct of the police investigation (DH 2003a). The third report considered the present system for death and cremation certification and for the investigation of deaths by coroners (DH 2003b). The fourth which is considered here looked at the regulation of CD (DH 2004a). The fifth report considered the monitoring of medical practitioners, disciplinary systems, whistle blowing and complaints (DH 2004b).

A finding of the Inquiry was that Harold Shipman probably killed 200 people in addition to the 15 deaths for which he was convicted. He managed to avoid any coronial investigation in all but two of the cases in which he had killed. He did this by claiming to be in a position to certify the cause of death and by persuading relatives that no autopsy (and therefore no referral to the coroner) was necessary. Most of the deaths were the result of the administration of morphine.

The fourth report made three major groups of recommendations (DH 2004a):

a) The setting up of an integrated and multidisciplinary inspectorate to monitor and audit the prescription, storage, distribution and disposal of CD.

b) A number of restrictions on the prescribing of CD to discourage or prevent health professionals from prescribing in circumstances in which it could be considered unsafe or unwise for them to do so – for example, prescribing for their own use or for that of their immediate families, prescribing outside the requirements of their normal clinical practice, or prescribing by professionals convicted of CD offences.

c) A series of measures should be put in place to tighten up the handling and safekeeping of CD, along each part of the supply chain from the supplier to the patient's home, and to provide a complete 'audit trail' to account for the movement of CD at each stage, both in the NHS and in the private sector.

The DH responded to the Inquiry Report by stating that these very significant recommendations were to be studied carefully and in consultation with existing inspectorates, patients, NHS and police organisations, and the healthcare professions. The views of the Advisory Council on the misuse of drugs would also be obtained (DH 2004c).

In the meantime the National Prescribing Centre published 'preview' guidance for NHS organisations and professionals summarising the legal requirements and best professional practice in the handling of CD. The National Programme for Information Technology was also considering the additional safeguards proposed in the report.

Safer management of controlled drugs

The fourth report of the Shipman Inquiry (see above) was concerned with the safety of CD (DH 2004a.) Following this report, the DH published in June 2006 its guidance on the safer management of CD (DH 2006b) (replacing interim guidance issued in March 2006). It sets out the action required to implement a series of changes to the way CD for human use are prescribed and dispensed and the monitoring of this activity. The main changes included special forms for private prescriptions, a new requirement for patients (or any one collecting drugs on their behalf) to sign for them with new forms gradually replacing the old forms, and prescriptions were to be only valid for 28 days for Schedule 2, 3, and 4 drugs (in place of 91 days for Schedule 2 and 3 drugs and 6 months for Schedule 4 drugs).

The Controlled Drugs (Supervision of Management and Use) Regulations (SI 2006/ 3148) which require accountable officers to be appointed and inspections to be undertaken are considered in Chapter 23.

Guidance from the Royal Pharmaceutical Society

The Royal Pharmaceutical Society of Great Britain (RPSGB) used to be both the regulatory body and professional organization for pharmacist until 2010 when it became the Royal Pharmaceutical Society (RPS) and divided the responsibilities with the General Pharmaceutical Council (GPC) which took over the registration obligations). The RPS has provided guidance on both CD and the community pharmacy as well as CD and hospital pharmacy. Both are available from the RPS website (www.rpharms.com). Information is also available from the GPC website (www.pharmacyregulation.org) about CD and community and hospital pharmacy.

Applying the law to the situation in Box 2.1

Under paragraph 7 of the Misuse of Drugs Regulations 1971:

Any person, other than a doctor or dentist, may administer to a patient, in accordance with the directions of a doctor or dentist, any drugs specified in Schedule 2, 3, or 4.

Morphine comes under Schedule 2 of the Regulations and one assumes that the staff nurse is drawing up the drug in accordance with a written prescription by the doctor. There is therefore no legal requirement that a second person should be present when the CD is drawn up, but guidelines recommend that this is the best practice. Mary should have another person, even if not registered, to be present and check with her the dosage and ensure that the correct entry is made in the CD Register. She should also ensure that before and after the CD is drawn up, the stock tallies with the Register.

Conclusions

There are serious criminal offences for the misuse of CD and strict precautions should therefore be followed in their storage and administration not only for the protection of patients but also for the protection of staff. In addition, the NMC has provided guidance for registered practitioners in the administration of CD. Both the Medicines Act 1968 and the Misuse of Drugs Act 1971 set up control machinery for overseeing the implementation of the legislation and it is to that which we turn in the next chapter. The Drugs Act 2005 makes amendments to the 1971 Act and provides tougher powers in relation to offenders. It is discussed in Chapter 28.

Key points

- The Misuse of Drugs Act 1971 provides controls for drugs which are liable to be misused or abused.
- The Act categorises Schedule 2 drugs into three Classes and penalties for offences are harsher for Class A drugs.
- Under the Misuse of Drug Regulations 2001 there are five schedules of drugs and powers and activities are regulated in accordance to the schedule in which the drug is listed.
- The regulations also cover the documentation which must be kept and the safe custody of CD.

References

Department of Health (2002) *Shipman Inquiry First Report: Death Disguised;* http://www.the-shipman-inquiry.org.uk/reports.asp. (19 July 2002). London

Department of Health (2003a) *Shipman Inquiry Second Report: The Police Investigation of March 1998*; http://www.the-shipman-inquiry.org.uk/reports.asp. (14 July 2003) London

Department of Health (2003b) S*hipman Inquiry Third Report: Death and Cremation Certification* http://www.the-shipman-inquiry.org.uk/reports.asp. (14 July 2003b) London

Department of Health (2004a) *Shipman Inquiry Fourth Report: The Regulation of Controlled Drugs in the Community*, Cm 6249 Stationery Office; http://www.the-shipman-inquiry.org.uk/reports.asp. (July 2004a) London

Department of Health (2004b) *Shipman Inquiry Fifth Report: Safeguarding Patients: Lessons from the Past – Proposals for the Future Command Paper* CM 6394, Stationery Office; http://www.the-shipman-inquiry.org.uk/reports. asp (December 2004b) London

Department of Health (July 2004c) S*tatement on the Shipman Inquiry Fourth Report* Press release 2004/0263, July 2004. London

Department of Health (2006a) *Improving Patients' Access to Medicines: A Guide to Implementing Nurse and Pharmacist Independent Prescribing within the NHS in England* Department of Health Gateway reference: 6429 (April 2006) London

Department of Health (2006b) *Safer Management of Controlled Drugs* London

Nursing and Midwifery Council (2007) *Standards for medicines management*. London

Websites

Royal Pharmaceutical Society website www.rpharms.com
General Pharmaceutical Council website www.pharmacyregulation.org

CHAPTER 3

Control mechanisms

> ## Box 3.1 Smith v. Secretary of State
>
> *In 2002 a case was brought against the Secretary of State (sued on behalf of the Committee on Safety of Medicines (CSM)) by a mother who in May 1986 gave aspirin to her daughter of six years when she was suffering from chickenpox. The child's health deteriorated, and following admission to hospital she was diagnosed as suffering from Reye's Syndrome. As a consequence the girl was left with serious neurological handicap and totally dependent upon others for her care. In June 1986 the Government issued a general public warning advising parents not to give aspirin in any form to a child under 12 years and told chemists to take all junior aspirin preparations off their shelves. This followed advice from the CSM that in this age group aspirin could trigger the potentially fatal Reye's Syndrome. The CSM had been aware of this danger in September 1982 following evidence from the USA. Further evidence was produced in 1985 and the CSM continued to monitor the situation. In April 1986 a meeting was held between the Department of Health (DH) and members of the aspirin industry. It was subsequently agreed that the producers would withdraw stocks and there would be cooperation between the industry and the DH rather than a public warning. In May 1986 the CSM recommended that the DH should give a general public warning, which was made on 10 June 1986. The mother's case was that there was an unreasonable delay in publishing a warning following the CSM meeting on 26 March 1986. It was accepted that the administration of aspirin was a contributory factor in the development of the girl's neurological condition and that had her mother been aware of the warnings prior to May 1986 she would not have given her aspirin. Was the Secretary of State and CSM liable? (Smith v. Secretary of State [2002] Lloyd's Rep Med 333)*

Introduction

Given everything that can go wrong in the production, distribution, prescription, dispensing and administration of medicines, and the many different professionals involved, it is important that the control mechanisms at every stage of the preparation and use of the medicines are carefully regulated and inspected and that those who work with medicines at each stage are properly trained and supervised. This chapter looks at the control mechanisms which have been set up by statute.

Department of Health responsibilities

Section 1 of the Medicines Act 1968 places the responsibility of administering the Act on the relevant Minister of State. Under sections 108–110 of the Medicines Act 1968 the primary duty of enforcing the provisions of the Medicines Act rests with the appropriate Minister or Secretary of State in England and Wales, Scotland and Northern Ireland. Some of the statutory responsibilities under the Act can be delegated, but the licensing requirements and provisions affecting hospitals or the premises of practitioners are solely the responsibility of the appropriate Minister.

The Commission for Human Medicines

The Medicines Commission, which had been established under section 2 of the Medicines Act 1968, was abolished and replaced by the Commission for Human Medicines (CHM) in October 2005. The CHM was established under the Medicines (Advisory Bodies) Regulations 2005 with members (of which there must be at least eight) appointed by the Secretary of State. The Secretary of State appoints one of the CHM members to be chairman.

The functions of the CHM under the replaced section 3 of the 1968 Act include giving advice to ministers on:
• The execution of the Act.
• The exercise of any power conferred by the Act.
• The execution of the Marketing Authorisation Regulations or the Clinical Trials Regulations.
• The exercise of any power conferred by those regulations or otherwise relating to medicinal products.
The CHM is also required to:
• Give advice with respect to safety, quality or efficacy in relation to medicinal products.

- Promote the collection and investigation of information relating to adverse reactions, for the purposes of enabling such advice to be given.
- Undertake the functions mentioned in section 4(4) of this Act (i.e. establishing a Committee in relation to the British Pharmacopoeia and other publications)

The Minister may establish Committees under section 4 (as amended) to:

- Give advice with respect to safety, quality or efficacy or with respect to all or any two of those matters.
- Promote the collection and investigation of information relating to adverse reactions, for the purpose of enabling such advice to be given.

A new Schedule 1A is added to the Medicines Act 1968 by the Regulations, which set out the rules relating to the function of the Commission and its Committees (all known as Advisory bodies). They can appoint subcommittees known as expert advisory groups, which must include the following:

- The Biological Expert Advisory Group
- The Chemistry, Pharmacy and Standards Expert Advisory Group
- The Pharamacovigilance Expert Advisory Group and such other groups as it considers appropriate.

Thus on 30 October 2005 the CHM was established which combined the functions of the CSM and the Medicines Commission.

The Medicines and Healthcare Products Regulatory Agency replaces the Medicines Control Agency

The Medicines Control Agency (MCA) was the licensing authority under the Act and the European Regulations. It had the function of monitoring the safety and quality of medicines. Its website provided access for health professionals, members of the public, academics, the pharmaceutical industry and journalists. It operated a Defective Medicines Report Centre. On 1 April 2003 the MCA was amalgamated with the Medical Devices Agency to form the Medicines and Healthcare Products Regulatory Agency (MHRA). The DH considered that this merger would provide the opportunity to build on the undoubted strengths of the MCA and would continue to be a world leader in terms of its scientific expertise and regulatory experience (DH 2003). A report by the National Audit Office's *Value for Money* study which was published in January 2003 showed that the MCA had made a major contribution to the protection of public health through an efficient and effective licensing regime. The Adverse Drug Reaction Scheme which it administers is considered below.

As an example of action taken by the MHRA, in January 2005 it announced that the painkiller co-proxamol was being placed on a phased withdrawal basis (DH 2005a). A consultation looking at evidence for the safety and effectiveness of co-proxamol found that the benefits of the medicine did not outweigh the risks and that it should be gradually withdrawn from clinical use. Co-proxamol is associated with 300–400 intentional and accidental fatal overdoses each year.

In April 2005 the Health Select Committee of the House of Commons recommended that the MHRA should be reviewed since too many drugs were being prescribed before their full side-effects were known. In July 2005 MHRA ordered the recall of certain heart drugs after counterfeit drugs were discovered.

Royal Pharmaceutical Society

The Royal Pharmaceutical Society (RPS) is the professional body for pharmacists and pharmaceutical technicians (comparable to the Royal College of Nursing). Previously the Royal Pharmaceutical Society of Great Britain (RPSGB), it had performed both roles of professional regulation and also professional advice for pharmacists. However in 2010 it shed its regulatory functions to become the new professional leadership body for pharmacists in England, Scotland and Wales. A Governance handbook which is updated annually is available on its website (www. rpharms.com). This sets out the rules, responsibilities and constitution of the Society.

General Pharmaceutical Council

In 2010 the General Pharmaceutical Council (GPC) was established as the registration body for pharmacists (comparable to the Nursing and Midwifery Council (NMC) for nurses, midwives and health visitors).

The functions of the RPSGB, which had been established under the Pharmacy Act 1954 to keep the Register for approved pharmacists and to regulate standards of education and entry onto and removal from the Register, were transferred to the GPC in 2010. In addition, the GPC now has the responsibility for maintaining the register of pharmacy premises and for disciplinary control over organisations and pharmacists which carry on retail pharmacy businesses. This was formerly the responsibility of the RPSGB under the Medicines Act 1968. The GPC also has an enforcement role under the Medicines Act of the law in relation to the following activities:

- Sale and supply of medicinal products which are not on a General Sales List (GSL).
- Sale and supply or administration of medicinal products on prescription only.
- Regulations restricting sale, supply or administration of certain medicinal products, except with the authority of specially certified practitioners.
- Regulations restricting sale or supply of medicinal products to persons in a specified class.
- Annual return of premises to the registrar.
- Restrictions on use of titles, descriptions and emblems.
- Regulations imposing further restrictions on titles.

The GPC sets standards to ensure the safe and effective practice of pharmacy. These standards include:

- Standards of conduct, ethics and performance.
- Standards for owners and superintendent pharmacists of retail pharmacy businesses.
- Standards for continuing professional development (CPD).
- Standards for the initial education and training for pharmacists and for pharmacy technicians.
- Ethics and performance standards in relation to retail pharmacy business.

The Minister also has a duty to ensure that the GPC and/or Food and Drug Authorities enforce other provisions of the Medicines Act in relation to specified medicinal products; adulterated medicinal products; regulations on labelling and marking of containers; distinctive colours, shapes and markings of medicinal products; regulations on information on automatic machines; leaflets to be supplied with medicinal products; false or misleading representations on advertisements; and many other regulations.

As an inspection authority the GPC has the right to authorize, in writing, for a person to enter and inspect, take samples and seize goods and documents.

In 2010 the GPC initiated a consultation on a new draft framework for CPD. Further information about the GPC can be found on its website (www. pharmacyregulation.org).

Other state registration bodies

The NMC, the General Medical Council (GMC), the General Dental Council (GDC) and the Health Professions Council (and other such registration bodies) have statutory responsibilities to ensure that medicines are prescribed and administered safely, through the identification of educational standards for entry onto the Register, through setting standards of professional conduct and fitness to practice and through control of the Register. Each registration body has published guidelines for good practice in handling medicines. Each registration body is empowered after due investigation and properly conducted proceedings to remove from the Register practitioners who are considered to pose a threat to public safety.

Criminal proceedings

The enforcement authorities have the power (sometimes after giving 28 days notice to the Minister) to bring criminal proceedings against a defendant for breach of the Medicines Act or statutory regulations.

Each Part of the Medicines Act 1968 creates offences and sets penalties in relation to breach of its provisions.

Advisory Council on Misuse of Drugs

This was established in February 1972 (S1 1971 No 2120) under the Misuse of Drugs Act 1971. Its role is to advise Ministers on the misuse of drugs and keep under review the situation with respect to drugs which are being, or appear to them likely to be, misused and to advise the Minister on action which could be taken. Its role is considered in Chapter 28.

European Medicines Agency

This acts as a drug regulator for Europe. It issued a warning on Cox-2 inhibitors anti-inflammatory drugs in 2005.

Adverse reactions

The system of notification of any adverse reactions is an extremely early warning system of any dangers. The Yellow Card Scheme was established in

1964 following the withdrawal of thalidomide. The DH in its guidelines for the implementation of extended formulary independent nurse prescribing states:

> *If a patient suffers a suspected adverse reaction to a prescribed, Over the Counter or herbal medicine, it should be reported immediately to the GP or consultant. The Yellow Card Adverse Drug Reaction (ADR) Reporting Scheme is a voluntary scheme through which doctors, dentists, coroners and pharmacists notify the Medicines Control Agency (MCA) (Now the MHRA)/Committee of the Safety of Medicines (now the Commission of Human Medicines) of suspected adverse drug reactions. The yellow cards for completion can be found at the back of the BNF/NPF. The MCA/CSM encourage the reporting of all suspected adverse drug reactions to newly licensed medicines that are under intensive monitoring (identified by a — symbol both on the product information for the drug and in the BNF and MIMS) and all serious suspected adverse drug reactions to all other established drugs. Serious reactions include those that are fatal, life threatening, disabling, incapacitating or which result in or prolong hospitalisation and/or are medically significant. Following pilot studies of ADR reporting by nurses, the MCA is currently exploring the possibility of extending the Scheme to give nurse and midwife prescribers the responsibility to report ADRs directly.*

(DH 2002)

As a consequence of the MCA inquiries, the Yellow Card Reporting Scheme was extended to nurses, midwives and health visitors in 2002. At the same time an electronic reporting system was introduced to enable quicker and easier submission of reports.

The Minister for Health, Lord Hunt, stated that a scheme to allow patients to report adverse reactions through NHS Direct and NHS Direct online would be introduced in 2003. Lord Hunt stated:

> *I want the new scheme rolled out across the country during 2003. NHS Direct plays a key role on the way patients access healthcare and it must be right that we use this point of access to be able to access information direct from patients.*

In April 2004 an independent review into access to the Yellow Card scheme chaired by Dr Jeremy Metters made significant recommendations for strengthening the scheme (Metters 2004). In May 2004, on the 40th anniversary of the Yellow Card scheme, the DH announced that patients would be able to directly report unexpected effects of drugs to the MHRA, the medicines watchdog (DH 2004). The MHRA set up different pilot methods of patient reporting, including the Internet and making forms available in GPs surgeries. Forms are available in 4000 GP surgeries and reports can be made online (www.yellowcard.gov.uk).

The MHRA describes the Yellow Card scheme in the following terms;

The Yellow Card Scheme is run by the MHRA and the Commission on Human Medicines (CHM), and is used to collect information from both health professionals and the general public on suspected side effects or ADRs to a medicine. Its continued success depends on the willingness of people to report suspected ADRs. We collect Yellow Card reports from anyone from the UK on both licensed and unlicensed medicines including: prescription medicines vaccines over-the-counter (OTC) medicines ,herbal remedies, swine flu antiviral medicines (Tamiflu or Relenza), swine flu vaccines (Pandemrix, made by GSK or Celvapan, made by Baxter).

There has been concern that there is under reporting of adverse reactions from GPs and in November 2010 the MHRA announced that there would be new arrangements for reporting:

From 3 November 2010, GPs will be able to report suspected adverse drug reaction (ADR) reports to the Yellow Card Scheme directly using their practice software. SystemOne, produced by The Phoenix Partnership, is used in 1,100 GP practices across the UK and is the first GP software to develop a Yellow Card reporting feature that interacts directly with the MHRA database. GPs will be able to quickly populate and securely send an electronic Yellow Card to the MHRA directly from their practice software.

See MHRA website www.mhra.gov.uk for announcement details.

Information to patients

In January 2005 the Health Minister announced that patients and researchers would be able to look at data on the safety of different medicines (DH 2005b). The intention was that the MHRA would publish anonymous data on suspected adverse drug reactions on their website. Researchers would also be able to access more detailed data and measures will be put in place to prevent potential abuse of the information. Every request would be reviewed by an independent committee to make sure that it is ethically and scientifically sound and protects patient confidentiality. In 2010 the MHRA initiated a consultation on on-line information to patients. It stated:

We have commissioned an online discussion site asking whether key information about medicines should be available online. The discussion site, aimed at healthcare professionals and the public, asks whether it is a good idea to make the MHRA's definitive database of patient information leaflets (PILs) and Summaries of Product Characteristics (SPCs)available online and, if so, what the site should look like.

Every medicine pack includes a PIL, which provides information on using the medicine safely. PILs are based on the SPCs - a description of a medicinal product's properties and the conditions attached to its use. We are considering making this information accessible via the internet, so that members of the public can look up key information about medicines, such as ingredients and side effects. We would also like to know the benefits to the public and healthcare professionals of having an authoritative, up-to-date database available at their fingertips.

(MHRA website www.mhra.gov.uk)

National Patient Safety Agency

The National Patient Safety Agency (NPSA) was established as a special health authority in 2001 following the publication of a report which recommended the setting up of a national system for the NHS to learn from its mistakes and problems which affect patient safety. The report entitled *An Organisation with a Memory* (DH 2000) was written by an expert group chaired by Professor Liam Donaldson, Chief Medical Officer. It recommended that the NHS and its constituent organisations should have the capability to learn from untoward incidents and service failures so that similar occurrences can be avoided in the future. The NPSA undertook the role of being the organisation to which a new NHS mandatory reporting system would report all failures, mistakes, errors and near-misses in healthcare. Since its establishment the NPSA has issued patient safety alerts including warnings about potassium chloride concentrate solutions; the misplacement of nasogastric feeding tubes; the standardisation of crash call numbers to 2222; and risks associated with oral methotrexate. It cooperates with other agencies such as the MHRA and the Royal College of Surgeons to make the NHS safer. Further information can be obtained from the NPSA website (www. npsa.org.uk). The NPSA welcomed the study conducted by the British Medical Journal (2004) into adverse drug reactions and is supporting the work of the MHRA in tracking adverse drug reactions. The NPSA is also looking at patient safety incidents where the outcome for the patient was unintended, but could have been prevented given knowledge of the likelihood of such reactions occurring. The NPSA will work with the National Programme for Information Technology in the NHS to establish safer systems for warning about when a drug should not be prescribed in certain combinations or conditions. (See also Chapter 6 and the figures on incidents of wrong administration and Chapter 19 on the NPSA alert about preventing accidental overdose with intravenous potassium.)

NHS Trusts were criticised by Sir Liam Donaldson, the Chief Medical Officer for the DH in his annual report on 2004 for failing to heed the warnings issued by the NPSA and MHRA (DH 2005c). NPSA has put great emphasis on being open about incidents in the NHS and the importance of communicating with patients and their families and carers. In 2009 it published guidance on being open entitled *Being open: communicating patient safety incidents with patients, their families and carers* (NPSA 2009).

Future developments

A review by the DH on *Liberating the NHS: Report of the Arm's Length Bodies* has made significant recommendations for changing some of the organisations considered in this chapter) in order to rationalise the numbers of ad hoc bodies and reduce expenditure. (DH 2010). The Medicines Products Healthcare Regulatory Authority will be retained as an executive agency of the DH and will be expected to undertake its regulatory duties in the most cost effective way. It is largely self-funding through the fees it charges. The NPSA is to be abolished. Its safety functions will transfer to the NHS Commissioning Board; its National Research Ethics Service functions will probably be transferred to a single research regulator and its National Clinical Assessment Service is to become self-funding over the next two to three years.

Application of the law to the situation in Box 3.1

The claimant failed in her claim. The judge ruled against her on the grounds shown in Box 3.2. Whilst this particular claimant failed because the judge held that no common law duty was owed to her on the facts, the judge did not rule out the possibility that in other circumstances a claim against the Secretary of State in respect of his statutory duties under the Medicines Act 1968 could succeed. It would of course be a very different situation if after the announcement, a doctor or nurse had prescribed aspirin to the child. That could clearly constitute negligence and give the mother a right to sue on the child's behalf.

Box 3.2 Smith v. Secretary of State: Judge's decision

1. The decision on 3 and 4 April 1986 to postpone issuing an interim warning was to be categorised in law as a discretionary policy decision as opposed to an operational one. Such a decision was not justiciable in private law cases and it would be contrary to the public interest to allow them to be so.

2. Accordingly, and on the facts of the case, neither the CSM nor the Secretary of State owed the claimant a common law duty in respect of the decisions allegedly negligent even if fault could be established.

3. This was not to say that the Secretary of State or CSM could never be liable at common law for breach of a duty of care to an individual member of the public for failure to properly exercise statutory powers and duties.

4. In any event the postponement on 3 and 4 April 1986 was reasonably justifiable. On one side of the equation there was the real risk of grave or fatal injury to two or three children from the delay; on the other the reasonable expectation of the undoubted benefit of a coherent coordinated campaign giving a clear message to both professionals and the general public.

Conclusions

The regulation, inspection and control of the medicinal products which are given to patients form a significant part of our laws relating to the care of the patient. Perhaps the most important control from the point of view of the registered practitioner is the fact that the individual health professional is personally and professionally accountable to her registration body for her conduct, and if there are therefore any concerns which she has about the safety of any products which she administers or prescribes she must follow reasonably acceptable practice in ensuring that the patient is not harmed.

Key points

■ The Secretary of State and his equivalent in Scotland and Northern Ireland have responsibility for the administration of the Medicines Act 1968.

■ The CHM is a statutory expert body to advise the Minister on matters arising under the Act.

■ Committees may be set up under section 4.

■ The MHRA has been formed from the amalgamation of the MCA and the Medical Devices Agency.

■ The GPC is the registration body for pharmacists and fulfills other statutory responsibilities of control and enforcement.

■ The RPS is the professional body for pharmacists. Other State registration bodies have responsibilities to ensure registered practitioners are educated in the supply and administration of medicines and comply with the law.

■ Healthcare professionals have responsibilities under the Yellow Card warning scheme of adverse drug reactions.

References

Department of Health (2000) *An Organisation with A Memory*. Report of an expert group chaired by Professor Liam Donaldson, Chief Medical Officer, London

Department of Health (2002) *Extending independent nurse prescribing within the NHS in England: A guide for implementation*. London

Department of Health (2003) press release No 2003/0018, Medicines Control Agency. 15 January 2003. London

Department of Health (2004) press release 2004/0163, *Patients to play central role in drug safety*, May 2004. London

Department of Health (2005a) press release No 2005/0034, *MHRA withdraws the pain killer co-proxamol*. January 2005. London

Department of Health (2005b) press release 2005/0015, *Patients set to benefit from better access to medicines safety data*, January 2005. London

Department of Health (2005c) *Annual report on 2004* by Donaldson L. Chief Medical Officer. London

Department of Health (2010) *Liberating the NHS: Report of the Arm's Length Bodies* London Crown.

Metters, J (2004) *Report of an Independent Review of Access to the Yellow Card Scheme* April 2004 London: TSO

National Audit Office (2003) *Value for Money (January 2003)*. London

NPSA news 1 July 2004. *British Medical Journal.*

National Patient Safety Agency (2009) *Being open: communicating patient safety incidents with patients, their families and carers*. London

Royal Society of Pharmacists (Annual Publication) *RPSA Governance Handbook* (www. rpharms.com). (Accessed March 2011)

Websites

DH website http://www.dh.gov. uk/

GPC website www.pharmacyregulation.org

MCA website www.open.gov.uk/mca/mcahome.htm.

MHRA The Yellow Card Scheme website www.yellowcard.gov.uk

MHRA website www.mhra.gov.uk

NPSA website www.npsa.org.uk.

CHAPTER 4

The *British National Formulary* and other sources

Box 4.1 A new drug

Brenda, a staff nurse on the children's ward, notices that a junior doctor has written a patient up for a drug of which she has never heard. She asks the ward sister whether she should administer it. The ward sister says 'Yes'. What is the law?

Introduction

It is essential that every registered practitioner has easy access to information about medicines and their contraindications and also knows how to obtain further advice when necessary. In the administration and prescribing of medicines, it is essential, as in so many areas of professional conduct, to know the limits of one's knowledge and competence; to know when to seek further advice and information; and how this can be accessed. This chapter seeks to set out some of the main sources of information available to a registered practitioner.

The *British National Formulary/Nurse Prescribers' Formulary*

The *British National Formulary* (BNF) is published by the British Medical Association (BMA) and the Royal Pharmaceutical Society (RPS) in association with the Community Practitioners and Health Visitors Association and the Royal College of Nursing (RCN). It is updated every six months and every registered practitioner should ensure that they have easy access to an updated copy. They are available from the Pharmaceutical Press with updates are also available via the BNF website (www.bnf.org). A BNF for children's medicines was first published in 2005, and is revised every 12 months, with updates online (see Chapter 15). A *Nurse Prescribers' Extended Formulary* had been prepared but this was discontinued in May 2006 under the Medicines for Human Use

(Prescribing) (Miscellaneous Amendments) Order, SI 2006 No 915. Qualified nurse independent prescribers are now able to prescribe any licensed medicine for any medical condition within their competence, including some controlled drugs.

Every drug which a healthcare professional is asked to administer or to prescribe would be contained in the BNF. The BNF gives details of the doses to be administered. It also lists side effects and contra-indications of which the nurse should be aware. The nurse should know her way through the BNF, being familiar with the categories of drugs and their different families. She should also be aware of any warnings about drugs. The BNF now includes the *Nurse Prescribers' Formulary* (NPF) which is set out at the beginning of the BNF. The book covers how to use the NPF/BNF; name changes following the EC directive (Directive 92/27/EEC) which requires the use of non-proprietary names; and then sets out guidance on nurse prescribing, the nurse prescribers' formulary for district nurses and health visitors and the nurse prescribers' extended formulary. The law relating to nurse prescribing is considered in Chapters 9 and 10, but as part of the information available to the registered practitioner, it is worth noting the following reports about nurse prescribing.

The initial report of June Crown relating to community nurse prescribing was published December 1989 and set out the recommendations of the report of the advisory group on nurse prescribing (known as the first Crown Report (DH 1989a)). Subsequently June Crown was asked to chair a further Committee and make recommendations on the Prescribing, Supply and Administration of Medicines to the Department of Health (DH 1989b). An interim report dealt with prescribing under patient group directions (PGD) or group protocols (DH 1998c). This was followed by the final Crown Report in 1999 (DH 1999).

Monthly Index of Medical Specialities

The *Monthly Index of Medical Specialities* (MIMS) is is available from MIMS Subscriptions and is a useful supplement to the NPF/BNF.

British Pharmacopoeia

Under section 4 (as amended) of the Medicines Act 1968, which enables committees to be set up under the Commission on Humans Medicines (CHM) (see Chapter 3), a British Pharmacopoeia Commission had been set up. This Commission prepares new editions of the *British Pharmacopoeia* (BP). This encyclopaedia sets out information on the descriptions and standards of the following:

- Substances and articles (whether medical products or not) which are or may be used in the practice of medicine, surgery, dentistry and midwifery.
- Substances and articles used in the manufacture of substances listed above.
- Lists of approved names for substances and articles (British Approved Names) which are placed at the head of monographs in the BP or in the compendium.

It is a criminal offence for a person to sell or supply a medicinal product by a particular name if that name is at the head of the relevant monograph in a specified publication and the product does not comply with the standard specified in that monograph. The product must also comply with the standard specified of any active ingredient named in the product.

A new BP website (www.pharmacopoeia.co.uk) described as a single authoritative source for information on the BP, was launched on 8 September 2008. The new website offers a cost-effective subscription service allowing access to new and revised monographs, omitted from previous editions of the BP and typical chromatograms published in the hard copy BP.

European Pharmacopoeia

This is published under the direction of the Council of Europe and sets standards for medicinal products. If there is any discrepancy between it and the BP, the European one takes precedence.

Textbooks

In addition to the official publications, there are some textbooks which are of interest and benefit to the registered practitioner. These include Martingdale *The Complete Drug* (2009); *Dale and Appelbe's Pharmacy Law and Ethics* (2005) and an annual publication by the Royal Pharmaceutical Society (RPS) M*edicines, Ethics and Practice: A Guide for Pharmacists*. In addition there are of course a wealth of books for registered practitioners covering medicines such as Tiziani's *Havard's Nursing Guide to Drugs* (2010). However very little in these books covers the law which applies to medicinal products (see Galbraith 2007 for further reading).

The hospital pharmacist

Most hospitals have instituted a system whereby a pharmacist visits the wards at regular intervals and checks the prescriptions written up for the patient. In addition the pharmacist is available to provide advice for all doctors and nurses on dosages of medicines, contra-indications and best practice in the prescribing and administration of medicines.

Poly-pharmacy and the interaction of the many drugs which may be taken by one patient is a developing science, and where unfavourable interactions are feared between different products the pharmacist should be consulted on the advisability of giving the patient these different preparations, and of the timing of the administration of them.

The community pharmacist employed by the primary care trust

Some Primary Care Trusts (PCT) and community trusts may have the services of a community pharmacist who can provide advice and help on the supply and administration of medicines to patients in the community. In addition, the community pharmacist is available to provide guidance to nursing homes and other residential care homes.

Retail pharmacists

Retail pharmacists provide a well-recognised advice service for patients seeking to buy General Sales List medicinal products as well as pharmacy-only products. They also have professional duties in relation to the dispensing of products to ensure that reasonable professional standards are followed. Nurse Prescribers in the community will find that the retail pharmacist will be a valuable source of information about the medicinal products they may wish to prescribe. The DH guidelines on the implementation of independent nurse prescribing (DH 2002) recognise that pharmacists are a useful source of help and advice to any prescriber, particularly on matters of pharmacology, drug usage and product selection. They will know the costs, availability and pack sizes of prescribed items. The DH reminds nurse and midwifery prescribers that pharmacists have legal and ethical obligations which mean that they may need to contact prescribers – sometimes urgently – to confirm an aspect of the prescription, return it for amendment or even to refrain from dispensing it. An up-to-date contact telephone number should be included (in the address box) on all prescriptions. (See Chapter 29 for further information on the role of retail pharmacists in primary healthcare.)

Drug warnings

The Yellow Card System and its expansion to nurses and midwives was considered in Chapter 3. All health practitioners should ensure that they receive notification from the Medicines and Healthcare Products Regulatory Agency (MHRA) of any adverse drug reaction warnings and that they know in turn how to bring adverse reactions to the attention of the MHRA.

Answering the situation in Box 4.1

No registered practitioner should ever administer a drug of which she has no knowledge. The nurse should check with the BNF details of the drug which has been prescribed. She should check the dosage against the prescription form and should look at the contra-indications listed in the BNF and compare them with what is known about the patient and what is in the patient's records. Finally, she should talk to the prescribing doctor to get further information and if necessary the hospital pharmacist until she is certain that she would be following sound professional practice in administering the medicine according to the prescription. If her inquiries do not resolve all her doubts then she should not administer the drug until she is satisfied that she is following sound professional practice. She would not be justified in taking the word of the ward sister that the drug was safe. If she administers a drug, then she must be personally satisfied that it is safe to do so. She is personally and professionally responsible for her actions and cannot rely upon the fact that she was obeying orders, whether from a doctor or senior nurse, unless the situation was an emergency one.

Key points

■ The administration of medicines requires up-to-date comprehensive knowledge of the medicinal product being given.

- The BNF/NPF provides essential guidance on all medicinal products which are to be administered or prescribed as well as guidance on prescriptions and special patient groups.
- The BP and EP provide definitions of the officially recognised medicinal substances in use.
- Textbooks on pharmacology provide useful background reading and can also be used for reference.
- Pharmacists, whether in hospital, the community or retail businesses, are an invaluable source of assistance.

References

Appelbe G, Wingfield J. (eds.) (2005) *Dale and Appelbe's Pharmacy Law and Ethics* 8th edn

British Pharmacopoeia Commission (Annual) *British Pharmacopoeia*

Department of Health (1989a) Advisory Group on Nurse Prescribing (chaired by June Crown) *Report of Nurse Prescribing and Supply.*

Department of Health (1998b) *Review of Prescribing, Supply and Administration of Medicines: A Report on the Supply and Administration of Medicines under Group Protocols* (Crown 1). London

Department of Health (1998c) Report on the *Supply and administration of medicines under group protocols* Crown first report. The Stationery Office.London

Department of Health (1999) *Review of Prescribing, Supply and Administration of Medicines Final Report* (Crown Report) London

Department of Health (2002) *Extending independent nurse prescribing within the NHS in England: A guide for implementation.* London

Galbraith A, et al (2007) *Fundamentals of Pharmacology: an applied approach for nurses and health* 2nd edn. Pearson Education

Harlow and Downie G et al (2007) *Pharmacology and Drug Management for Nurses* 4th edn. Churchill Livingstone, Edinburgh

Martingdale (2009) *The Complete Drug Reference* 36th edition March 2009

Tiziani A (2010) *Havard's Nursing Guide to Drugs*. Mosby Elsevier Edinburgh.

CHAPTER 5

Administration of medicines I

Box 5.1 IV drugs out of date

Heather was drawing up antibiotics which were to be given intravenously to a patient suffering from a severe chest infection. She had to mix the antibiotic with a saline solution and then administer it to the patient. She had a lot of patients to care for and failed to notice that the expiry date on the antibiotic had passed. The patient subsequently suffered harm. Is Heather to blame?

Introduction

Even the most simple, the most common, medicine can cause harm if given to the wrong patient or by the wrong means. Aspirin, which many people may take daily to prevent heart attacks (and more recently, cancer), could cause an allergic reaction in those who are sensitive to it and since 1986 should not be given to children. This chapter looks at the principles for the administration of medicines and at some of the common errors in the administration of medicines. The Nursing and Midwifery Council (NMC) in its guidelines for the administration of medicines had warned against the mechanistic administration of medicines:

The administration of medicines is an important aspect of the professional practice of persons whose names are on the Council's register. It is not solely a mechanistic task to be performed in strict compliance with the written prescription of a medical practitioner (now independent/supplementary prescriber). It requires thought and the exercise of professional judgement... (NMC 2007)

This quote is from the NMC's *Standards for medicines management* published in 2007 which replaced the 2004 *Guidelines for the administration of medicines*.

Standards for the administration of medicines

The NMC in its *Standards for medicines management* (2007) has set out Standards 8 to 16 for the practice of administration of medicines which are shown in Box 5.2.

Box 5.2 NMC standards for the practice of administration of medicines

SECTION 4

Standard 8

As a registrant, in exercising your professional accountability in the best interests of your patients:

- You must be certain of the identity of the patient to whom the medicine is to be administered.
- You must check that the patient is not allergic to the medicine before administering it.
- You must know the therapeutic uses of the medicine to be administered, its normal dosage, side effects, precautions and contra-indications.
- You must be aware of the patient's plan of care (care plan/pathway).
- You must check that the prescription or the label on medicine dispensed is clearly written and unambiguous.
- You must check the expiry date (where it exists) of the medicine to be administered.
- You must have considered the dosage, weight where appropriate, method of administration, route and timing.
- You must administer or withhold medicine in the context of the patient's condition (e.g. digoxin not usually to be given if pulse below 60) and co-existing therapies e.g. physiotherapy.
- You must contact the prescriber or another authorised prescriber without delay where contra-indications to the prescribed medicine are discovered, where the patient develops a reaction to the medicine, or where assessment of the patient indicates that the medicine is no longer suitable (See Standard 25).

- You must make a clear, accurate and immediate record of all medicine administered, intentionally withheld or refused by the patient, ensuring the signature is clear and legible; it is also your responsibility to ensure that a record is made when delegating the task of administering medicine.

In addition:

- Where medication is not given, the reason for not doing so must be recorded.
- You may administer with a single signature any Prescription Only Medicine (POM), General Sales List (GSL) or Pharmacy (P) medication.

In respect of Controlled Drugs (CD):

- These should be administered in line with relevant legislation and local standard operating procedures.
- It is recommended that for the administration of CD a secondary signatory is required within secondary care and similar healthcare settings.
- In a patient's home, where a registrant is administering a CD that has already been prescribed and dispensed to that patient, obtaining a secondary signatory should be based on local risk assessment.
- Although normally the second signatory should be another registered health care professional (for example doctor, pharmacist, dentist) or student nurse or midwife, in the interest of patient care, where this is not possible a second suitable person who has been assessed as competent may sign. It is good practice that the second signatory witnesses the whole administration process.

For Guidance, go to www.dh.gov.uk and search for Safer Management of Controlled Drugs: Guidance on Standard Operating Procedures (DH 2011).

- In cases of direct patient administration of oral medication from stock in a substance misuse clinic, it must be a registered nurse who administers, signed by a second signatory (assessed as competent), who is then supervised by the registrant as the patient receives and consumes the medication.
- You must clearly countersign the signature of the student when supervising a student in the administration of medicines.

Standard 9

As a registrant you are responsible for the initial and continued assessment of patients who are self-administering and have continuing responsibility for recognising and acting upon changes in a patient's condition with regards to safety of the patient and others.

Standard 10

In the case of children, when arrangements have been made for parents/carers or patients to administer their own medicinal products prior to discharge or rehabilitation, the registrant should ascertain that the medicinal product has been taken as prescribed.

Standard 11

In exceptional circumstances, where medication has been previously prescribed and the prescriber is unable to issue a new prescription, but where changes to the dose are considered necessary, the use of information technology (such as fax, text message or email) may be used but must confirm any change to the original prescription.

Standard 12

As a registrant, you must ensure that there are protocols in place to ensure patient confidentiality and documentation of any text received including: complete text message, telephone number (it was sent from), the time sent, any response given, and the signature and date when received by the registrant.

Standard 13

Where medication has been prescribed within a range of dosages, it is acceptable for registrants to titrate dosages according to patient response and symptom control and to administer within the prescribed range.

Standard 14

Registrants must not prepare substances for injection in advance of their immediate use or to administer medication drawn into a syringe or container by another practitioner when not in the presence of the patient.

Standard 15

Registrants should never administer any medication that has not been prescribed, or acquired over the internet without a valid prescription.

Standard 16

Registrants must assess the patient's suitability and understanding of how to use an appropriate compliance aid safely.

Who can administer?

Only a nurse who has knowledge and competence should be administering different medicinal products to patients. In addition, the nurse should ensure that she has the necessary skill and training to administer the medicinal products required. Where the nurse delegates the activity to another person she should ensure that the delegation and supervision are appropriate. The nurse would be personally and professionally responsible for any inappropriate delegation and supervision.

Common errors in administration

Box 5.3 sets out a check list for nurses to use before a drug is administered.

The correct patient

Chapters 12–16 consider the issues relating to consent and the capacity to consent: and the differences in law between the mentally competent adult, the child,

Box 5.3 Checklist for the administration of drugs

A) The correct patient. Consent?
- Capacity to consent:
- Child
- Mentally ill or handicapped
- Pre-existing disability or contra-indications
- Warnings about side-effects; drowsiness, etc.

B) Correct drug
- Side-effects
- Timing
- Special precautions
- Any contra-indications
- Expiry date

C) Correct dose
- Type of patient
- Physique of patient
- Allergy frequency

D) Correct site and method of administration
Injection: skin, muscular, vein, artery, site on body

E) Correct procedure
- Level of competence of nurse
- Skill, training
- Appropriate delegation
- Safe equipment, sound sterile procedure
- Correct gauge of needle, form of drug and transport

F) Correct record-keeping of dose, time, drug and method

mentally ill detained patient or mentally incapacitated patient. In this chapter we discuss how the nurse should ensure that she is giving the medication to the correct person and whether there are any contra-indications. In a busy ward with a high turnover of patients a nurse might not get to know the patients very well and the safest way of ensuring that the medication is being given to the correct person is to check the patient's identity tag. Even asking the patient if she is Beryl Jones might not be a safe method of checking: patients, fearful of hospitals and slightly deaf, may be only too willing to agree to any question asked by a nurse. Even using the name on the bed may not be safe, since patients may sometimes sit on beds other than their own, and name labels attached to the beds are sometimes not changed.

The nurse should also check that the particular drug is suitable for that particular patient and that there are no pre-existing disabilities or contra-indications which would make the drug inappropriate.

The nurse must also ensure that she gives the necessary information to the patient about the possible side-effects (e.g. drowsiness or minor headaches) and what the patient should do to minimise them. Giving information to the patient is considered in Chapter 13.

Correct drug

Once the nurse is satisfied that she is dealing with the correct patient, she must be sure that she is giving the correct drug to the patient. This means that she must be familiar with that particular medicinal product. If necessary, she must look it up in the *British National Formulary* (BNF) (see Chapter 4). She should check whether there are any side-effects of that particular medicine of which the patient should be warned. She should check against the prescription and the BNF whether the drug is being given at the right time and whether there are any special precautions in how the drug should be administered. For example, some drugs should be given with liquid, others before or after a main meal. She should once again check whether there are any contra-indications why that particular drug should not be given to that patient. She should also note the expiry date on the label and ensure that it is within that date.

Correct dose

Having satisfied herself that the medicinal product is correct and is being given to the correct patient, the nurse should ensure that she is giving the correct dose. It is important that she understands metric measurements, especially where she has to make up the preparation in any way (see below). She should check the prescription requirements against the BNF standards and the type, physique and age of patient. Where there is an incompatibility, check this with the prescribing doctor and if necessary the pharmacist until she is satisfied that the dose is correct. She should also check whether there is any history of allergies and whether the patient has had this preparation before.

Correct site and method of administration

The nurse must check the prescribed route of the medicinal product against the instructions on the label and ensure that these are in agreement and that she is following the correct instructions.

- Is the drug to be given by injection, and if so is it through the skin or is it intramuscular?
- Should it be given as an intravenous infusion, or should it be by an arterial route?
- If it is to be given through the skin or muscle, on which part of the body should it be given?
- If it is an oral preparation, is it at the right time, at the right interval from the last administration of the drug and given in the correct format?

Correct procedure

The nurse is required to ensure that she is personally competent to administer the particular product. She should also ensure that she is using safe equipment and following sound sterile procedure. Where she is giving the drug by injection she should ensure that she is using the correct gauge of needle for that particular patient and that particular product and that the form of drug and transport are appropriate.

Documentation

Finally it is the duty of the nurse who has administered the drug to ensure that she makes a correct record of the dose, the time, the drug and the method of administration. Record keeping and medicines are considered in detail in Chapter 25.

Innumeracy

The United Kingdom Central Council for Nursing, Midwifery and Health Visiting (UKCC), (which has since been replaced by the NMC), advised in 2000 that student nurses should be given more mathematics training following claims that drug calculation errors could be putting patients at risk (Coombes 1999). Professor Bryn Davis, a UKCC member, stated that the GCSE maths exam which is a compulsory entry requirement for training, is failing to prepare nurses for complex drug calculations. An example of the fatal effects of miswriting decimals was seen in October 2000, when it was alleged that a baby in a neo-natal unit died when a decimal point in a drug prescription was entered in the wrong place (Hurst 2000). The death was reported to the coroner.

In its guidance on Standard 8 in its *Standard for medicines management*, the NMC (2007) states:

Drug calculations

Some drug administrations can require complex calculations to ensure that the correct volume or quantity of medication is administered. In these situations, it is good practice for a second practitioner (a registered professional) to check the calculation independently in order to minimise the risk of error. The use of calculators to determine the volume or quantity of medication should not act as a substitute for arithmetical knowledge and skill.

PRN medication

PRN medication (*pro re nata* – 'as required, whenever necessary') enables a doctor to write the patient up for medication, but leave to the nurse the discretion as to when, if at all, the drug should be administered, depending on the patient's condition. The value of the system is that it allows the patient to have a drug when necessary, without calling the doctor for the specific purpose of prescribing the drug for it to be administered immediately. Thus pain relief drugs, sleeping tablets, and indigestion drugs can be prescribed in case the patient might need such help. Unfortunately, the doctor does not always ensure that sufficient information is given on the drugs sheet. Thus the doctor might fail to give the maximum amount

51

that can be given in any 24-hour period. The doctor might also fail to specify the dose and the intervals at which it can be given. The hospital pharmacist should check the drugs sheets regularly to ensure that all the relevant information is present, and the nurse should not administer these drugs without first checking the limitations. It is also essential that every drug that is administered PRN should be recorded when given, as overdoses could easily occur if a record is not kept. Each hospital should have a policy relating to PRN medication.

Answering the situation in Box 5.1

Heather is at fault in not ensuring that the antibiotic had not gone beyond its expiry date. Even though it is easy to see how she could have missed that information, since she is under pressure to care for so many patients, it is no defence to a patient who is harmed by negligence that the ward was too busy to provide a reasonable standard of care for her or him (see Chapter 20). In addition, there would also appear to be others at fault, since there should have been a system in place to ensure that the drugs cupboard should be regularly checked to ensure that medicines close to their expiry date were removed and dealt with separately. Hospital policy should identify whether the checking of ward stocks was the responsibility of the ward sister or the pharmacy department.

Conclusions

The number of occasions when a nurse has looked back after a tragedy arising from mistakes in administration and thought 'If only I had...' are countless. Sadly, once the error has occurred, it is often too late then to repair the harm to the patient. Strategies are essential to improve mathematical skills (Wright 2004). Chapters 6 and 7 considers some of the tragedies which have occurred through mistakes in prescribing and in administration and also look at the action which should be taken when the nurse is aware of an error.

Key points

- The NMC has provided *Standards for medicines management.*
- A check list should be closely followed to ensure that the correct medicine is given to the correct patient, in the correct format, in the correct site, at the correct time, following the correct procedure.
- PRN medication administration should conform with local policies.
- The nurse should ensure that documentation on the administration of medicines is completed as soon as possible.

References

Coombes, R. (1999) Nurses need a dose of maths. *Nursing Times*, **96**(24), 4–5.

Department of Health (2000) *An Organisation with A Memory.* Report of an expert group chaired by Professor Liam Donaldson, Chief Medical Officer. London

Department of Health (2011) *Safer Management of Controlled Drugs: Guidance on Standard Operating Procedures* (www.dh.gov.uk) Accessed 17.3.2011. London

Hurst, G. (2000) Baby dies after one decimal point drug dose error. *The Times*, 11 October.

Nursing and Midwifery Council (2004) *Guidelines for the administration of medicines.* London

Nursing and Midwifery Council (2007) *Standards for medicines management.* London

Wright, K. (2004) An investigation to find strategies to improve student nurses' maths skills. *British Journal of Nursing*, **13**(21), 1280–1284. London

Websites

Department of Health website www.dh.gov.uk

CHAPTER 6

Administration of medicines 2

Box 6.1 Situation: error in administration

Julia, a staff nurse on the ophthalmic ward, unfortunately administered the patient's eye medicine to the wrong eye. She panicked when she realised her mistake and simply carried on and put the medicine in the correct eye. The patient noticed what had happened and said 'Two lots today then'. Julia did not report it. What is the law?

Introduction

The last chapter considered the principles to be followed in the administration of medicines. This chapter looks at some of the cases which have arisen as a result of errors in the administration of medicines, the Nursing and Midwifery Council (NMC) guidelines on managing errors and at the difference between the use of ward stocks and medication dispensed on a personal basis.

Illegible writing on the prescription

Many cases of harm to patients have resulted from the person administering the drug failing to read the prescription correctly as a result of bad handwriting. The following is an example of a tragedy which need never have occurred if more care had been taken. The nurse should always check with the prescribing doctor, or if necessary the pharmacist, if there are any doubts about the content of the prescription and if anything is illegible.

Daonil or Amoxil

One of three items on a prescription was for 21 Amoxil tablets. The pharmacist misread this as Daonil. The patient suffered hypoglycaemia and sustained permanent brain damage. The pharmacist said that he had read the 'A' for a 'D' and the 'x' for an 'n'. There were other indications from which the pharmacist should have realised that his interpretation was for the wrong drug: the other drugs which were also prescribed, the dosage and the fact that the patient paid for his prescription (Daonil is a drug used by diabetic patients who do not have to pay prescription charges.). Both doctor and pharmacist were held liable for the harm which befell the patient. The doctor was held 25% liable. Damages totalled £137,547 (Prendergast v. Sam & Dee Ltd [1989] 1 Med LR 36).

Dealing with illegible handwriting

Nurses often complain that they are unable to read the doctors' writing on the drug charts. If they have any doubt about the drug prescribed they should not administer it unless they have checked it with the doctor who wrote it, his superior, or in certain circumstances, the pharmacist. If the nurse fails to double-check illegible writing she could herself become liable. Clinical governance is concerned with the quality of care provided to patients; good standards of documentation, including handwriting, are essential if effective communication is to take place between health professionals. It therefore follows that bad handwriting could become a problem for those responsible for clinical governance to rectify through its management processes.

Instructions by telephone

Box 6.2 Night instructions

Ward Sister Dury was the night sister at a small geriatric hospital which was served by GPs. One night she was very worried about the condition of a frail patient whose blood pressure and temperature were raised. She telephoned the duty GP and expressed her anxieties to him. He was of the opinion that she need not be concerned and suggested that the patient should be given paracetamol. She was reluctant to take instructions over the telephone, but decided that, since he would not visit, there was little else she could do for the patient. She gave the dose of paracetamol, but unfortunately the patient's condition deteriorated and she again telephoned the GP, who did not visit until 9.00 a.m., by which time the patient had died.

The situation shown in Box 6.2 is not uncommon. What is the position of the ward sister in Box 6.2? Should she have taken instructions over the telephone? The NMC *Standards on medicines management* (2007) states:

Administering medication from a remote prescription/direction to administer
Standard 11

In exceptional circumstances, where medication (NOT including Controlled Drugs (CD)) has been previously prescribed and the prescriber is unable to issue a new prescription, but where changes to the dose are considered necessary, the use of information technology (such as fax, text message or email) may be used but must confirm any change to the original prescription.

Guidance on standard 11 states that a verbal order is not acceptable on its own. The fax or email prescription/direction must be stapled to the patient's existing medication chart.

Standard 12 covers text messaging and states:

As a registrant, you must ensure that there are protocols in place to ensure patient confidentiality and documentation of any text received include: complete text message, telephone number (it was sent from), the time sent, any response given, and the signature and date when received by the registrant.

The Guidance on standard 12 recognises that an order to administer medication by text messaging is an increasing possibility and states that:

A second signature – normally another registrant but where this is not possible another person – should sign to confirm the documentation agrees with the text message.

It would now be possible for PGD to be drawn up so that following appropriate training, the ward sister could prescribe and administer against an agreed protocol. (PGD are considered in Chapter 8.)

The wrong drug

A coroner called for the urgent introduction of measures which would make it impossible to inject patients with the wrong drug during routine surgery (A Correspondent' (2001) Coroner calls for drug error safeguard. The Times, 2 May 2001). A consultant anaesthetist had intended to inject replacement body fluids into a 74-year-old patient, who was undergoing an operation to repair an aortic aneurysm. Instead, he attached a bag of Bupivicaine, a powerful painkiller, to an intravenous drip, which led to a cardiac catastrophe. The drug should only have been given via an epidural catheter inserted into the spine. An internal report by the Brighton Health Care NHS Trust and a report by the Royal College of Anaesthetists (available at www.rcoa.ac.uk) recommended that drugs given intravenously be kept separate from those injected into the spine.

National Patient Safety Agency

In 2007 the National Patient Safety Agency (NPSA) issued an alert in relation to epidural injections as a result of three deaths being reported. It gave the following advice to all healthcare organisations to minimise risk when administering epidural injections and infusions, including:
- Labelling infusion bags and syringes.
- Minimising the likelihood of confusion between different types and strengths.
- Reducing the risk of the wrong medicine being selected. Using clearly labelled epidural administration sets and catheters that distinguish them from those used for intravenous and other routes.
- Using infusion pumps and syringe driver devices for epidural infusions that are easily distinguishable from those used for intravenous and other types of infusion.
- Ensuring all staff involved in epidural therapy are adequately trained.

A *Rapid Response Report* published in 2008 by the NPSA alerted all healthcare professionals to the risks of prescribing, dispensing or administering intravenous heparin flush solutions to NHS patients. It set out the actions which healthcare organisations should take.

A report published in 2009 by the NPSA calculated that at least 100 patients are dying or suffering serious harm each year after healthcare workers give them the wrong medication (available at www.npsa.nhs.uk). There were 860,000 incidents regarding medication being reported in 2007, the number doubling in two years. However only 4% had caused serious harm. Causes of the mistakes were workload pressures, long hours, fatigue and reduced staff levels. These figures related to voluntary reports of incidents and the actual figure could be much higher. Over 82% of the incidents occurred in the administration or dispensing of medicines by nurses or pharmacists. Of the 100 deaths, 41 were caused in the administration of drugs to patients by nurses and 32 were due to prescribing (David 2009). Agyemang, Owusu and White (2010) analyse medication errors by nursing staff and suggests ways in which nursing practice can be improved to prevent their occurrence.

Managing errors

There is a danger that if a nurse knows that she has made a mistake in administering medication, her fear of the repercussions might lead her to ignoring the mistake and hoping that it will never come to light. This is, however, a dangerous and unprofessional attitude to take, since if she is prepared to admit her mistake and take immediate action to mitigate any harm to the patient, she may be able to limit the danger to the patient and also lessen the repercussions to herself, personally and professionally. The NMC in Section 9 of its *Standards for medicines management* (2007) on the management of adverse events states:

> *Standard 24*
>
> *As a registrant, if you make an error you must take any action to prevent any potential harm to the patient and report as soon as possible to the prescriber, your line manager or employer (according to local policy) and document your actions. Midwives should also inform their named Supervisor of Midwives.*

In the Guidance on standard 24 the NMC states:

> *The NMC supports the use of a thorough, open and multi-disciplinary approach to investigating adverse events, where improvements to local practice in the administration of medicinal products can be discussed, identified and disseminated. It is important that an open culture exists in order to encourage the immediate reporting of errors or incidents in the administration of medicines. The NMC believes that all errors and incidents require a thorough and careful investigation at a local level, taking full account of the context and circumstances and the position of the practitioner involved. Such incidents require sensitive management and a comprehensive assessment of all the circumstances before a professional and managerial decision is reached on the appropriate way to proceed. If a practicing midwife makes or identifies a drug error or incident, she should also inform her Supervisor of Midwives as soon as possible after the event.*

The NMC also made it clear that it distinguishes between two different situations:

When considering allegations of misconduct arising from errors in the administration of medicines, the NMC takes great care to distinguish between those cases where the error was the result of reckless or incompetent practice and/or was concealed, and those that resulted from other causes, such as serious pressure of work, and where there was immediate, honest disclosure in the patient's interest. The NMC recognizes the prerogative of managers to take local disciplinary action where it is considered to be necessary but urges that they also consider each incident in its particular context and similarly discriminate between the two categories described above.

Ward stocks and individual patient medication

In hospitals and nursing homes it is customary for there to be a mix of medicinal products held on the ward or department. Some are there as part of the basic stock held by that ward or department. Other medicinal products are received and held in respect of a particular patient and dispensed by the pharmacist against a written prescription for that particular patient. Recommendations were given in the Aitken Report (1958) and in the Roxburgh Report (Scotland)(1972) on ward stocks that the pharmacist should agree with the ward or department a list of medicines which it could hold as a standard stock list in addition to a specialist list of medicines appropriate to the ward specialty. The original system was for ward stocks to be ordered by the person in charge of the ward or department from the pharmacy on a printed requisition form.

A more recent system adopted in some hospitals is for the pharmacist to take responsibility for requisitioning ward stocks and to make sure that stocks are kept up to the standard agreed list. Whether the registered practitioner is administering medicinal products to the patient from the ward stocks or from the patient's individual dispensed package, she should ensure that the same care is taken over checking the drugs and following the checklist set out in the last chapter.

Dispensing faults

A helpful fact sheet for pharmacists on dispensing errors has been issued by the Royal Pharmaceutical Society (RPS 2004) which sets out the procedure which should be followed if a patient complains about a dispensing error. Much of its guidance would be relevant to nurses. It suggests the mnemonic of HELP for the final check:

H - How much has been dispensed.

E - Expiry date.

L - Label checks for the correct patient's name, the correct product name, the correct dose and the correct warning.

P - Product check, i.e. check that the correct medication of the correct strength has been supplied.

Applying the law to the situation in Box 6.1

Clearly Julia is at fault, and doubly so: first with the error in administration to the incorrect eye; then secondly in her failure to report it. She cannot be sure that the incorrect administration has not caused any harm to the eye. She should ensure that immediate notification of her error is made to a pharmacist or doctor who can advise on any action which should be taken to reduce the effects of any possible harm. The fact that the patient has not complained does not affect Julia's responsibility to admit her mistake and ensure that any possible harm is reduced. Julia has failed to follow the guidance of the NMC. She therefore faces potential fitness to practice proceedings of the NMC and disciplinary proceedings brought by the employer.If the patient has been harmed, her employer may face a civil action for compensation brought by the patient because of its vicarious liability for the negligence of Julia. Her failure to take the correct action following her error will be taken into account by the NMC in its Conduct and Competence proceedings.

Conclusions

There are considerable responsibilities upon the nurse or midwife who is administering a medicinal product. In addition, the practitioner must ensure that there are no errors in the prescription which has been written and it is to the writing of prescriptions that we turn in the next chapter.

Key points

- Illegible writing on a prescription should be queried with the prescriber and if necessary with the pharmacist.
- NMC guidance on instructions about medicines over the telephone should be followed.
- Where an error occurs in the administration of medicine, the practitioner should immediately admit the fault and ensure that remedial action is taken to prevent harm to the patient.
- Disciplinary action against a practitioner should take note of immediate admission that a fault has occurred.

References

Agyemang, E., Owusu R, and White A, (2010) Medication errors: types, causes and impact on nursing practice *British Journal of Nursing* vol 19 no 6 : 381-385 London

A Correspondent' (2001) Coroner calls for drug error safeguard. *The Times*, 2 May 2001

David, R. (2009) Wrong medication kills or harms 100 a year and it may be a great many more. *The Times* 4 September 2009.

Joint Sub-Committee of the Standing Medical Nursing and Pharmaceutical Advisory Committees (Aitken Report 1958) *Control of Dangerous Drugs and Poisons in Hospitals.*

NPSA (2008) *Rapid Response Report.* London

Nursing and Midwifery Council (2007) *Standards for medicines management.* London

Royal Pharmaceutical Society of Great Britain (2004) F*act Sheet 11: Dealing with Dispensing Errors.*

Scottish Home and Health Department (Roxburgh Report 1972); 1979 (GEN)11 A report on *Control of Medicines in Hospital Wards and Departments.*

Website

National Patient Safety Agency website www.npsa.nhs.uk

Royal College of Anaesthetists website www.rcoa.ac.uk

CHAPTER 7

Prescriptions: Basic principles

> ## Box 7.1 An epidural dose
>
> *A woman in a private hospital was prescribed a top-up epidural following a hysterectomy. The junior doctor mistook a dose of 3 ml of diamorphine for 30 ml. The woman collapsed following its administration and the doctor was unable to use the resuscitation equipment as he had not had the necessary training. Although the Consultant was able to revive her, she died a few days later (Kennedy 2000). Who is liable?*

Introduction

The word 'prescription' means a written instruction by an appropriate health professional for the dispensing and administration of the medicinal products set out in it. There are some medications which under the Medicines Act 1968 can only be supplied under a prescription (see below). Often, however, the appropriate health professional may write a prescription for many different medicinal products, many or even all of which are not by law required to be provided under a prescription and could be obtained by the patient directly from a supermarket as a general sale or from a chemist shop by a sale under the supervision of a registered pharmacist. In the two latter cases, however, the patient or carer would have to pay for the product. When the medicines are provided under a prescription in the community or from out-patient department of a hospital, the patient will have to pay the cost of the prescription or nothing at all if the patient comes under one of the categories of exemption from prescription charges. (In Wales the Welsh Assembly has exercised its devolutionary powers to exempt persons from paying prescription charges).

Prescription only medicines

Under section 58 of the Medicines Act 1968, apart from specified statutory exceptions, Perscription Only Medicines (POM) can only be sold or supplied in accordance with a prescription given by a specified practitioner.

A Statutory Instrument (SI) lays down the requirements for a prescription to be lawful (SI 1997 No 1830). These requirements are shown in Box 7.2.

Box 7.2 Legal requirements for a prescription

a) Signed in ink, by and with the practitioner's name who is prescribing.

b) Written in ink, or otherwise so as to be indelible, unless it is a health prescription which is not for a Controlled Drug (CD), specified in Schedule 1, 2 or 3 to the Misuse of Drugs Regulations, in which case it may be written by means of carbon paper or similar material.

c) Shall contain the following particulars:
   i. the name and address of the practitioner giving it
   ii. the appropriate date (see below).
   iii. such particulars as indicate whether the practitioner giving it is a doctor, a dentist, an appropriate nurse practitioner, a veterinary surgeon or a veterinary practitioner.
   iv. where the practitioner giving it is a doctor, dentist or an appropriate nurse practitioner, the name and address and the age, if under 12, of the person for whose treatment it is given.

d) Shall not be dispensed after the end of the period of six months from the appropriate date, unless it is a repeatable prescription, in which case it shall not be dispensed for the first time after the end of that period nor otherwise than in accordance with the direction contained in the repeatable prescription.

e) In the case of a repeatable prescription that does not specify the number of times it may be dispensed, shall not be dispensed on more than two occasions unless it is a prescription for oral contraceptives in which case it may be dispensed six times before the end of the period of six months from the appropriate date..

The appropriate date is the date on which the prescription was signed by the practitioner, or in the case of a health prescription only, the date indicated by him or her as being the date before which it shall not be dispensed. Where a health prescription bears both dates, the later of those dates is the appropriate date.

Mistakes in prescription or fraudulent prescriptions

If the pharmacist has exercised due diligence and believes on reasonable grounds that the necessary conditions for the prescription have been fulfilled or that the prescription is genuine, then the sale or supply of the medicinal product is not rendered unlawful by its failure to satisfy the conditions or by the fact that it is forged.

Exemptions to these prescription requirements

The particulars set out in Box 7.2 apply to the giving of prescriptions in the community and their dispensing through a retail pharmacist.

They are not legally required in hospitals, although the principles set down by the NMC for prescriptions (see Box 7.3) are clearly of value.

The Aitken Report (1958) recommended that medicines should not be administered to a patient without a written authority from a doctor on the prescription sheet.

Hospitals and health centres

The legal requirements shown in Box 7.2 do not apply to hospitals and health centres where POM are supplied for the purpose of being administered (whether in the hospital or elsewhere) to a particular person in accordance with the written directions of a doctor or dentist relating to that person. Nor do they apply to medicines given under a Patient Group Direction (PGD), which is considered in the next chapter.

Box 7.3 NMC Standards for the validity of a prescription

Check that the prescription or other direction to administer is:
• Not for a substance to which the patient is known to be allergic or otherwise unable to tolerate.
• Based, whenever possible, on the patient's informed consent and awareness of the purpose of the treatment.
• Clearly written, typed or computer-generated and indelible.
• Specifies the substance to be administered, using its generic or brand name where appropriate and its stated form, together with the strength, dosage, timing, frequency of administration, start and finish dates and route of administration.
• Is signed and dated by the authorised prescriber.
• In the case of CD, specifies the dosage and the number of dosage units or total course; and is signed and dated by the prescriber using relevant documentation as introduced e.g. Patient Drug Record Cards.

Check that you have:
• Clearly identified the patient for whom the medication is intended.
• Recorded the weight of the patient on the prescription sheet for all children, and where the dosage of medication is related to weight or surface area (e.g. cytotoxics) or where clinical condition dictates recorded the patient's weight.

The law relating to the patient's consent is considered in Chapters 12 to 16.

The guidance published by the NMC on record keeping should also be followed (NMC 2007).

Prescriptions for Controlled Drugs

The Misuse of Drugs Act 1971 identifies in Schedule 2 certain medicinal products known as Controlled Drugs (CD) to which special controls and offences apply. The Misuse of Drug Regulations 2001 have five schedules which set out the CD in order of their seriousness and the penalties relating to their misuse. These rules relating to prescriptions of CD are considered in Chapter 2.

Guidelines from the Nursing and Midwifery Council

The NMC in its *Standards for medicines management* (2007) has set out principles for the POM which are shown in Box 7.3. These are for the nurse who is administering a medicine to use to check the validity of the prescription, but are also of value when it is the nurse who is the appropriate registered practitioner for prescribing purposes. It should be stressed that not all of the guidelines set out in Box 7.3 are required as a matter of law, but it is good practice to ensure that the principles are followed in the interests of patient safety.

Dividing responsibility

It may happen that several different practitioners are involved in an incident which causes harm to a patient. The court has to determine the respective responsibility of each person and their employer (if any). Under the Civil Liability (Contribution) Act 1978, a successful claimant can obtain compensation from any one of several defendants, and that defendant can then claim from the others reimbursement according to their responsibility for the harm. An example of this is given below. The case does not involve a nurse, but if the situation was in a hospital context rather than in the home, one can imagine a nurse being involved.

Overprescribing

It was alleged by Mrs Dwyer that Dr Roderick prescribed a particular drug (Migril) and was negligent in choosing the number and frequency with which the relevant tablets should be taken, so that within a relatively short time she had received a dangerous overdose. The manufacturers had warned that not more than four tablets should be taken for any one attack of migraine and that no more than 12 tablets should be taken in the course of one week. Dr Roderick's prescription was for two tablets to be taken every four hours as necessary. He prescribed a total of 60 tablets. Dr Roderick admitted that this was utterly wrong: 'I have no satisfactory explanation. It was a mental aberration'. When the prescription was taken for dispensing there were two qualified pharmacists in the shop, neither of whom noticed the error and simply repeated Dr Roderick's instructions on the label. They in turn accepted some liability. Over the next six days Mrs Dwyer took 36 Migril tablets. As a result of this overdose she suffered serious personal injuries due to irreversible ergotamine poisoning, which resulted in constriction of the blood vessels and gangrene of her toes and lower limbs. As well as suing the chemists and Dr Roderick, Mrs Dwyer sued as second defendant Dr Roderick's partner, Dr Jackson, who saw her three days after the prescription had been given and who failed to discover the fact that his partner had overprescribed the drug and failed to stop her taking it (Dwyer v. Roderick, 20 June 1984 QBD). The trial judge decided that each defendant was liable: Dr Roderick was 45% liable, Dr Jackson was 15% liable and the pharmacists were 40% liable. The Court of Appeal held by a majority that Dr Jackson was not negligent. It accepted his evidence that it was his usual practice to enquire what medication a patient was on. Liability was thus divided between Dr Roderick and the pharmacists. Mrs Dwyer received £92,000 compensation.

One of the very interesting aspects of this case was that the incident occurred in November 1973 but did not come to court until 1982; thus the actual evidence of what happened was scanty and undoubtedly made Mrs Dwyer's case against Dr Jackson very difficult. The court commented adversely on the delay and suggested that the time might be ripe for changes designed to enable the court and the judiciary to play a greater part in encouraging the parties and their advisers to speed up the process of litigation. These changes have now taken place (known as the 'Woolf Reforms'). Cases may still only commence many years after an incident and therefore nurses must be aware of the importance of record keeping. In any such incident, the nurse is likely to have very little personal recall, but will be heavily dependent on the clarity and comprehensiveness of the records. (The Woolf Reforms are considered in Chapter 20, which looks at accountability and the civil law.)

Prescription errors

Research reported in *The Times*, which was carried out by Bryony Dean at an unnamed London hospital, found that about one in 200 prescriptions written by doctors contain errors likely to cause significant harm to patients (Wright 2002). Public health officials considered that a similar problem occurred across the UK. The study looked at all prescriptions for a month in the 550 bedded hospital and found that 36,200 drug orders were written, amounting to almost 1,300 a day. Mistakes were detected by pharmacists in 1.5% of the drug orders. The mistakes included:

- Prescribing 10 times the recommended dose of a drug for heart failure omitting a drug to treat stomach ulcers on the medical chart for a patient with a peptic ulcer.
- Four out of 10 errors involved the choice of drug.
- Almost two-thirds (61%) concerned the dose and/or timing of the medication.

Paracetamol, morphine, diamorphine and metoclopramide were the drugs most likely to be the subject of error. Senior House Officers made 56% of the mistakes and Junior House Officers one in three.

In 2003 the National Patient Safety Agency (NPSA) established a confidential reporting system for drug errors so that the lessons can be shared across the country (see Chapter 3 on the NPSA). In March 2007 the NPSA published *Safety in doses: improving the use of medicines in the NHS* which is available on its website (www.npsa.nha.uk). The Audit Commission identified errors in prescribing and administration of medicines as a major cause of preventable death and illness in hospitals.

Medical defence organisations say that 25% of all negligence claims in general practice are related to prescribing problems. In a letter to the editor of *The Times*, Tom Walley, Chairman of the Clinical Section of the British Pharmacological Society suggested that in the light of these figures 'a demonstration of competency in prescribing should be a specific mandatory requirement before doctors qualify' (Walley 2001).

In the NPSA report published in 2009 on medication errors (see Chapter 6) of the 100 deaths a year caused by medication errors, 41 were caused in the administration of drugs to patients by nurses and 32 were due to prescribing (David 2009).

The labelling of medicines is considered in Chapter 13.

The Yellow Card Reporting scheme for Adverse Drug Reactions (ADR) has now been extended by the Medicines and Healthcare Products Regulatory Agency (MHRA) to patient reporting (see Chapter 3).

Application of the law to the situation in Box 7.1

The report of this case was taken from the account of the proceedings of the inquest before the coroner. It is likely, however, depending on what facts were established, that the private hospital would accept vicarious liability for its employees who were negligent in administering the drug to the patient. If there is evidence that the prescription was not written clearly enough, then there might also be an acceptance of some liability by the medical defence organisation representing the Consultant (if the Consultant was acting as a self-employed practitioner). In the circumstances, any claim by the relatives of the deceased might be settled without being disputed in court. In addition, disciplinary action and professional conduct proceedings could take place against any practitioners involved in this tragedy. The extent of liability of the staff nurse is not clear, but if she had queried the dose of 30 ml being given to the patient and the junior doctor had noted her concerns, the tragedy might never have occurred.

Conclusions

In this chapter we have considered the basic principles which apply to the writing of prescriptions. In the next few chapters we look at PGD and the role of the nurse prescriber.

Key points

- Certain medicines – POMs – can only be supplied on a prescription.
- Prescriptions may however be written for other medicines from the General Sales List or medicines which can only be supplied under the supervision of a pharmacist.
- The legal requirements for writing prescriptions do not apply in hospitals, but do apply to community prescribing.
- The NMC guidelines for prescription writing should be followed as a matter of good practice.
- Where several different defendants are to blame for harm, the Civil Liability (Contribution) Act 1978 enables one defendant to pay the claimant and then recover a proportion of the compensation from the other defendants.
- Research indicates that prescription errors account for a significant proportion of harm suffered by hospital patients.

References

Aitken Report Joint Sub-Committee of the Standing Medical Nursing and Pharmaceutical Advisory Committees (1958) *Control of Dangerous Drugs and Poisons in Hospitals.*

David, R. (2009) Wrong medication kills or harms 100 a year and it may be a great many more. *The Times.* 4 September 2009

Kennedy, D. (2000) Hospital blamed in report on overdose drug. *The Times*, 3 July 2000, p. 4.

NPSA (2007) *Safety in doses: improving the use of medicines in the NHS* (www.npsa. nha.uk).

Nursing and Midwifery Council (2007) *Standards for medicines management.* London

Nursing and Midwifery Council (2009) *Record keeping: Guidance for nurses and midwives.* London

Walley, T. (2001) Chairman, Clinical Section, British Pharmacological Society. Letter to the Editor, *The Times*, 28 December 2001.

Wright, O. (2002) Harmful errors in one in 200 prescriptions. *The Times*, 5 December 2002.

CHAPTER 8

Patient Group Directions

Box 8.1 Nurse prescribing

Sarah is a nurse specialist for accident and emergency (A&E). She is told by the consultant that as a nurse specialist she would be able to supply certain Prescription Only Medicines (POM), including painkillers, for patients who are only seen by the clinical nurse specialist in A&E. She feels that this is the equivalent of prescribing and considers that there should be a more formal procedure. What is the law?

Introduction

The first Crown Report in 1989 recommended that community nurses should, after the appropriate training, be eligible to prescribe specified medications (DH 1989). It was necessary to introduce amending legislation to the Medicines Act 1968 to authorise nurses to prescribe and also to the NHS legislation to enable pharmacists to dispense against a prescription signed by a registered nurse. Following these legislative changes it became apparent that many nurses working in hospitals appeared able to supply medicines to patients under what was called a trust protocol, even though the patient had not been seen by a doctor. There were concerns about the legality of this process. June Crown was asked to chair a committee to review the prescribing and supply of medicines.

Group protocols or Patient Group Directions

The Crown Committee first considered the arrangements for and legality of group protocols and reported in March 1998 (DH 1998) (see Box 8.2) and recommended legislation to ensure that their legal validity was clarified. The criteria against which the Crown Report suggested that any group protocol should be tested are shown in Box 8.3. It recommended that certain products should be excluded from group protocols. These included:

- New drugs under intensive monitoring and subject to special adverse reaction reporting requirements (this includes the Black Triangle scheme which refers to newly introduced drugs, still subject to special monitoring for potential side-effects by the Medicine Control Agency (so called because they are identified by a black triangle symbol in the *British National Formulary*.
- Unlicensed medicines.
- Medicines used outside their licensed indications.
- Medicines being used in clinical trials.

Box 8.2 Crown recommendations on group protocols

1. The majority of patients should continue to receive medicines on an individual basis. However, there is likely to be a continuing need for supply and administration under group protocols in certain limited situations.

2. Current safe and effective practice using group protocols which are consistent with criteria defined in the Report should continue (see Box 8.3).

3. The law should be clarified to ensure that health professionals who supply or administer medicines under group protocols are acting within the law.

4. All group protocols should comply with specified criteria.

5. Current protocols should be reviewed in the light of those criteria.

6. The Department of Health (DH) should disseminate widely the criteria.

7. An evaluation study should be undertaken on the use of the group protocols.

8. These recommendations should apply to all sectors of healthcare, including the private and charitable sectors

---

Box 8.3 Criteria for group protocols

- Should ensure that patient safety is not compromised or put at risk.
- Should specify clear arrangements for professional responsibility and accountability.
- Should contribute to the effective use of resources.
- Should be consistent with the Summary of Product Characteristics which is part of the marketing authorisation granted for the product.
- The content of the protocol should state the clinical need which it is intended to address and the objectives of care which it will provide.
- The characteristics of staff authorised to take responsibility for the supply or administration of medicines under a group protocol.
- The description of treatment available; the management and monitoring of group protocols.
- The development of group protocols: by whom? Approval; employer's final approval; date and signature and monitoring.
- Implementation of group protocols.

Patient Group Directions

As a consequence of the Crown Report on group protocols, new regulations came into force on 9 August 2000 (POM (Human Use) Amendment Order 2000 SI 2000 No 19170). These provide for PGD to be drawn up to make provision for the sale or supply of a POM in hospitals in accordance with the written direction of a doctor or dentist. A PGD is defined in the Regulations as:

a) In connection with the supply of a prescription only medicine as referred to in article 12A(2), 12B, or 12C, a written direction relating to the supply and administration of a description or class of prescription only medicine or

b) in connection with the administration of a prescription only medicine as referred to in article 12A(2), 12B or 12C, a written direction relating to the administration of a description or class of prescription only medicine and which

> *i. is signed by a doctor or dentist and by a pharmacist and*
>
> *ii relates to the supply and administration, or to administration, to persons generally (subject to any exclusions which may be set out in the Direction).*

An electronic prescription service between general practitioners and pharmacists is gradually being established and further details can be found on the website of NHS Connecting for Health www.connectingforhealth.nhs.uk/.

Box 8.4 Particulars for Patient Group Directions as set out in the Regulations

a) the period during which the Direction shall have effect

b) the description or class of POM to which the Direction relates

c) whether there are any restrictions on the quantity of medicine which may be supplied on any one occasion, and if so, what restrictions

d) the clinical situations which POM of that description or class may be used to treat

e) the clinical criteria under which a person shall be eligible for treatment

f) whether any class of person is excluded from treatment under the Direction, and if so, what class of person

g) whether there are circumstances in which further advice should be sought from a doctor or dentist and, if so, what circumstances

h) the pharmaceutical form or forms in which POM of that description or class are to be administered

i) the strength, or maximum strength, at which POM of that description or class are to be administered

j) the applicable dosage or maximum dosage

k) the route of administration

l) the frequency of administration

m) any minimum or maximum period of administration applicable to POM of that description or class

n) whether there are any relevant warnings to note, and if so, what warnings

o) whether there is any follow up action to be taken in any circumstances, and if so, what action and in what circumstances

p) arrangements for referral for medical advice

q) details of the records to be kept of the supply or the administration of medicines under the Direction.

In addition the PGD must be authorised by one of the following:

• The Common Services Agency

• The Health Authority

• The Special Health Authority

• The NHS trust.

To be lawful the PGD must cover the particulars which are set out in Part 1 of Schedule 7 of the Statutory Instrument (SI) (See Box 8.4)

The registered health professionals shown in Box 8.5 may supply medicines under a PGD.

Procedure

Where it is considered that a PGD would meet the needs of patients and could be safety implemented, a design group would be set up comprising a pharmacist, a doctor and a nurse or other relevant registered health professional (e.g. a physiotherapist or orthoptist, as shown in Box 8.5). They would identify the drugs which could be safely prescribed for patients suffering from a specific condition by a non-doctor. Each requirement of the regulations as set out in Box 8.4 would be

---

Box 8.5 Registered health professionals who are authorised to supply medicines under a Patient Group Direction

- Pharmacists
- Registered health visitors
- Registered midwives
- Registered nurses
- Registered ophthalmic opticians
- State registered chiropodists
- State registered orthoptists
- State registered physiotherapists
- State registered radiographers
- Individuals who hold a certificate of proficiency in ambulance paramedic skills issued by the Secretary of State or state registered paramedics
- Registered dieticians*
- Registered occupational therapists*
- Registered orthotists and prosthetists*
- Registered speech and language therapists*
- *added by a subsequent SI ((POM (Human Use) Amendment (No 2) Order 2004 SI 2004 No 1189)

---

checked to ensure that the direction took account of it. Categories of patients who should be excluded from the direction because they would need to be personally seen by a doctor would be identified. Arrangements would be made for a regular audit of the PGD to ensure that it was working safely and that any necessary amendments to the direction should be identified and implemented.

Guidance from the Department of Health

The DH issued guidance on PGD for England in 2000 and further details are given in its concise guide Medicines Matters (DH 2005). A dedicated website provides model forms of PGD covering a wide variety of medicines, including patient information leaflets. The NHS National electronic library holds information on PGDs (www.nelm.nhs.uk/PGD).

Guidance from the Nursing and Midwifery Council

In its *Standards for medicines management* the NMC (2007) emphasises that the registered practitioner must follow the guidance provided by the appropriate government health department regarding implementation of PGD. It further states that:

> Patient group directions are drawn up locally by doctors, dentists, pharmacists, and other health professionals where relevant. They must be signed by a doctor or dentist and a pharmacist, both of whom should have been involved in developing the direction, and must be approved by the appropriate health care organisation. The NMC would consider it good practice that a lead practitioner from the professional group using the PGD and senior manager where possible, are also involved and sign off a PGD.

The NMC does not see PGD as a form of prescribing, but only of supply.

Patient Group Direction and Controlled Drugs

In general, Controlled Drugs (CD) cannot be the subject of PGD, but there are some exceptions to this statement. These exceptions result from amendments made to the Misuse of Drugs regulations in October 2003 and include the following:

1. A registered nurse may, when acting in her capacity as such, supply or administer diamorphine under a PGD for the treatment of cardiac pain to a person admitted as a patient to a coronary care unit or accident and emergency department of a hospital.

2. A registered nurse or pharmacist or any of the other named healthcare professions listed in Box 8.5, may when acting in their capacity as such, supply or administer any Schedule 5 CD in accordance with a valid PGD.

3. A registered nurse, pharmacist or any of the other named healthcare professions listed in Box 8.5 may, when acting in their capacity as such, supply and administer any Part 1 Schedule 4 CD in accordance with a valid PGD provided that it is not a drug in parenteral form for the treatment of addiction. For the purposes of the Regulations a person is considered to be addicted to a drug if, and only if, he has as a result of repeated administration become so dependent on the drug that he has an overpowering desire for the administration of it to be continued.

Unlicensed drugs

Medicines without a UK marketing authorisation are not considered appropriate for inclusion in a PGD.

Practice nurse and Patient Group Directions

The practice nurse could be the identified health professional who is able to supply and prescribe medicines under a PGD. Controversy has however arisen as to when a PGD is required. The General Practitioners Committee in its newsletter on 20 September 2002 stated that:

> There has been a tendency for Primary Care Trusts to put pressure on GPs to sign up to PGDs due to a misunderstanding of this measure. This has created uncertainty among GPs and their practice nurses alike, to the point where some practice nurses are being encouraged to believe that it is illegal to carry out routine immunisations, such as influenza, on their practice patients without a PGD being signed by their employing GP for each and every medication. Our clear legal advice is that this is not the case.

For independent contractor GPs and, in particular, their practice nurses, there is no requirement to sign up to PGDs. Such PGDs are often very complex and bureaucratic. The circumstances of GP practices are quite different to those pertaining for the PCT itself. GP patients are already individually identified before presentation for treatment by virtue of being registered, either permanently or temporarily. Moreover, in general practice, relevant medical records will be available to the nurse at the time of presentation. GPs are already permitted to delegate the supply and administration of medication to their practice nurses, provided a clear instruction has been given, preferably in the form of a simple written practice protocol.

GPs and practice nurses should therefore be assured that they may continue to supply and administer to their registered patients medications such as influenza vaccine provided a clear written instruction or protocol exists, without the need to sign up to a PGD.

Patient Specific Direction and Patient Group Direction contrasted

Clearly there is a difference between a Patient Specific Direction (PSD) and a PGD. As the DH clarifies in its *Medicines Matters* guide (DH 2005):

The Patient Specific Direction is the traditional written instruction, from a doctor, dentist or nurse prescriber, for medicines to be supplied or administered to a named patient. The majority of medicines are still prescribed, supplied or administered using this process. As a Patient Specific Direction is individually tailored to the needs of a single patient, it should be used in preference to a Patient Group Direction.

Patient Group Directions and the private sector

A doctor can write a patient specific written direction to allow the supply of a POM within the course of business of a private hospital. Since April 2003, PGDs can now be supplied for use within the private sector, subject to specified conditions.

The conditions on which PGDs can be used in the course of a business of an independent hospital, clinic or medical agency are:

• The PGD must be in effect at the time of supply.

- It must relate to medicines that have a marketing authorisation or a homoeopathic certificate of registration.
- It must contain all the particulars listed in Box 8.4 above.
- It must be signed on behalf of the registered provider and by the relevant manager for the clinic, hospital or medical agency if there is one.
- It must designate in writing by or on behalf of the registered provider or the relevant manager if there is one, the individuals supplying or administering under the PGD, who must belong to one of the classes of persons specified in the Regulations.

Similar conditions apply to the use of PGDs in the provision of healthcare by or on behalf of the police, prison service or armed forces and also by a person lawfully conducting a retail pharmacy (RPSGB 2004).

Extension to scope of Patient Group Directions

In August 2009, the MHRA and the DH issued consultation MLX 362, which contained proposals to expand the scope of PGDs to enable the sale, supply and administration of certain medicines by dental therapists and dental hygienists. The proposals aimed to enable dental therapists and dental hygienists to administer local anaesthesia and to sell or supply fluoride supplements and toothpastes with high fluoride content of 2800 and 5000 parts per million (ppm). As a consequence of the consultation amendments were made to the regulations which came into effect in June 2010 (SI 2010/ 1136).

Application of the law to the situation Box 8.1

Sarah is right to be concerned. She is being asked by the Consultant to prescribe POMs to patients and she should ask for a PGD to be drafted and authorised and then implemented as described above. After the appropriate training and supervision, she would then be empowered to implement the PGD. Regular audit should take place to ensure that it is working safely and that no problems have arisen. As an alternative, Sarah could ask to be recognised as an independent or supplementary prescriber for certain preparations, and this is considered in the next two chapters.

The DH has provided a concise guide to the current mechanisms for the prescribing, supply and administration of medicines (DH 2005).

Key points

■ Following the implementation of community nurse prescribing, it was apparent that many hospital nurses were supplying medicines under trust protocols without clear legal authority.

■ The Crown Committee was set up to make recommendation on the prescription, supply and administration of medicines.

■ Its interim report made recommendations on PGD.

■ Regulations came into force in 2000 enabling designated health professionals to supply medicines under a PGD.

■ The NMC has issued guidance on PGDs.

References

Department of Health (1998) Review of Prescribing, Supply and Administration of Medicines: A Report on the *Supply and Administration of Medicines under Group Protocols* (Crown 1). London

Department of Health (2000) *Patient Group Directions* HSC 2000/026 DH 2000. Londn

NHS Modernisation Agency (2005) *Medicines Matters: A Guide to Current Mechanisms for the Prescribing, Supply and Administration of Medicines*. London

Nursing and Midwifery Council (2007) *Standards for medicines management*. London

Royal Pharmaceutical Society of Great Britain (2004) *Fact Sheet 10: Patient Group Directions*.

General Practitioners Committee (2002) *Newsletter* 20 September 2002

Websites

NHS Connecting for Health website www.connectingforhealth.nhs.uk/

NHS National electronic library holds information on PGDs website www.nelm.nhs.uk/ PGD

CHAPTER 9

Non medical prescribing I

Box 9.1 Situation

Community nurses hold a children's clinic to which mothers bring their children and those nurses who have prescribing powers are able, where appropriate, to give the mothers a prescription for any necessary medicinal products. Mavis Robson decided that one child required a preparation for head lice and asked the mother if the child was asthmatic. The mother said no and the nurse wrote a prescription. Mavis said that she had been unable to refer to the child's records since they were not available at this clinic. She subsequently learnt that because of an allergic reaction, the child had suffered considerable harm. Is she liable?

Introduction

Prescribing by community nurses follows a long history of recommendations for its introduction. It was first recommended in the Cumberlege Report on Community Nursing in 1986. The Report suggested that a limited list of items and simple agents should be approved by the Department of Health and Social Security (as it was then) for prescription by nurses as part of a nursing care programme (Cumberlege 1986). This recommendation was followed in Wales by the Report of the Committee under the chairmanship of Noreen Edwards to review community services in Wales (Welsh Office 1987). It made similar recommendations. An advisory group under the chairmanship of June Crown was then set up to advise the Secretary of State for Health and it reported in 1989, supporting limited prescribing by nurses in the community (DH 1989).

Legislation to implement community nurse prescribing

Prescribing by community nurses could only take place after changes had been made to the Medicines Act for nurses to be authorised as prescribers and then for changes to the NHS legislation so that pharmacists could lawfully dispense against a prescription written by a nurse.

Medicinal Products (Prescription by Nurses etc.) Act 1992

This Act made two changes to the existing legislation to give specific practitioners the right to prescribe. The first change was the addition of a new section to the Medicines Act 1968 adding a subsection d to section 58 to enable the following to prescribe:

> *d. registered nurses, midwives and health visitors who are of such description and comply with such conditions as may be specified in the order, are to be appropriate practitioners for the purposes of this section*

As a consequence of this change the provisions of section 58 enable a registered pharmacist lawfully to dispense prescription only medicines for those professions listed in subsection 1.

The second change brought about by the 1992 Act is to section 41 of the NHS Act 1977. As a result of this new subsection, Family Health Service Authorities and subsequently health authorities and primary care trusts (PCT) have a duty to make arrangements for the provision of medicinal products prescribed by nurses etc. and are empowered to pay the pharmacists for their services in so providing. Similar amendments are made in legislation covering Scotland and Northern Ireland. Section 5 of the 1992 Act states that there shall be paid out of money provided by Parliament any increase attributable to this Act in the sums so payable under any other enactment.

Which nurses can prescribe under these changes?

In the consultation document on the implementation of nurse prescribing in the community issued by the Medicines Control Agency (MCA) of the DH in July 1994 it is stated that in order to be eligible to prescribe, once the regulations are in force, a nurse must be (DH 1994):

- suitably qualified
- appropriately trained
- authorised by her/his employers

Box 9.2 Criteria for nurses to prescribe set in 1994

- Nurses who are registered on parts 1–12 of the UKCC (now Nursing and Midwifery Council (NMC)) register.
- Have a district nurse qualification and be employed by a District Health Authority (DHA) or fundholding practice.
- Be registered on part 11 as a health visitor and be employed by a DHA, trust or fundholding practice.
- Be named on the professional register and marked as qualified to prescribe.

Following the consultation document, a Statutory Instrument (SI) was issued which set out the necessary training and qualifications of nurses to prescribe (SI 1994 No 2402). These are shown in Box 9.2.

The criteria set in 1994 were updated in 1997 when the definition of 'appropriate nurse practitioner' and the medicines in relation to which they are such a practitioner was set out (SI 1997 No 1830 POM (Human Use) Order). The appropriate nurse practitioner now means:

1. A person who:
   a) is registered in the register maintained by the NMC; and
   b) has a district nursing qualification additionally recorded in the professional register; or
2. A person registered in the professional register as a health visitor.

In August 2004 the Nursing and Midwifery Council's new register was introduced with responsibility for registration for nurses, midwives and community specialist public health nurses. Special provision is made for specific qualifications including that of being eligible to prescribe to be noted on the register.

The *Nurse Prescribers' Formulary*

The *Nurse Prescribers' Formulary* (NPF) was originally published by the British Medical Association (BMA) and the Royal Pharmaceutical Society of Great Britain (RPSGB) in association with the Health Visitors' Association and the Royal College of Nursing (RCN). This pilot edition was printed in 1994 and was designed to operate in the eight pilot fundholding districts. The pilot edition also included guidance on prescription writing and notes on various preparations. Subsequently the medicinal products which a nurse can prescribe under this legislation was included in the NPF, which was shown as a supplement to the *British National Formulary* (BNF). In May 2006 the NPF was discontinued and a nurse independent prescriber is able to prescribe medicines which come within his or her competence (see Chapter 4).

Implementation of community nurse prescribing

Once the legislation had been enacted, community nurse prescribing was introduced in eight pilot schemes in England. After these had been evaluated, it was gradually introduced across the whole of the United Kingdom. The prescribing course is now integrated into university based specialist practitioner programmes for new district nurses and health visitors. It is also provided as a post-registration training and development programme for registered nurses.

Practice nurses and Walk-in Centres

In February 2000 prescribing powers were given to nurses employed by a doctor on the medical list (i.e. a GP) and also to nurses working in Walk-in Centres, as defined in the NHS (Pharmaceutical Services) Amendment Regulations 2000 SI 2000 No 121 (see below).

Under these amending regulations, nurses who are defined as nurse prescribers who may issue prescription forms are those who at the time of ordering the listed drug or medicine or listed appliance are:

- Employed as a district nurse by a health authority or NHS trust.
- Employed as a nurse by a doctor whose name is included in a medical list.
- Assisting in the performance of persons' medical services under a pilot scheme.
- Assisting, in the capacity of a nurse, in the provision of services in a Walk-in Centre, which in this regulation means a Centre at which information and treatment for minor conditions is provided to the public under arrangements made by or on behalf of the Secretary of State. The regulations also include health visitors.

At the time the revised regulations were published the DH issued a press release giving further details of the changes being made which will be considered in the next chapter (DH 2000).

Answering the question in Box 9.1

Mavis is personally and professionally responsible for her actions in prescribing and therefore must take reasonable precautions to prevent any reasonably foreseeable risk arising. In this situation she did not have access to the records of the child, from which she might have discovered that the child had a history of chest problems and therefore possibly suffered from an asthmatic condition. It is true that Mavis asked the mother if the child had asthma and the mother denied that. However, the mother might not have identified her child's problems by that name and Mavis should have been able to have access to the child's medical record before prescribing a preparation which could lead to allergic reactions. The question which would be asked is: 'Would any reasonable community nurse have checked with the child's records to ensure that there were no contra-indications against the medicinal product which she was intending to prescribe?'. If the answer, given by experts in the field of community nursing, to that question would be 'Yes', then Mavis is at fault, and if the harm suffered by the child can be traced to these failures of Mavis then compensation may be payable by Mavis's employers to the child because of her employer's vicarious liability for the actions of an employee in the course of employment.

Conclusions

The activity of prescribing should not be taken on lightly. Even the most apparently harmless product can be devastating to a patient if there are contra-indications. Wisely, the introduction of community nurse prescribing was brought in very slowly and after careful scrutiny.

In addition to these original prescribing powers in the community, district nurses and health visitors may have powers under PGD (see Chapter 8) and may also have powers under Extended Formulary Nurses Independent Prescribing and Supplementary Prescribing (which were introduced following the final Crown Report) (DH 1999 and 2006). These are considered in the next chapter.

Key points

■ Following the Crown recommendations in 1989 pilot schemes were established to enable appropriately trained district nurses and health visitors to prescribe in the community.

■ The scheme was extended to the rest of the country and subsequently to practice nurses and nurses working in Walk-in Centres.

■ A nurse who is recognised as an independent nurse prescriber is able to prescribe medicines in the BNF which come within her sphere of competence.

References

Cumberlege, J. (1986) *Neighbourhood Nursing – a Focus for Care (Review of Community Nursing Services)*. Department of Health and Social Security. London

Department of Health (1989) Advisory Group on Nurse Prescribing (chaired by June Crown) Report of *Nurse Prescribing and Supply*. London

Department of Health (1994) Medicines Control Agency *Implementation of nurse prescribing in the community*. MLK 208. London

Department of Health (1999), *Review of Prescribing, Supply and Administration of Medicines Final Report* (Crown Report), March 1999 London

Department of Health (2000) press release 2000/0146: *Go-ahead for plans to allow nurses to prescribe more medicines*, 13 March 2000. London

Department of Health (2006) *Improving Patients' Access to Medicines: A Guide to Implementing Nurse and Pharmacist Independent Prescribing within the NHS in England* Department of Health Gateway reference: 6429 April 2006. London

Welsh Office (1987) *Report of the Review of Community Nursing in Wales, Nursing in the Community –a team approach for Wales*.

CHAPTER 10

Non medical prescribing 2

Box 10.1 Situation

A clinical nurse specialist in accident and emergency (A&E) prescribed a painkiller for a patient suffering from a minor injury. She was unaware that the patient was allergic to this medicine. The patient suffered serious liver damage and the relatives are urging her to sue. What is the liability of the clinical nurse specialist?

Introduction

In the previous chapter we considered the implementation of community nurse prescribing and its extension to practice nurses and nurses working in Walk-in Centres. In this chapter we consider the final Crown Report and the subsequent developments in nurse prescribing.

The final Crown Report

In March 1999 the final Crown Report was published (DH 1999). It proposed a new framework for the prescribing, supply and administration of medicines inside and outside the NHS in which:

- The majority of patients continue to receive medicines on an individual patient-specific basis.
- The current prescribing authority of doctors, dentists and certain nurses (in respect of a limited list of medicines) continues.
- New groups of professionals would be able to apply for authority to prescribe in specific clinical areas, where this would improve patient care and patient safety could be assured.

The report's recommendations are shown in Box 10.2 and they cover the first three terms of reference:

1. To develop a consistent policy framework to guide judgements on the circumstances in which health professionals might undertake new responsibilities with regard to prescribing, supply and administration of medicines;
2. To advise on the likely impact of any proposed changes;
3. To consider possible implications for legislation, professional training and standards.

Box 10.2 Recommendations of the final Crown Report

1. The legal authority in the UK to prescribe, including authorising NHS expenditure, should be extended beyond currently authorised prescribers.

2. The legal authority for new professional groups to prescribe or to authorise NHS expenditure, should be limited to medicines in specific therapeutic areas related to particular competence and expertise of the group and may include prescription only medicines.

3. Two types of prescribers should be recognised: the independent prescriber and the dependent prescriber. (The dependent prescriber is now known as the supplementary prescriber)

4. A UK-wide advisory body, provisionally entitled the 'New Prescribers Advisory Committee', should be established under section 4 of the Medicines Act to assess submissions from professional organisations seeking powers for suitably trained members to become independent or dependent prescribers.

5. Newly authorised groups of prescribers should not normally be allowed to prescribe specified categories of medicines including controlled drugs, unlicensed drugs, black triangle drugs, drugs over which there is continuing professional concerns and drugs with public health concerns about safeguards,

Box 10.2 continued

6. The current arrangements for the administration and self-administration of medicines should continue to apply. Newly authorised prescribers should have the power to administer those parenteral prescription only medicines (POM) which they are authorised to prescribe.

7. Repeatable prescriptions should be available on the NHS, with limits to the number of repeats and the duration of its validity.

8. There should be thorough evaluation of the likely costs and benefits to the NHS before general adoption of extensions to prescribing authority if significant costs are likely.

9. There should be primary legislation which permits ministers, through regulations, to designate new categories of dependent.

10. The new arrangements should be subject to evaluation and monitoring.

Other recommendations are made to the DH and to professional bodies on the criteria to be followed in making proposals for extensions to prescribing and the arrangements they should make for training to the General Medical Council (GMC) and postgraduate deans. It also recommended that employers and manager in all sectors who are responsible for staff who supervise or undertake the administration of any medicines should ensure that those staff have the right training and skills to do so safely and regular opportunities for updating their knowledge.

Independent and dependent (supplementary) prescribers

Perhaps the most significant recommendation of the Crown Report (DH 1999) is that there should be two types of prescriber:
1) The independent prescriber is defined as the person who is responsible for the assessment of patients with undiagnosed conditions and for

decisions about the clinical management required, including prescribing. This group would include doctors, dentists and certain nurses who are already legally authorised prescribers. Other health professionals may also become newly legally authorised independent prescribers.

2)   The dependent prescriber (now known as the supplementary prescriber) is defined as the person who is responsible for the continuing care of patients who have been clinically assessed by an independent practitioner. The continuing care can include prescribing which will be informed by clinical guidelines and will be consistent with individual treatment plans. Dependent prescribers may also be involved in continuing established treatments by issuing repeat prescriptions, with authority to adjust the dose or dosage form according to the patients' needs. There should be provision for regular clinical review by the assessing clinician.

Individual practitioners

The final recommendation of the Crown Report (DH 1999) is to individual practitioners:

All legally authorised prescribers should take personal responsibility for maintaining and updating their knowledge and practice related to prescribing, including taking part in clinical audit, and should never prescribe in situations beyond their professional competence.

The situation following the final Crown Report

Legislation implementing the final Crown Report is contained in section 63 of the Health and Social Care Act which amends the Medicines Act 1968. It amends section 58 of the Medicines Act to enable 'other persons who are of such a description and comply with such conditions as may be specified in the order' to be eligible to write prescriptions for medicinal products. Section 63(3) lists those persons who are eligible as including persons who are registered by a board established under the Professions Supplementary to Medicine Act 1960. The list includes 'persons who are registered in any register established, continued or maintained under an Order in Council under section 60(1) of the Health Act 1999'.

Extension of nurse prescribing

On 25 October 2000 the DH issued a consultation paper to extend nurse prescribing. It proposed training about 10,000 nurses to prescribe treatment for a broader range of medical conditions, including:

- Minor injuries and ailments such as cuts, burns and hayfever.
- Promoting healthier lifestyles such as help with giving up smoking.
- Chronic diseases including asthma and diabetes.
- Palliative care.

Extended formulary nurse prescribing

Following the consultation, a Statutory Instrument (SI) was issued in 2002, which came into force on 1 April 2002 (POM (Human Use) Amendment Order 2002 SI 2002 No 549). This enabled nurses who met certain conditions and who were to be known as 'extended formulary nurse prescribers', to be able to prescribe certain POM. The Extended Formulary means the *Nurse Prescribers' Extended Formulary supplement* which was to be found in the *British National Formulary*.

An extended formulary nurse prescriber meant a person:

- who is registered in parts 1, 3, 5, 8, 10, 11, 12, 13, 14 or 15 of the professional register* and
- against whose name is recorded in that register an annotation signifying that he is qualified to order drugs, medicines and appliances from the Extended Formulary.

---

*Note that in August 2004 a new NMC register was introduced with only three sections: nurses (divided into two subparts), midwives and specialist community public health nurses (Nurses and Midwives (Parts of and Entries in the Register) Order of Council SI 2004 No 1765). In the case of a first level nurse, a midwife or a specialist community public health nurse, the register can indicate a qualification to order drugs, medicines and appliances in the following categories:

a) from the District Nurse and Health Visitor Formulary

b) from the Extended Formulary

c) as a supplementary prescriber

Schedule 3A to the Statutory Instrument (SI) lists substances which may be prescribed, administered or directed for administration by extended formulary nurse prescribers and the conditions for such prescription or administration. This list sets out the substance in column one, and the requirements as to use, route of administration, or pharmaceutical form in column two.

Under this extended nurse prescribing, appropriately trained practitioners were able to prescribe all General Sales List and Pharmacy medicines currently prescribable by GPs under General Practitioner Medical Services (GPMS) regulations, with the exception of those products which contain certain Controlled Drugs (CD), together with a list of POM. A sum of £10 million in central funding was allocated over the period 2001–2004 to train around 10,000 nurse prescribers.

Additional criteria for eligibility to become an independent nurse prescriber

In its guidance on implementation the DH (2002) has advised that in addition to fulfilling the legal criteria, applicants for the prescribing preparation will need:
- The ability to study at level 3 (degree level).
- At least three years post-registration clinical nursing experience (or part-time equivalent); nominees will usually be at E grade or above.
- A medical prescriber willing to contribute and to supervise the nurse's 12 day learning in practice element of preparation.
- The support of the employer and confirmation of certain conditions.

The three key principles to prioritise potential applicants for training as independent nurse prescribers are seen by the DH as being:
- Patient safety.
- Maximum benefit to patients in terms of quicker and more efficient access to medicines for patients.
- Better use of nurse's skills.

Department of Health guidance on extending independent nurse prescribing within the NHS

In March 2002 the DH issued guidance for the implementation of extended independent nurse prescribing which was later updated in 2004. The guidance was then replaced by a publication in 2006 entitled *Improving Patients' Access to Medicines: A Guide to Implementing Nurse and Pharmacist Independent Prescribing within the NHS in England* (DH 2006a). This has been followed by similar guidance from the other constituent countries of the UK. The DH guidance covers:

- Scope of this guidance and effect of devolution
- Nurse independent prescribing and pharmacist independent prescribing in England
- Implementation strategy
- Training and preparation for independent prescribing
- Medicines prescribable under independent prescribing arrangements
- Clinical governance in independent prescribing good practice, ethics and issues for all independent prescribers
- Patient records: Access and updating
- Adverse drug reaction reporting
- Legal and clinical liability
- Dispensing of prescribed items
- Verification of prescribing status
- Dispensing by appliance contractors
- Urgent dispensing
- Dispensing of items in Scotland, Wales and Northern Ireland
- Dispensing items against a Nurse or Pharmacist
- Independent Prescriber's prescriptions in hospital pharmacies
- Independent prescribing monitoring information
- Annexes
  - Annex A - History
  - Annex B - Standards for prescribing and outline curricula for training Nurse and Pharmacist Independent Prescribers
  - Annex C - Maintaining competency in prescribing – Outline Frameworks
  - Annex D - Notification of prescriber details to the Prescription Pricing Division of the NHS Business Services Authority
  - Annex E - Prescription forms
  - Annex F - Good practice examples of non-medical prescribing clinical governance frameworks
  - Annex G - Controlled drugs
  - Annex H - Prescribing information and advice
  - Annex I - Web links for further information

The DH guidance on the records to be kept of prescriptions by independent nurse prescribers is considered in Chapter 25.

Training

The Nursing and Midwifery Council (NMC) has laid down the criteria for eligibility to become an independent prescriber. In 2006 the NMC published its *Standards of proficiency for nurse and midwife prescribers*. The NMC states that:

> Under the new legislation prescribers must have sufficient knowledge and competence to:
>
> • Assess a patient/client's clinical condition
>
> • Undertake a thorough history, including medical history and medication history, and diagnose where necessary, including over-the-counter medicines and complementary therapies
>
> • Decide on management of presenting condition and whether or not to prescribe
>
> • Identify appropriate products if medication is required
>
> • Advise the patient/client/client on effects and risks
>
> • Prescribe if the patient/client agrees
>
> • Monitor response to medication and lifestyle advice.

The NMC groups the standards into the following domains:
- Clinical pharmacology, including the effects of co-morbidity.
- Consultation, history-taking, diagnosis, decision-making and therapy, including referral.
- Influences on, and psychology of, prescribing.
- Prescribing in a team context and sharing information.
- Evidence-based practice and clinical governance in relation to nurse/midwife prescribing.
- Legal, policy and ethical aspects of prescribing.
- Professional accountability and responsibility.
- Prescribing in the public health context.

There are four sections, the first covering education and training provision to prepare nurses and midwives to prescribe. The second section on standards for prescribing practice sets 21 practice standards on:
- Licence as a prescriber
- Accountability
- Assessment
- Need

- Consent
- Communication
- Record keeping
- Clinical management plans (supplementary prescribing)
- Prescribing and administration/supply
- Prescribing and dispensing
- Prescribing for family and others
- Computer-generated prescribing by nurses or midwives
- Evidence-based prescribing
- Delegation
- Continuing professional development
- Controlled drugs
- Prescribing unlicensed medicines
- Prescribing medicines for use outside the terms of the licence
- Repeat prescribing
- Remote prescribing via telephone, email, fax, video link or website
- Gifts and benefits.

The final sections cover additional guidance and further information which includes a glossary, legal classification of medicines and resources.

Prescribing controlled drugs

The NMC in its practice standard 16 on Controlled Drugs (CD) states:

16.1 You must only prescribe CD for which you are legally entitled to. Midwives may supply and administer CD via Exemption Orders as this is not a form of prescribing

16.2 Legally you must include clear dosage instructions on a prescription to avoid uncertainty on administration. Extra care must be given when syringe drivers are being used

16.3 You must ensure you do not prescribe beyond your limits of competence and experience 16.4 You must inform anyone who needs to know about any restrictions placed on your prescribing practice, particularly pharmacists with dispensing responsibilities

16.5 You may use computer-generated prescriptions for all CD, providing the necessary software is in place and that there is an audit trail of your prescribing practice

16.6 The quantity of any CD prescribed (excluding those in schedule 5) should not exceed 28 days supply per prescription. A new prescription is required where a patient/client has continuing clinical need

16.7 You must not prescribe a CD for yourself

16.8 You may only prescribe a CD for someone close to you if:

> *a) No other person with the legal right to prescribe is available*
>
> *b) And only then, if that treatment is immediately necessary to:*
>> *i) Save life*
>>
>> *ii) Avoid significant deterioration in the patient/client's health*
>>
>> *iii) Alleviate otherwise uncontrollable pain*

16.9 You must be able to justify your actions and must document your relationship and the emergency circumstances that necessitated your prescribing a CD for someone close to you.

The DH in its guidance in 2006 on independent nurse prescribers states that Nurse Independent Prescribers (formerly known as Extended Formulary Nurse Prescribers) are able to prescribe any licensed medicine for any medical condition, including some CD (See Chapter 3).

Supplementary prescribing

In April 2002 the DH announced its intention of introducing supplementary prescribing by a nurse or pharmacist in 2003 (DH 2002a). The aim was to enable the pharmacists and nurses to work in partnership with doctors and to help treat such conditions as asthma, diabetes, high blood pressure and arthritis. The doctor would draw up a plan with the patient's agreement, laying out the range of medicines which can be prescribed and when to refer back to the doctor. This early announcement was followed by a press release in November 2002 which gave further details of the patient conditions and the medicinal products which would be the subject of supplementary prescribing (DH 2002b). In commenting on these changes, Sarah Mullally, the Chief Nursing Officer for England, is reported as saying that:

> *This type of prescribing will be a very useful addition to the practice of nurses, many of whom already manage a variety of long term conditions and health needs for their patients. Nurses often advise doctors on prescribing decisions in their specialist area, and the introduction of supplementary prescribing will allow nurses to write many of those prescriptions themselves. I believe that nurses will welcome the opportunity to develop these skills for the benefit for their patients.*

Subsequent developments on supplementary prescribing

In March 2003 the DH issued a guide for the implementation of supplementary prescribing by nurses and pharmacists within the NHS in England (DH 2003). (The Welsh Assembly has issued its own guidance (2004)) This covers the topics shown in Box 10.3.

Supplementary prescribing is defined in the guidance as:

A voluntary partnership between an independent prescriber (a doctor or dentist) and a supplementary prescriber to implement an agreed patient- specific Clinical Management Plan with the patient's agreement.

The aim of supplementary prescribing is to provide patients with quicker and more efficient access to medicines and to make the best use of the skills of trained nurses and pharmacists. The DH considers that over time it is likely to reduce doctors' workloads, freeing up their time to concentrate on patients with more complicated conditions and more complex treatments.

The legal basis for supplementary prescribing is section 63 of the Health and Social Care Act 2001 and the subsequent statutory instruments (.The NHS (Amendments Relating to Prescribing by Nurses and Pharmacists etc) (England) Regulations 2003 SI 2003 No 699.) Under SI 2003 No 699, where a doctor employs a supplementary prescriber the conditions under which she/he can prescribe prescription only medicines, can administer a prescription only medicine for parenteral administration or give directions for the administration of a prescription only medicine for parenteral administration are that:

a. The person satisfies the applicable conditions set out in article 3B(3) of the POM order (POM (Human Use) Order 1997 SI 1997 No 1830 (amended by SI 2002/549 and 2003/696) unless those conditions do not apply by virtue of any of the exemptions set out in the subsequent provisions of that Order.

b. The medicine is not a controlled drug within the meaning of the Misuse of Drugs Act 1971.

c. The medicine is not specified in Schedule 10 to the Medical Regulations (drugs and other substances not to be prescribed for supply under pharmaceutical services). (SI 1992/635 as amended by AI 1992/2412; SI 1993/2421; 1994/2620; 1995/3093; 1997/981; 1998/682 and 2838; 1999/326 ad 1627; 2000/1645; 2001/1178, 3386 and 37742; 2002/554, 881, 1768, 1920 and 2469; and 2003/26)

d. The medicine is not specified in an entry in column 1 of the Schedule 11 to

Box 10.3 Department of Health guidance on supplementary prescribing

Background

- How supplementary prescribing will work
- Who can undertake supplementary prescribing
- Training and preparation for supplementary prescribing
- Evaluation audit and clinical governance of supplementary prescribing
- The clinical management plan
- Medicines prescribable under supplementary prescribing
- The patient review
- Good practice, ethics and issues common to all supplementary prescribers: stock items, informing patients prescribing for self, family and friends
- Patient records
- Adverse reaction reporting
- Legal and clinical liability
- Dispensing of prescribed items
- Verification of prescribing status
- Dispensing by appliance contractors
- Urgent dispensing and dispensing of items in Wales, Scotland and Northern Ireland.

Budget setting and monitoring
Annexes

A) NMC requirements for extended and supplementary prescribing
B) Royal Pharmaceutical Society of GB Outline curriculum
C) CMP template for teams that have full co-terminus access to patient records
D) CMP template for teams lacking full co-terminus access
E) Notification of prescriber details to PPA
F) Prescription forms.

(DH 1999)

the Medical Regulations (drugs to be prescribed under pharmaceutical services only in certain circumstances).

Where a doctor employs a supplementary prescriber the conditions on which he or she can give a prescription for an appliance or a medicine which is not a POM include:

a. He acts in accordance with a clinical management plan (which may be amended from time to time) which is in effect at the time he acts, which has been agreed by the patient to whom the plan relates, the doctor or dentist who is a party to the plan and any supplementary prescriber who is to prescribe, give directions for the administration or administer under the plan and which contains the following particulars:

i. the name of the patient to whom the plan relates

ii. the illness or conditions which may be treated by the supplementary prescriber

iii. the date on which the plan is to take effect, and when it is to be reviewed by the doctor or dentist who is a party to the plan

iv. reference to the class or description of medicines or types of appliances which may be prescribed or administered under the plan

v. any restrictions or limitations as to the strength or dose of any medicine which may be prescribed or administered under the plan, any period of administration or use of any medicine or appliance which may be prescribed or administered under the plan

vi. relevant warnings about known sensitivities of the patient to, or known difficulties of the patient with, particular medicines or appliances

vii. the arrangements for the notification of suspected or known adverse reactions; incidents occurring with the appliance which might lead to the death or serious deterioration of the patient and

viii. the circumstances in which the supplementary prescriber should refer to, or seek the advice of, the doctor or dentist who is a party to the plan.

b. He has access to the health records of the patient to whom the plan relates which are used by any doctor or dentist who is a party to the plan.

c. If it is a prescription for a medicine, the medicine is not a controlled drug within the meaning of the Misuse of Drugs Act 1971

d. If it is a prescription for a medicine, the medicine is not specified in Schedule 10 to the Medical Regulations (drugs and other substances not to be prescribed for supply under pharmaceutical services).

Registered optometrists were added to the list of eligibility to be supplementary prescribers in June 2005 (SI 2005 No 1507).

NMC standards on extended independent nurse prescribing and supplementary prescribing

In November 2002 the NMC published a copy of new NMC standards for the extension of independent prescribing by nurses, midwives and health visitors and supplementary prescribing (NMC 2002). Successful completion of a course meeting these standards can lead to an entry on the register which will enable the practitioner to prescribe independently or as supplementary prescribers. The NMC requirements cover:

- The standard of programme
- The kind of programme
- The content of the programme.

The NMC identifies the principal areas, knowledge and competencies required to underpin the practice of prescribing.

Recent changes

Under a SI in 2004 the permitted use or route of administration for specified substances when prescribed or administered by an extended formulary nurse prescriber was changed; for example, erythromycin is to include oral use (POM (Human Use) Amendment Order 2004 No 2). The SI also adds diamorphine and morphine to the list of substances that may be parenterally administered by registered nurses. A change brought into force on 19 November 2004 extended the exemption for administration for the purposes of saving life in an emergency to specified medicinal products (SI 2004 No 2693).

It was inevitable that the range of medicinal products which nurses and other healthcare professionals would be allowed to prescribe would continue to grow. In April 2004 the DH announced that a further 60 medicines were to be added to the 180 Prescription Only Medicines (POM) which nurses could prescribe (DH 2004). In February 2005 the DH initiated a consultation on further developments to prescribing by nurses and pharmacists (DH 2005a). At that time there were 28,000 district nurses and health visitors who could prescribe, and over 4,000 extended formulary nurse prescribers prescribing for chronic conditions such as dermatitis, conjunctivitis and back pain. Under the new proposals nurses were able to prescribe for such conditions as asthma and diabetes and pharmacists were able to prescribe for a range of common conditions from acne to tonsillitis and took on duties including patient admission and discharge reviews, acute pain management and medication reviews. The options for independent nurse prescribing being consulted upon in 2005 were:

- No change – maintain a nurse Prescribers' Extended Formulary for specified medical conditions
- Prescribing for any medical condition from a specified Formulary Prescribing for specific medical conditions from a full Formulary
- Advanced practice nurses with a higher level of competencies.

There were seven similar options for pharmacists. Annex A to the consultation document contained a list of medication conditions for which the appropriately trained nurse was currently entitled to prescribe and Annex B a list of the preparations in the nurse prescribers' Extended Formulary.

The consultation ended on 23 May 2005. Following the consultation, statutory changes were achieved by amendment to the POM (Human Use) Order 1997 and NHS Regulations (Medicines for Human Use (Prescribing) Order 2005, SI 2005/765 and Medicines for Human Use (Prescribing) (Miscellaneous Amendments) Order 2005, SI 2005 No 1507 and No 1520).

An overview and guide to the current mechanisms for the prescribing, supply and administration of medicines was published by the DH in 2005 (DH 2005b). The DH reported in June 2005 that independent nurse prescribing is viewed positively by patients, doctors and nurses (DH 2005c).

In 2006 the DH published *Improving Patients' Access to Medicines:A Guide to Implementing Nurse and Pharmacist Independent Prescribing within the NHS in England* (DH 2006a). This supersedes the 2004 discussed earlier. (See above). In 2006 the DH also published *Medicines Matters: A guide to the mechanisms for the prescribing, administration and supply of medicines*. It describes itself as a brief guide to good practice and is helpful in setting out the basic principles of prescribing (DH 2006b).

In 2006 the concept of the extended formulary for nurse prescribers was discontinued and instead independent nurse prescribers are able to prescribe medicines which come within their professional competence (Medicines for Human Use (Prescribing) (Miscellaneous Amendments) Order, SI 2006 No 915).

In 2007 the NMC published its *Standards for medicines management* which set standards on both the administration of medicines and also both independent and supplementary prescribing. These, together with the NMC *Standards of proficiency for nurse and midwife prescribers*, which was published in 2006, provide set standards and provide guidance for nurses and midwives in all aspects of medicines supply and administration.

Mixing of medicine

Legislative changes which came into force in December 2009 enable nurse and pharmacist independent prescribers to mix medicines themselves and to direct others to mix. Supplementary prescribers can also mix medicines themselves and direct others to mix, but only where that preparation forms part of the Clinical Management Plan for an individual patient. Nurse and pharmacist independent prescribers can prescribe unlicensed medicines for their patients, on the same basis as doctors and dentists (and supplementary prescribers if that is part of a Clinical Management Plan) (MHRA 2010). 'Mixing' is defined as 'the combination of two or more medicinal products together for the purposes of administering them to meet the needs of a particular patient.'

The DH has also provided guidance (DH 2010). It quotes the principles set by the Commission on Human Medicines (CHM) on the mixing of medicines:

• *Mixing should be avoided where possible. It must only be undertaken when clinically appropriate and essential to meet the needs of the patient. It should not be undertaken for the convenience of a health professional.*

• *The instruction/ direction to mix must be in writing.*

• *The prescriber takes responsibility for satisfying himself or herself that clinical governance arrangements are in place to ensure that the "mixer" is competent to undertake the task safely and effectively - especially within a non-hospital environment.*

• *The person mixing the medicines must be competent.*

• *No-one should be obliged to mix and administer medicines if they do not feel competent or content to do so.*

Other healthcare professionals

The powers to prescribe have been given to other healthcare professions and there is constant extension of those registered practitoners who are able to prescribe. An appendix to *Medicines Matters* (DH 2006b) contains a matrix setting out which health professionals are able to prescribe and under which mechanism together with any exemptions. In 2010 the MHRA consulted on amendments to the range of medicines which can be sold, supplied or administered by podiatrists. The Consultation ended on 17 January 2011.

Applying the law to the question in Box 10.1

Whether or not the clinical nurse specialist is guilty of a failure to follow the reasonable standard of professional practice will depend upon a lot of information which is not given in this scenario. What questions did she ask about any possible allergies? How capable was the patient in terms of her ability to answer any questions? What was the accepted approved practice in this situation? If the answer to these questions is that the clinical nurse specialist followed reasonable practice, it is unlikely that she would be found guilty of professional misconduct or that the patient would win a claim for compensation against the NHS trust.

Conclusions

The Crown Report in a sense gave its approval to a controlled development of professional competence in areas formerly the sole reserve of medical staff. However, clear checks are in place to ensure that these developments take place with well-defined precautions to secure patient safety and also to secure efficient use of resources (DN 1999). Whilst nurses are likely to be the most numerous group to develop prescribing skills, other professionals, such as physiotherapists, radiographers, orthoptists, dieticians, speech therapists and many others have found that the legislation has facilitated professional development or at the minimum validated activities already taking place. The need to obtain a doctor's personal attendance on a patient in order that a specific drug could be prescribed has placed an unnecessary obstacle in the advancement of professional practice for many health professionals and also in the efficient and speedy care of patients, this obstacle is now being increasingly lifted. In order to ensure that patient safety is not compromised it is essential that this development is accompanied by the warning contained in the final Crown Report and set out above. It probably cannot be too frequently repeated:

All legally authorised prescribers should take personal responsibility for maintaining and updating their knowledge and practice related to prescribing, including taking part in clinical audit, and should never prescribe in situations beyond their professional competence.

The dangers from even commonly prescribed drugs should not be underestimated. A study suggests that prescription drugs are linked to 15,000 deaths a year (Hawkes 2005).

Key points

■ The final Crown Report recommended the introduction of independent and dependent (now known as supplementary) prescribers.
■ Following the successful implementation of community nurse prescribing legislation has been introduced to enable appropriately trained nurses to prescribe against an extended formulary.
■ The extended nurses formulary was initially published as a supplement within the BNF but was discontinued in 2006.
■ Further development of supplementary prescribing by nurses, pharmacists and other heath professionals has continued.

References

Department of Health (1999) Review of Prescribing, Supply and Administration of Medicines Final Report (Crown Report). London.

Department of Health (2000) *Consultation paper on extending nurse prescribing*. 25 October 2000 London

Department of Health (2002 (updated 2004)) *Extending independent nurse prescribing within the NHS in England: A guide for implementation*. London.

Department of Health (2002) press release 2002/0189: *Groundbreaking new consultation aims to extend prescribing powers for pharmacists and nurses*. London.

Department of Health (2002) press release 2002/0488: *Pharmacists to prescribe for the first time Nurses will prescribe for chronic illness*, 21 November. London.

Department of Health (2003) *Supplementary prescribing by nurses and pharmacists within the NHS in England*. London.

Department of Health (2004a) press release 2004/0141: *Nurses' prescribing powers to be expanded even further*, April 2004. London.

Department of Health (2005a) *Consultation on options for the future independent prescribing by extended formulary nurse prescribers; Consultation on options for the future independent prescribing by pharmacists*, February 2005. London.

Department of Health (2005b) NHS Modernisation Agency *Medicines Matters: A Guide to Current Mechanisms for the Prescribing, Supply and Administration of Medicines*.

Department of Health (2005c) press release 2005/0223: *Patients positive about nurse prescribing*, June 2005. London.

Department of Health (2006a) *Improving Patients' Access to Medicines: A Guide to Implementing Nurse and Pharmacist Independent Prescribing within the NHS in England* (Department of Health Gateway reference: 6429 April 2006). London.

Department of Health (2006b) *Medicines Matters: A guide to mechanisms for the prescribing, supply and administration of medicines* July 2006. London

Hawkes, N. (2005) Prescription drugs linked to 15,000 deaths each year. *The Times*, 11 May 2005.

Medicines Healthcare Protection Regulatory Agency (2010) *Mixing of medicines*

Nursing and Midwifery Council circular 25/2002: *Extended independent nurse prescribing AND supplementary prescribing*.

Nursing and Midwifery Council (2007) *Standards for medicines management*. London.

Nursing and Midwifery Council (2006) *Standards of proficiency for nurse and midwife prescribers*. London.

CHAPTER II

Midwives and medicines

> **Box II.I Situation**
>
> *Miriam, a student midwife, was called to attend a home birth and arrived before the registered midwife. The woman was in considerable pain and had in her possession pethidine which had been left by the general practitioner. She asked the student midwife to inject her with it. What is the legal position?*

Introduction

Registered midwives have specific statutory powers in relation to medicines and Controlled Drugs (CD). The restrictions on retail sale or supply of Prescription Only Medicines (POM) do not apply to the supply or sale of certain medicinal products by a registered midwife in the course of her professional practice.

By Statutory Instrument (SI) 1997 No 1830 the midwife can supply:

- All medicines that are not POM.
- POM containing any of the following substances but no other POM:
  - Choral hydrate
  - Ergometrine maleate (only when contained in a medicinal product which is not for parenteral administration
  - Pentazocine hydrochloride
  - Phytomenadione (SI 1998 No 2081)
  - Triclofos sodium.

The midwife can also administer parenterally in the course of professional practice POM containing any of the following substances (SI 1997 No 1830.):

- Ergometrine maleate
- Lignocaine
- Lignocaine hydrochloride
- Naloxone hydrochloride
- Oxytocin, natural and synthetic

      –   Pentazocine lactate
      –   Pethidine hydrocloride
      –   Phytomenadione
      –   Promazine hydrocloride.

Lignocaine, lignocaine hydrocloride and promazine hydrocloride may only be administered by a midwife while attending a woman in childbirth.

Midwives and Controlled Drugs

A registered midwife who has notified the local supervising authority of her intention to practise may, as far as is necessary for the practice of her profession or employment as a midwife, possess and administer any CD which the Medicines Act 1968 permits her to administer. (Regulation 11 of the Misuse of Drugs Regulations 2001 No 3998 amending and re-enacting the Misuse of Drugs Regulations S I 1985 2066).

Supplies may only be made to her or possessed by her, on the authority of a midwife's supply order. This supply order must specify the name and occupation of the midwife, the purpose for which it is required and the total quantity to be obtained. The supply order must be signed:

- By a doctor who is authorised by the local supervising authority for the region or area in which the CD was, or is, to be obtained, or
- By the supervisor of midwives appointed by the local supervising authority for that area.

The Regulation defines a midwife's supply order as:

an order in writing specifying the name and occupation of the midwife obtaining the drug, the purpose for which it is required and the total quantity to be obtained.

Disposal of unwanted stocks

A midwife may surrender any stocks of CD in her possession which she no longer requires to the doctor as identified above (Reg. 11) or any doctor, or pharmacist (Reg. 6).

Documentation

The midwife must keep a CD book in which she must record the following:

- the date
- the name and address of the person from whom the drug was obtained
- the amount obtained
- the form in which it was obtained
- the name and address of the patient to whom the drug was administered
- the amount administered
- the form in which it was administered.

When the midwife receives the CD from the pharmacist, she must sign the pharmacist's CD register and the pharmacist must keep the midwife's supply order for two years.

Midwives Rules: administration of medicines

The Midwives Rules (UKCC 1998) were replaced in 2004 by new rules and standards published by the Nursing and Midwifery Council (NMC 2004), and they specify additional rules in relation to the supply and possession of medicines by midwives.

Rule 7 on the administration of medicines sets out the following requirements:

A practising midwife shall only supply and administer those medicines, including analgesics, in respect of which she has received the appropriate training as to use, dosage and methods of administration.

Standards

Standards specified by the NMC in relation to rule 7 are:

- A midwife must abide by the regulations relating to the destruction of CD
- A midwife must respect the right of individuals to self-administer substances of their choice.

Guidance

The following guidance is issued by the NMC in relation to rule 7:

You are able to supply and administer all non-prescription medicines, which include all pharmacy and general sales list medicines without a prescription. The list of medicines are all those in the British National Formulary that are not prescription only medicines. These medicines do not need to be in a Patient Group Direction for you to be able to supply and/or administer them as part of your professional practice.

Local policies, sometimes referred to as 'standing orders', have frequently been developed to supplement legislation on medicines that practising midwives may supply and/or administer. There is no legal requirement to replace these with Patient Group Directions.

You should expect your supervisor of midwives to audit your records related to drug administration from time to time.

Some medicines, which are normally only available on a prescription issued by a medical practitioner, may be supplied to you for use in your practice either from a retail chemist or hospital pharmacy. Further details can be found on page 37 of this document under supplementary information and legislation.

You should advise a woman who has not used a controlled drug, which has been prescribed by her GP, to destroy it and suggest she does so in your presence. Alternatively, you can advise the woman to return the unused controlled drug to the pharmacist from where it was obtained. You must not do that for her.

If you are aware that a woman is self-administering illegal substances you should discuss the health implications for her and her baby with her.

You should also assist her by liaison with others in the multi-professional team to gain further support or access to detoxification programmes.

(NMC guidance on homoeopathic and herbal medicines is discussed in Chapter 24.)

Midwives Rules: records

Under the rules revised by the NMC in 2004, Rule 9(4) makes it a statutory duty for the self-employed midwife to transfer her official records to the local supervising authority (LSA) immediately before she ceases to practice. This would include her documentation on medicines.

Midwives Rules: inspection of premises and equipment

Rule 10(1) requires the practising midwife to give to a supervisor of midwives, a LSA and the Council, every reasonable facility to monitor her standards and methods of practice and to inspect her records, her equipment and any premises that she is entitled to permit them to enter, which may include such part of the midwife's residence as may be used for professional purposes.

Rule 10(2) states:

A practising midwife shall use her best endeavours to permit inspection from time to time of all places of work in which she practises, other than the private residence of a woman and baby she is attending, by persons nominated by the Council for this purpose, one of whom shall be a practising midwife.

In its guidance on this rule the NMC makes it clear that it is the midwife's responsibility to let the LSA and the NMC monitor her standards and methods of practice. This may include allowing access to records, equipment and place of work.

Midwives standards and guidance

The Midwives Code of Practice has been replaced by standards and guidance set by the NMC (2004). Unlike the Rules, these paragraphs are not part of the law of the country, but they provide standards for and guidance to registered midwives, and failure to conform to these standards and guidance could be used in evidence in fitness to practise investigations and proceedings.

NMC guidance on legislation with regard to the supply and administration of medicines

Registered midwives are able to supply and administer, as appropriate, on their own initiative and as part of their professional practice certain medicinal products covered by legal 'exemptions'. The relevant pieces of legislation are as follows.

Pharmacy and General Sales List medicines

The Medicines (Pharmacy and General Sale – Exemption) Order 1980 SI 1980 No 1924 deals with Pharmacy and General Sales list exemptions thus:

Exemption for products used by midwives in the course of their professional practice.

4. There are hereby specified for the purposes of section 55(2)(b) (exemptions for certified midwives) the following classes of medicinal products:

> *a. all medicinal products that are not prescription only medicines, and*

> *b. prescription only medicines which, by virtue of an exemption conferred by an order made under section 58(4)(a), may be sold or supplied by a certified midwife otherwise than in accordance with a prescription given by a practitioner.*

Prescription Only Medicines

These are covered by the POM (Human Use) Order 1997 SI 1997 No 1830. The two relevant exemptions from the POM order are contained in Schedule 5:

- Article 11(1)(a) Part I covers exemptions from restrictions on the sale and supply and
- Article 11(2) Part III covers exemptions from the restrictions on administration or POM.

The supply and administration of all non-Prescription Only and General Sales List medicines by registered midwives in the course of their professional practice

The NMC issued guidance in March 2003 following its concern that the supply and administration of some non-prescription medicines such as nitrous oxide and oxygen have been wrongly written into PGD (NMC 2003). In its guidance for employers and registered midwives it emphasises that under SI 1980 No 1924 a registered midwife can supply and administer all non-POM, including pharmacy and General Sales List medicines. A student midwife during the course of her programme of education, can administer those medicines under the guidance of a practising midwife, for which the registered midwife remains accountable.

The NMC feared that including medicines unnecessarily in PGD would have implications for student midwives gaining experience in the administration of nitrous oxide and oxygen to women in the course of their education.

Prescribing of diamorphine and morphine

An amendment was made to the POM (Human Use) Order 1997 in January 2004. It states that in Schedule 5 to the principal order (exemption for certain persons from section 58(2) of the Medicines Act 1968), diamorphine and morphine are to be added to the list of drugs which midwives can administer without the requirement of a patient-specific prescription. The NMC emphasised that there is no requirement for a Patient Group Direction (PGD) for such medicines.

The NMC in its guidance in 2004 provides an updated list of the midwives exemption drugs as follows:
- Diamorphine
- Ergometrine maleate
- Lignocaine
- Lignocaine hydrochloride
- Morphine
- Naloxone hydrochloride
- Oxytocins, natural and synthetic
- Pentazocine lactate
- Pethidine hydrochloride
- Phytomenadione
- Promazine hydrochloride.

The list that the midwives can also supply as well as administer can be obtained from the SI (POM (Human Use) Amendment Order 2004) which is available from the HMSO website (www.hmso.gov.uk).

Management or errors or incidents in the administration of medicines

Standard 24 of the standards set by the NMC suggest sensitive management of any incidents relating to the administration of medicines and require the registered practitioner to report the error or incident immediately to the line manager or employer (see Chapter 6). In addition, midwives should inform their named supervisor of midwives.

Routine antenatal anti-D prophylaxis for RhDnegative women

A position statement issued by the UKCC on 11 February 1999 was withdrawn by the NMC in March 2003. It followed guidance from the National Institute for Clinical Excellence (NICE 2002) which recommended that pregnant rhesus negative women should be offered anti-D prophylaxis as a preventative treatment (to haemolytic disease in the new born) routinely, unless they already have antibodies to the D antigen in their blood. NICE also recommended that healthcare professionals should explain the options available to rhesus negative mothers so that they can make an informed choice about treatment.

Medicines during pregnancy

A team from the University of Bristol found that only 17% of mothers did not take any conventional medicine throughout pregnancy (NMC 2004). Some 39% of women took analgesics – mostly paracetamol and aspirin – during the early stages of pregnancy. One in four took indigestion medicines in mid- to late pregnancy. Minor ailments were often self-medicated with over-the-counter products, without the woman consulting a doctor. In response to this study, the *British National Formulary* (BNF) has issued new advice on medication use during pregnancy (www.bnf.org).

The BNF guidance emphasises that women need to take special care about their entire lifestyle during pregnancy: this means taking care with eating, drinking, exercising and, indeed, taking medicines.Women should consult their doctor or pharmacist before embarking on any treatment with medicines or herbal remedies during pregnancy.

The BNF advises that medicines should be avoided during pregnancy as far as possible. Drugs which have been extensively used in pregnancy and appear to be usually safe should be prescribed in preference to new or untried drugs; and the smallest effective dose should be used. The BNF advises caution and not overstating the potential for harm. It suggests that:

> Before we get too concerned about the level of medicine taking during pregnancy, we need to have a clearer idea of whether the clinical outcome of the pregnancy in women who have taken medicines is statistically different from those who have not.

Patient Group Directions and independent/ supplementary prescribing

Midwives may also be identified as the appropriate registered health professional to supply medicinal products to patients under a PGDs and would have to ensure that the statutory requirements for such authorisation have been complied with. These were considered in Chapter 8. Midwives may also be identified as independent prescribers or supplementary prescribers (see Chapter 10), so after the appropriate training, the range of medicinal products which midwives are authorised to supply to their patients could be vastly expanded.

NMC and consultation on changes to midwives rules

The NMC commissioned Alpha Research to conduct a review of the midwives rules and standards which was published in April 2009 and available on the NMS website (www.nmc-uk.org/). At the time of writing the NMC is consulting on changes to the midwives rules. Any changes to the rules will have to be approved in Parliament. Following any rule changes, the NMS will publish draft standards and guidance and consult on any changes in May 2011.

Extension of student midwives powers

In 2010 the Medicines and Healthcare products Regulatory Agency (MHRA) launched a consultation on proposals to allow student midwives access to the parenteral medicines which can currently be administered by registered midwives under an exemption in medicines legislation. The consultation ended on November 2010 and at the time of writing the outcome is awaited. Consultation has ended but no further information as yet from the MHRA

Applying the law to the situation in Box 11.1

In this situation, the student nurse is not the supplier of pethidine, since the patient has that in her own right from the general practitioner. Ideally it would be preferable for the student midwife to wait for the registered midwife to arrive.

117

However, if her arrival were to be delayed, the student could act as the agent of the woman in ensuring the safe administration of the drug. She should read the directions on the label, ascertain when the woman last had a dose and ensure that all directions were complied with. The student should also be aware of any local policies and guidelines which cover the situation. This situation is very different from one where a registered midwife brings her own supplies of CD to a domiciliary visit. A student would not be able to have supplies as described above, but only work under the direct supervision of the registered midwife.

Conclusions

In spite of the developments in the extension of independent nurse prescribing, the midwife is in a very different legal situation since she has specific statutory powers which give her extensive powers in relation to CD. She therefore has considerable responsibilities in ensuring that the statutory requirements and the Midwives Rules are followed and that note is taken of the standards and guidance issued by the NMC. In addition, she should ensure that she is acquainted with local guidelines and policies on the safe prescription, supply and administration of medicines.

Key points

■ Registered midwives have specific statutory powers in relation to medicines and CD.
■ They are legally bound to follow the Midwives Rules and are advised to follow the standards and guidance set by the NMC.
■ Rules also relate to her record keeping, equipment and premises.
■ Guidance on medicines to pregnant women is provided in the BNF.
■ An extension to the powers of student midwives is currently the subject of consultation by the MHRA.

References

British National Formulary (2004) *British National Formulary Extra*: News 6 October 2004; http://www.bnf.org/.

National Institute for Clinical Excellence (2002) *Guidance for rhesus negative women during pregnancy*, 2002/024 http://www.nice.org.uk/. London

Nursing and Midwifery Council (2003) Circular 8/2003, March 2003. London

Nursing and Midwifery Council (2003) *Routine antenatal anti-D prophylaxis for RhD-negative women*. Circular 5/2003, 5 March 2003.

Nursing and Midwifery Council 2004. *Revised UKCC Midwives Rules and Code of Practice*. London

Nursing and Midwifery Council (2004) Circular 10/2004 *Addition of diamorphine and morphine to the list of exemptions for midwives*. 27 April 2004. London

Nursing and Midwifery Council (2004) NMC Council News, 8 October 2004. Reporting research by J. Headley, K. Northstone, H. Simmons, J. Golding et al.: Medication use during pregnancy: data from the Avon longitudinal study of parents and children. Eur. J. Clinical Pharmacol.

Nursing and Midwifery Council (2007) *Standards for medicines management*.

Nursing and Midwifery Council (2009) *Alpha Research review of the midwives rules and standards April 2009* (available on the NMS website (www.nmc-uk.org/).

UKCC (1988) *Midwives Rules and Code of Practice*. London

Website

British National Formulary website http://www.bnf.org
HMSO website http://www.hmso.gov.uk/.

CHAPTER 12

Consent by the mentally capacitated patient

Box 12.1 Situation

Roy Dawes was diagnosed as diabetic, but was not prepared to keep to the necessary diet which should have been able to control his condition. In particular, he was a heavy drinker. He was therefore advised that he would require insulin and regular blood testing. He failed to comply with this regime and the community nurse wondered if he could be compelled to have his medication. What is the law?

Introduction

It is a basic principle of law that a mentally capable adult has the right to refuse even life-saving treatment for a good reason, a bad reason or no reason (Re MB (adult: Medical treatment) [1997] 2 FLR 426.). Under the Mental Capacity Act 2005 there is in law a presumption that a person over 16 years has the requisite mental capacity to make decisions. However this presumption can be rebutted (i.e removed) on a balance of probabilities (the civil law test) if there is evidence to the contrary. It is therefore an essential requirement for the legality of prescribing and administration of medicines that the patient gives consent. This in law consists of two aspects:

1. Failure by the patient to give effective consent when the medicine is administered could be seen as **a trespass to the person**, which is actionable as a civil wrong without proof that the patient has suffered harm.
2. The patient must be given sufficient information to make a decision on whether or not to have the medication. Giving this information is part of the **duty of care** of the registered practitioner. It is only actionable if the patient suffers from harm which was not disclosed to her or him.

The first aspect of consent, trespass to the person, will be considered in this chapter in relation to the administration and prescribing of medicinal products. The second aspect, breach of the duty of care to inform, will be considered in the next chapter.

Trespass to the person

An action for trespass (which belongs to a group of civil wrongs known as 'torts') is one of the oldest remedies in law (known as a right of action in law); it includes an assault and a battery. An action for assault arises where the employee of the defendant (in this context it is normally the employer of the health professional that would be sued because of its vicarious liability for the actions of the employee) causes a claimant reasonable apprehension of the infliction of a battery upon him/her; a battery arises where there is intentional and direct application of force to another person.

Assault and battery are also used to describe possible criminal actions, but when we are using the terms in relation to a trespass to the person we are referring to a civil action brought in the civil courts (i.e. County Court or High Court) for compensation by a claimant.

Unlike an action for negligence, harm does not have to be proved. The mere fact that a trespass has occurred is sufficient to bring an action. The action is known as actionable *per se*, i.e. actionable without proof of harm having been suffered. Trespass can also exist in relation to land and to goods. The mere touching of another person's property or possessions can constitute in law an actionable trespass. Any deliberate touching of another person may constitute an assault or battery (Box 12.2). An action can still constitute a trespass even when it is performed in the best interests of a person who is mentally capable but has not given consent.

Valid consent

To be valid, consent must be given by a person who has the necessary mental capacity. This could include a child of 16 or 17 who has a statutory right to give consent, or a child under 16 years who has a right recognised at common law (i.e. judge-made law) to give consent, provided the child is 'Gillick competent' (this is considered in Chapter 15). Consent must be given voluntarily – there must be no coercion, deceit or fraud.

Box 12.2 The case of Re F (Re F (A mental patient: sterilisation) [1990])

In this case, Lord Goff said:

A prank that gets out of hand, an over-friendly slap on the back, these things may transcend the bounds of lawfulness, without being characterised as hostile....Any touching of another's body is, in the absence of lawful excuse, capable of amounting to a battery and a trespass. Furthermore, in the case of medical treatment, we have to bear well in mind the libertarian principle of self-determination, which, to adopt the words of Cardozo J [an American Judge], recognises that:

Every human being of adult years and sound mind has a right to determine what shall be done with his own body; and a surgeon who performs an operation without his patient's consent commits an assault for which he is liable in damages.

(*Schloendorff v. Society of New York Hospital 211 NY 125 (1914)*)

Sufficient information must be given to the person so that he/she understands the basics of what is proposed. There are advantages in ensuring that the consent is evidenced in writing (the Department of Health has recommended that certain forms should be completed to provide evidence that consent has been given (DH 2007)) but the writing is not the consent – the consent is the actual agreement by the person that what is proposed can go ahead. Consent can be given in general terms to a particular procedure, without every single aspect being explained to the patient, but failure to warn of the significant risks of substantial harm could constitute an action for breach of the duty of care to inform (see Chapter 13).

Miss B case

In the recent case of Re B (re) (consent to treatment: capacity) ([2002] 2 ALL ER 449), the President of the Family Division stated that a mentally competent patient could ask for her ventilator to be switched off and that it was a trespass to her person to treat her without her consent. The facts are shown in Box 12.3.

Box 12.3 Facts of Re B [2002]

Miss B suffered a ruptured blood vessel in her neck which damaged her spinal cord. As a consequence she was paralysed from the neck down and was on a ventilator. She was of sound mind and knew that there was no cure for her condition. She asked for the ventilator to be switched off. Her doctors wished her to try out some special rehabilitation to improve the standard of her care and felt that an intensive care ward was not a suitable location for such a decision to be made. They were reluctant to perform such an action as switching off the ventilator without the court's approval. Ms B applied to court for a declaration to be made that the ventilator could be switched off.
(Re F (Re F (A mental patient: sterilisation) [1990])

The main issue in the case was the mental competence of Miss B. If she were held to be mentally competent, then she could refuse to have life-saving treatment for a good reason, a bad reason or no reason at all. She was interviewed by two psychiatrists who gave evidence to the court that she was mentally competent. The judge therefore held that she was entitled to refuse to be ventilated. The judge, Dame Elizabeth Butler-Sloss, President of the Family Division, held that B possessed the requisite mental capacity to make decisions regarding her treatment and thus the administration of artificial respiration by the trust against her wishes amounted to an unlawful trespass. It was reported on 29 April 2002 that Miss B had died peacefully in her sleep after the ventilator had been switched off. The definition of capacity will be considered in Chapter 14.

Refusing medication

It follows therefore that when a nurse is administering medicines and a mentally competent patient refuses to take it, then that is the right of the patient. The nurse should clearly explain the advantages to the patient of following the recommended course of treatment, but if the patient refuses the nurse must accept that refusal. If the nurse has reason to doubt the mental capacity of the patient, then she must take further advice (this is considered in Chapter 14). She must ensure that she documents the patient's records and the prescription sheet with the fact that she was unable to administer the medicine because of the patient's refusal.

Application of law to the scenario in Box 12.1

The crucial issue in this situation is the mental capacity of Roy. If he is considered to have the necessary mental capacity and the situation has been explained to him carefully, then he can make his own decision on whether or not to inject the insulin himself (or whether or not to receive injections) and keep to the correct diet. The community nurse may well wish to bring in a colleague with the appropriate skills to assist in the determination of his competence. Once the decision is made that he is mentally competent, then it is Roy's right in law to make decisions over whether or not he will take the recommended medicinal products.

Conclusions

As pointed out above, where the patient has given a valid consent, he or she cannot sue for trespass to the person. However, if the registered practitioner has failed to give the appropriate information to the patient then the patient may have an action in negligence for breach of the duty of care to inform. It is to this duty of providing information about medication that we turn in the next chapter.

Key points

- A mentally competent patient has the right to give or refuse consent to the treatment.
- A trespass to the person can arise when treatment has not been obtained.
- It is actionable without proof of harm.

References

Department of Health (2007) *Good Practice in Consent Implementation Guide*. London

CHAPTER 13

Giving information to the patient

> ## Box 13.1 Unwanted side-effects
>
> *Roy was advised that a new drug which had just come on the market would assist his chronic depression. He was not given any further information, but after taking it for a few days found that it had a strong effect on his personality and he became aggressive and violent. As a consequence of a fight at work he has lost his job and now he claims that had he known of these effects he would not have taken the new drug?*

Introduction

In the previous chapter we considered the law relating to consent and trespass to the person. In this chapter we consider the law relating to the giving of information to patients and the law of negligence in relation to breach of the duty of care to inform the patient of the significant risks of substantial harm.

Giving information: breach of the duty of care

If a valid consent by a mentally competent person has been given for a particular medicinal product, then that will be a defence against a possible action for trespass to the person. The patient may, however, allege that he/she was not told about specific risks associated with the medication. If these risks subsequently occur and harm is caused, and the patient can show that he/she would probably not have agreed to the procedure had he/she known of these risks, then he/she may succeed in an action for negligence against the professional or the professional's employer. The latter is vicariously liable for any negligence by its employees committed in the course of their employment. Unlike an action for trespass to the person, where harm does not have to be established, an action for negligence will only succeed if harm can be shown. As in any other action for negligence, there are four elements which the claimant will have to establish:

- A duty of care is owed by the defendant (or the defendant's employee), including the duty to inform.
- There has been a breach of this duty of care by a failure to follow the reasonable standard of care, as defined in the Bolam Test (Bolam v. Friern Barnet Management Committee, [1957] 1 WLR 582).
- A reasonably foreseeable consequence of this breach of duty is that harm has occurred.

All four elements must be established by the claimant on a balance of probabilities.

Chatterton v. Gerson

A case where the clear distinction was drawn between an action for trespass to the person and an action for breach of the duty of care to inform was the case of Chatterton v. Gerson [1981] QB 432. In this case, Judge Bristow said:

In my judgment once the patient is informed in broad terms of the nature of the procedure which is intended, and gives her consent, that consent is real, and the cause of the action on which to base a claim for failure to go into risks and implications is negligence, not trespass.

The duty of care

The duty of care to diagnose, advise and treat also includes the duty to inform the patient. The courts have held that the duty of care is not divisible: it includes all the above components (Sidaway v. Bethlem Royal Hospital Governors and others [1985] 1 ALL ER 643 [1985] AC 871).

The standard of care

How much information are doctors, nurses and other health professionals expected to give the patient? In America, there is a concept of informed consent, and it is a requirement that any relevant information in the knowledge of the health professionals should be given to a patient before consent is given to a particular procedure.

In the Sidaway case (Sidaway v. Bethlem Royal Hospital Governors, [1985]), the House of Lords held that the English Courts do not recognise a concept of informed consent. The facts of this case were that Amy Sidaway agreed to undergo an operation to relieve pain in her neck. She was informed about the possibility of disturbing a root nerve, but not about the risk of damage to the spinal cord. Unfortunately, the latter occurred and she became severely disabled. She sued for negligence on the basis that there was a breach of the duty of care to inform her about the possibility of such a risk. The trial judge held that the surgeon had told her about the possibility of damage to the nerve root, and that he had not told her of the danger of damage to the spinal cord (the aggregate risk of damage to the nerve root or spinal cord occurring was estimated at between 1-2%); nor did he tell her that it was an operation of choice rather than necessity. However, in refraining from informing her of these facts, he was following a practice at that time (1974) which would have been accepted as proper by a responsible body of skilled and experienced neurosurgeons. The judge thus applied what has become known as the Bolam Test (Bolam v. Friern Barnet Management Committee, [1957]) to the case. In the Bolam case Judge McNair stated that:

> The standard of care was that of the ordinary skilled man exercising and professing to have that special skill.... A doctor was not guilty of negligence if he acted in accordance with the practice accepted at that time as proper by a responsible body of medical opinion notwithstanding that other doctors adopted different practices.

As a consequence, Amy Sidaway lost her case in the High Court and appealed to the Court of Appeal unsuccessfully and thence to the House of Lords. The judges in the House of Lords all had different bases for their views, but they agreed that in general she had failed in her action. Lord Diplock applied the Bolam Test to the duty of care to inform. Lord Bridge distinguished between two extremes: warning the patient of all possible risks once the treatment has been decided upon in the patient's best interests, and not warning the patient of any risks in order not to alarm the patient. Between these two extremes, Lord Bridge suggested that the Bolam Test should be applied, but this did not mean handing over to the medical profession the entire question of the scope of the duty of disclosure. There will be circumstances where the judge could come to the conclusion that disclosure of a particular risk was so obviously necessary to an informed choice on the part of the patient that no reasonably prudent medical person would fail to make it.

Lord Templeman stated that:

In my opinion if a patient knows that a major operation may entail serious consequences, the patient cannot complain of lack of information unless the patient asks in vain for more information or unless there is some danger which by its nature or magnitude or for some other reason required to be separately taken into account by the patient in order to reach a balanced judgment in deciding whether or not to submit to the operation.

Lord Scarman supported a 'prudent patient test', a concept derived from an American case, Canterbury v. Spence 464 F 2d 772 (DC, 1972). In this case, it was recognised that there were four principles, as listed in Box 13.2.

Box 13.2 The four principles of the Canterbury v. Spence 464 F 2d 772 (DC, 1972) case

1. Every human being of adult years and of sound mind has a right to determine what shall be done with his/her own body.

2. The consent is the informed exercise of a choice, and that entails an opportunity to evaluate knowledgeably the options available and the risks attendant on each.

3. The doctor must therefore disclose all 'material risks'. What risks are 'material' is determined by the 'prudent patient' test, which is as follows:

   a risk is... material when a reasonable person, in what the physician knows or should know to be the patient's position, would be likely to attach significance to the risk or cluster of risks in deciding whether or not to forgo the proposed therapy.

4. The doctor has, however, a therapeutic privilege. This exception is that a reasonable medical assessment of the patient would have indicated to the doctor that disclosure would have posed a serious threat of psychological detriment to the patient.

Bolam Test

The Bolam Test does not assume that there is only one way to inform patients or to carry out treatment procedures. As McNair said:

> *a doctor was not guilty of negligence if he acted in accordance with the practice accepted at that time as proper by a responsible body of medical opinion, notwithstanding that other doctors adopted different practices.*

This conforms with the ruling given by the House of Lords in the Maynard case, where the House of Lords emphasised that:

> *It was not sufficient to establish negligence for the plaintiff (i.e. claimant) to show that there was a body of competent professional opinion that considered the decision was wrong, if there was also a body of equally competent professional opinion that supported the decision as having been reasonable in the circumstances.*

(Maynard v W Midlands RHA [1984] 1 WLR 634;[1985] 1 ALL ER 6350)

However, the House of Lords (Bolitho v. City Hospital Hackney HA [1997] 4 ALL ER 771) has urged that experts must give responsible and reasonable evidence.

Causation and the Chester case

Where the claimant is alleging that he or she was not given all the necessary information, then the claimant must prove that had the appropriate information been given, including information about the risks of harm, then failure to provide that information caused the claimant to suffer from that harm. What, however, if there is no evidence that the claimant would have refused that particular treatment had he or she known of the problems? This is the issue which has recently been considered by the Court of Appeal which held that there was negligence by the doctor even if the claimant had not shown that she would have followed the advice anyway (Chester v. Afshar [2002] 3 ALL ER 552 CA). The facts of the case are shown in Box 13.3.

Box 13.3 Facts of Chester v. Afshar [2002] CA [2004] HL

The defendant, a neuro-surgeon, advised the claimant to undergo lumbar surgery. She consented, and following the operation suffered partial paralysis. The judge found that although the defendant had not performed the operation negligently, he had failed to warn the claimant of the small risk of partial paralysis inherent in the operation.

The judge also found that, had she been warned, the claimant would not have consented to the operation taking place then, but would have sought further advice before deciding what to do.

The House of Lords, in a majority ruling, dismissed the appeal against the Court of Appeal decision. The House of Lords held that the defendant owed a duty to the claimant to inform her of the risks inherent in the proposed surgery, including that of paralysis, so that she could make her own decision. Lord Hope stated:

This duty to inform gave the claimant a right to be informed before she consented to it (the operation). It was unaffected in its scope by the response she would have given had she been told of those risks. The problem of causation arose in the present case, since how could causation be established when the patient could not have refused absolutely ever to undergo the operation if told of the risks but would have postponed her decision until later? The matter raised an issue of legal policy which a judge had to decide whether justice required the normal approach to causation to be modified. The law which imposed the doctor's duty to warn had at its heart the patient's right to make an informed choice as to whether and if so when and by whom to be operated on. Patients may have, and were entitled to have, different views about those matters. All sorts of factors might be at work: the patient's hopes and fears and personal circumstances, the nature of the condition to be treated and, above all, the patient's own views whether the risk was worth running for the benefits which might come if the operation was carried out. For some the choice might be easy: simply to agree or to decline the operation. But for many it would be difficult, requiring time to think, to take advice and to weigh up the alternatives.

The duty was owed as much to the patient who, if warned, would find the decision difficult as to the patient who would find it simple and could give a clear answer to the doctor one way or the other immediately.

To leave the patient who would find the decision difficult without a remedy, as the normal approach to causation would indicate, would render the duty useless in the cases where it might be needed most. That would discriminate against those who could not honestly say that they would have declined the operation once and for all if they had been warned. The result would be unacceptable. The function of the law was to enable rights to be vindicated and to provide remedies when duties had been breached. Unless that was done the duty was a hollow one, stripped of all practical force and devoid of all content.

On policy grounds therefore, the test of causation was satisfied and justice required that the claimant be afforded the remedy she sought, as the injury she suffered at the defendant's hands was within the scope of the very risk which he should have warned her about when obtaining her consent to the operation which resulted in that injury.

(Chester v Afshar HL; [2004] UKHL 41; [2004] 3 W.L.R. 927)

The effect of the House of Lords ruling is that it is easier for a claimant to establish that compensation should be payable following failure to inform him or her of the risks of a particular procedure, if those risks actually occur and the patient is harmed. Only in clear-cut cases where the patient makes it clear that they agree to an operation proceeding whatever the untold risks may be would the patient fail.

Information about medicinal products

It is likely that in hospitals insufficient information may be given to the patient about known side-effects of the medication they are prescribed. Significant risk of serious harm should usually be notified to the patient, who could also be shown the manufacturer's leaflet about side-effects and contra-indications.

Explanatory leaflets must be provided by pharmaceutical companies as a result of a European Directive 92/27/EEC. A guidance note on the provision of patient information with dispensed medicine was published by the Medicines Control Agency (MCA) in August 2002. This pointed out that the law required all medicines with marketing authorisations in the UK to have an approved leaflet which would be included in the packaging before the medicine is sold or supplied, except where this information is already in the packaging. This legal requirement does not apply when the patient has medicines administered to her or him in hospital, but it is recommended that the leaflet should be available in the pharmacy or on the ward so that it can be supplied to the patient on request.

Systems should be in place to ensure that patients are aware of the availability of patient information leaflets.

An investigation by the National Audit Office found that safety warnings and information about medicines fail to get through to the public (Wright 2003). It considered that the Medical Control Agency (since 1 April 2003 the Medicine and Healthcare Products Regulatory Agency (MHRA)) needs to do more to communicate directly with the public and improve its safety messages. Only 33% of people read all the information provided with prescribed medication, while 10% never read the leaflet at all.

The forms recommended by the DH for completion by the patient in relation to consent to treatment require the health professional to outline significant risks which the treatment entails (DH 2007). However, there is no evidence that these forms are used for consent to medication, as opposed to invasive treatments such as surgery.

Where a doctor prescribes an unlicensed medicinal product to a patient, good practice would ensure that the patient was notified that the product had not obtained a marketing authorisation under the Medicines Act 1968 (see Chapter 1).

New regulations on false or misleading information about medicines came into force on 1 August 2005 (Medicines (Provision of False or Misleading Information and Miscellaneous Amendments) Regulations 2005, SI 2005 No 1710).

In 2009 the Pharmaceutical Labelling (Warning of Cognitive Function Impairment) Bill 2009 was put down for a second reading but withdrawn by its sponsor Andrew Dismore. If enacted it would have made it a criminal offence not to label psychoactive pharmaceuticals, specified by the Secretary of State, with a warning symbol that it could lead to the impairment of the consumer's ability to drive a motor vehicle or operate machinery such that the consumer is a danger to himself and others.

In 2010 the MHRA commissioned an online discussion site asking whether key information about medicines should be available online. The discussion site, aimed at healthcare professionals and the public, asks whether it is a good idea to make the MHRA's definitive database of patient information leaflets (PILs) and Summaries of Product Characteristics (SPCs) available online and, if so, what the site should look like.

Clearer labelling on medicines was recommended following research undertaken by the University of Leeds (Smyth 2002). It is suggested that instead of 'this medicine may cause drowsiness' should be 'this medicine may make you sleepy' and instead of 'do not operate machinery' should be 'do not drive or use tools or machines'.

Application of the law to the situation in Box 13.1

The answer to the legal issue posed by this situation depends upon what information was known (or should have been known) to the clinician at the time that the drug was prescribed. If it was known that a consequence of the new medicine was a significant effect on the personality of the patient, and any reasonable doctor would have given that information to Roy, then Roy would have a prima facie case of a breach of the duty of care to inform. He might not be able to prove that he would not have taken the drug had he known of the warning, but if he could show that he would have delayed making a decision in the light of information about side-effects, he would satisfy the requirement of causation laid down by the House of Lords. It is clear that in recent years the law has moved towards greater openness towards the patient and the information which must be disclosed. Roy might also have a possible claim against the manufacturers under the Consumer Protection legislation, where he would only have to show that there was a defect in the product, not that there was any negligence in its production. (A & others v National Blood Authority & another (2001), TLR 4 April 2001.). If other information were to come to light which suggested that there had been negligence in the production and marketing of the product, he might also be able to sue the manufacturers for breach of the duty of care they owe to him in the law of negligence.

He might find that he could join up with others who have suffered as a consequence of the drug in a class action.

Conclusions

There is a presumption that a person over the age of 16 years has the necessary mental capacity to make any decision which is now set out in the Mental Capacity Act 2005, the presumption can be rebutted (i.e. removed) on a balance of probabilities. Where there is evidence that this capacity is lacking, then the law empowers a health professional to act in the best interests of that person. It is to this topic we turn in the next chapter.

Key points

- A duty of care is owed to give information about significant risks of substantial harm.
- The Bolam Test of reasonable practice has been used to determine how much information the professional should give the patient.
- A European Directive requires pharmaceutical companies to provide explanatory leaflets with their products.

References

Department of Health (2007) *Good practice in consent implementation guide*. London

Medicines Control Agency (2002) Guidance note: Provision of patient information with dispensed medicine August 2002.

Smyth C (2002) Medicine labels are given dose of plain English *The Times* 4 March 2011:21)

Wright, O. (2003) Medicine warnings criticised. *The Times*, 16 January.

CHAPTER 14

Consent and the mentally incapacitated patient

Box 14.1 Situation

Agnes Daily is on the medical ward of Roger Park Hospital following a stroke. She is aggressive towards the nurse and frequently refuses her medication. Can she be forced to receive it?

Introduction

In the last two chapters we considered the law relating to consent by the mentally competent adult and medication and the giving of information to the patient. In this chapter we consider the law relating to the mentally incapacitated adult and the administration of medicines. The law relating to the administration of medicines to detained patients is considered in Chapter 16.

Capacity

Box 14.2 Case scenario 1

Doctors advised a patient (C) from Broadmoor Special Hospital, who was suffering from chronic paranoid schizophrenia, that he had gangrene in his foot. He was transferred to Heatherwood Hospital where the doctor diagnosed a grossly infected right leg with a necrotic ulcer covering the whole of the dorsum. The consultant vascular surgeon considered that C would die imminently unless he had a below-knee amputation. His chances of survival were assessed as being no better than 15% if he just had conservative treatment. Patient C stated that he would prefer to die with two feet than live with one. He therefore refused to give consent to the operation and he sought an injunction from the High Court to stop the amputation from going ahead.

(Re C (adult: refusal of medical treatment), [1994] 1 WLR 290)

The three-stage test of mental capacity

In Box 14.2, the sole issue before Judge Thorpe was did patient C have the requisite capacity to give a valid refusal, i.e. was his right of self determination to be upheld? If the answer to the question was 'yes', then he had the right in law to refuse any treatment, 'for a good reason, a bad reason or for no reason at all' (words used by the Court of Appeal in Re MB (an adult: medical treatment) (1997) 2 FLR 426). On the other hand, if the effect of his chronic paranoid schizophrenia was to render him incapable of making a valid decision, then action could be taken in his best interests and his refusal overruled.

Judge Thorpe stated that there were three stages in determining whether the requisite mental capacity existed:

1. Could the patient comprehend and retain the necessary information?
2. Was he able to believe it?
3. Was he able to weigh the information, balancing risks and needs, so as to arrive at a choice?

In future, comparable cases will be determined by the statutory definition in the Mental Capacity Act 2005 set out below.

Box 14.3 Case scenario 2

Miss MB required a Caesarean section in order to save her foetus. However, while she gave consent to the operation, she suffered from a needle phobia which caused her to panic and refuse the preliminary anaesthetic. The trust applied for a declaration that the Caesarean section could take place on the grounds that the needle phobia rendered her mentally incapacitated and therefore the operation should proceed in her best interests.

(Re MB (an adult: medical treatment), [1997] 2 FLR 426)

In the above case of MB, the judge held that the woman was mentally incapacitated as a result of the phobia and the operation could therefore proceed in her best interests. The same day the Court of Appeal upheld that decision. In a reserved judgment it set out how capacity was to be determined (Box 14.4).

Box 14.4 Determining capacity: Re MB

A person lacks the capacity if some impairment or disturbance of mental functioning renders the person unable to make a decision whether to consent to or to refuse treatment. That inability to make a decision will occur when:

a) The patient is unable to comprehend and retain the information which is material to the decision, especially as to the likely consequences of having or not having the treatment in question

b) The patient is unable to use the information and weigh it in the balance as part of the process of arriving at the decision.

(Re MB (an adult: medical treatment) [1997] 2 FLR 426)

This is very similar to the new statutory definition given below.

Lack of mental capacity

Common law powers

Prior to the bringing into force of the Mental Capacity Act 2005, in the absence of statutory provision for decision making on behalf of mentally incapacitated adults, the courts have been obliged to fill the vacuum and lay down the principles which apply. However since October 2007 and the implementation of the Mental Capacity Act 2005, the common law principles have been replaced by the statutory provisions.

The leading case on common law powers was Re F, the facts of which are shown in Box 14.5. In this case, the judge granted the declaration sought by F's mother. The official solicitor (who acts on behalf of the mentally incapacitated adult) appealed against the declaration to the Court of Appeal, which upheld the judge's order. The official solicitor then appealed to the House of Lords. The House of Lords held that there was at common law (i.e. judge-made law or case law) the power for a person to act in the best interests of a mentally incapacitated adult. This power is derived from the principle of necessity.

Box 14.5 Sterilisation of a mentally incapacitated adult (Re F (mental patient: Sterilisation), [1990])

F was 36 years old and had severe learning disabilities, with the mental age of a small child. She lived in a mental hospital and had formed a sexual relationship with a male patient. The hospital staff considered that she would be unable to cope with a pregnancy and recommended that she should be sterilised, considering that other forms of contraception were unsuitable. Her mother supported the idea of a sterilisation operation, but because F was over 18 years did not have the right in law to give consent on her behalf.

The mother therefore applied to court for a declaration that an operation for sterilisation was in her best interests and should be declared lawful.

(F v West Berkshire HA & Another F(re) (a mental patient: sterilisation) [1989] 2 ALL ER 545 [1990] 2 AC 1)

The principle of necessity

Necessity may arise in an emergency situation, e.g. when an unconscious person comes into hospital, and the health professionals should do no more than is reasonably required in the best interests of the patient, before he/she recovers consciousness. Necessity may also arise in a situation where a person is permanently or semi-permanently lacking mental capacity. In such a situation, there is no point in waiting for the patient to give consent. According to Lord Goff:

The need to care for him [the patient] is obvious; and the doctor must then act in the best interests of his patient just as if he had received his consent so to do. Were this not so, much useful treatment and care could, in theory at least, be denied to the unfortunate.

The doctor must act in accordance with a responsible and competent body of relevant professional opinion (Bolam v. Friern Hospital Management Committee, [1957] 1 WLR 582.).

The House of Lords issued a declaration that sterilisation was in the best interests of F and could proceed. It did recommend that in future such cases of sterilisation for social reasons (as opposed, for example, to sterilisation which resulted from an operation to remove a cancerous growth) should be brought before the courts for a declaration to be made.

Bournewood judgment

In 1998 the House of Lords held that there were powers at common law to act out of necessity in the best interests of a mentally incapacitated person by treating him or her in a psychiatric hospital without placing that person under the detention provisions of the Mental Health Act 1983. The facts of the case are shown in Box 14.6. The decision of the House of Lords was overruled by the European Court of Human Rights (see below).

European Court of Human Rights

The decision by the House of Lords that L had been lawfully admitted as an informal patient on the basis of the common law doctrine of necessity, was challenged before the European Court of Human Rights.

The ECHR held that the absence of procedural safeguards to protect an applicant against arbitrary deprivation of liberty on the ground of necessity after he had been compulsorily detained breached his right to liberty guaranteed by article 5.1 of the European Convention on Human Rights. The ECHR also held unanimously that article 5.4 had been breached in that the applicant's right to have the legality of his detention reviewed by a court had not been ensured.

Subsequently the Department of Health (DH) issued a consultation paper on options to fill the gap in statute law made evident by the Bournewood case.

Deprivation of Liberty Safeguards

As a consequence of the decision of the ECHR in the Bournewood case, the UK was compelled to change the law to ensure that there was statutory provision covering the loss of liberty of those who were not detained under the Mental Health Act 1983. The Deprivation of Liberty Safeguards (DoLS) were enacted by changes to the Mental Capacity Act 2005 contained in the Mental Health Act 2007. Under these provisions the managers of a care home or hospital must apply to the local authority or to the primary care trust if it is necessary to deprive

Box 14.6 Bournewood case

L was a UK national born in 1949 and lived in Surrey. He was autistic and unable to speak, and his level of understanding was limited. He was frequently agitated and had a history of self-harming behaviour. He lacked the capacity to consent or object to treatment. For over 30 years he was cared for in Bournewood Hospital, an NHS Hospital trust hospital. He was an in-patient at the hospital's intensive behavioural unit from around 1987 until March 1994, when he was discharged on a trial basis to paid carers, with whom he successfully stayed until 22 July 1997.

In 1995 he started attending a day-care centre on a weekly basis. On 22 July 1997, while at the day centre, he became particularly agitated, hitting himself on the head with his fists and banging his head against the wall. Staff could not contact his carers, so they called a local doctor, who gave him a sedative. L remained agitated and on the recommendation of his social worker was taken to hospital. A consultant psychiatrist diagnosed him as requiring in-patient treatment. With the help of two nurses, he was transferred to the hospital intensive unit as an 'informal patient'. Dr M, the medical officer responsible for L since 1977, considered detaining him compulsorily under the Mental Health Act 1983, but concluded that it was not necessary, as he was compliant and had not resisted admission or tried to run away.

In or around September 1997 L sought leave to apply for judicial review of the hospital's decision to admit him. The High Court rejected his application, finding that he had not been detained but had been informally admitted in accordance with the common law doctrine of necessity. The applicant appealed. Following an indication from the Court of Appeal on 29 October 1997 that the appeal would be decided in his favour, L was admitted for treatment as an involuntary patient under the 1983 Act. The Court of Appeal held that his detention under common law powers was unlawful. The hospital authorities appealed to the House of Lords which ruled in 1998 that he had been lawfully admitted as an informal patient on the basis of the common law doctrine of necessity. (In the meantime L had applied to a Mental Health Review Tribunal and an independent psychiatric report recommended his discharge. He was released from hospital on 5 December 1997 and officially discharged to his carers on 12 December 1997.) (R. v Bournewood Community and Mental Health NHS Trust ex parte; [1999] AC 458) a person of their liberty. To obtain authorisation they must carry out several assessments including;

- An age assessment (the person must be over 18 years)
- A mental health assessment – (client/patient must be suffering a mental disorder).
- A mental capacity assessment – (client/patient must lack the capacity to decide whether to be admitted to or remain in the hospital or care home).
- An eligibility assessment – the client/patient must not be detained under or subject to the Mental Health Act 1983 (as amended).
- A best interests assessment – (it would be in the person's best interests and it would be a proportionate response to the likelihood of suffering harm and the seriousness of that harm.

There must be no conflict between the authorisation sought and a valid decision by a donee of a power of attorney. Further information on DoLS can be obtained from the DH and Ministry of Justice websites (www.dh.gov.uk and www.justice.gov.uk). The Court first considered the operation of the DoLS in the case of GJ v the Foundation Trust (GJ v The Foundation Trust [2009] EWHC 2972 (Fam)). In this case the court had to consider whether GJ was 'ineligible to be deprived of liberty by the MCA' and the relationship between the Mental Health Act 1983 (as amended by the MHA 2007) and the Mental Capacity Act 2005. The case details can be accessed on the bailii website (www.bailii.org).

Law Commission and statutory powers

In 1995 the Law Commission (an independent body which reviews UK laws), published its proposals on decision making on behalf of mentally incapacitated adults (Law Commission, 1995). The report followed five years of consultation and consultation papers on all aspects of mentally incapacitated adults and included a draft Mental Incapacity Bill. This Bill proposed a statutory framework for decisions to be made on behalf of the mentally incapable adult, day-to-day decisions being made by a statutory decision maker, and special courts for making decisions in more complex situations such as abortions and sterilisations. No legislative action was taken in the light of the report.

In December 1997 a consultation document was issued by the Lord Chancellor (Lord Chancellor's Office 1997) covering much of the ground already consulted upon by the Law Commission. Following this consultation, a White Paper (Lord Chancellor's Office 1999) giving the Government's proposals on decision making on behalf of the mentally incapacitated adult was published in 1999. Based on these proposals a draft Mental Incapacity Bill was published which was subjected to pre-legislative scrutiny by a Joint Committee of the Houses of Parliament. A revised Bill was introduced in the light of the Joint Committee's recommendations.

The Mental Capacity Act 2005 recognises as a basic principle that:

A person must be assumed to have capacity unless it is established that he lacks capacity.

It then provides a statutory definition for mental capacity as follows:

A person lacks capacity for the purposes of the MCA in relation to a matter if at the material time he is unable to make a decision for himself in relation to the matter because of an impairment of, or a disturbance in the functioning of, the mind or brain.

The impairment or disturbance can be permanent or temporary.

In any proceedings the question of whether a person lacks capacity must be decided on the balance of probabilities.

The phrase 'unable to make decisions for himself' used in section 2 is subsequently defined in section 3:

A person is unable to make a decision for himself if he is unable:

a) to understand the information relevant to the decision

b) to retain that information

c) to use or weigh that information as part of the process of making the decision, or

d) to communicate his decision (whether by talking, using sign language or any other means)

Subsection 3(2) provides that:

A person is not to be regarded as unable to understand the information relevant to the decision if he is able to understand an explanation of it given to him in a way that is appropriate to his circumstances (using simple language, visual aids or any other means).

Subsection 3(3) provides that:

The fact that a person is able to retain the information relevant to a decision for a short period only does not prevent him from being regarded as able to make the decision.

The information relevant to a decision includes information about the reasonably foreseeable consequences of deciding one way or another or failing to make the decision (S.3(4)).

In Scotland the Adults with Incapacity (Scotland) Act 2000 enables decisions to be made on behalf of mentally incapacitated adults. It covers both the making of medical decisions and also decisions relating to property and finance. The bulk of the provisions came into force in April 2002. The Act introduces a new regime of intervention and guardianship orders and reforms the law on powers of attorney. Former powers under the Mental Health (Scotland) Act 1984 are repealed. A new court jurisdiction is set up. The first section sets out the principles which are to apply, including the principle that:

there shall be no intervention in the affairs of an adult, unless the person responsible for authorising or effecting the intervention is satisfied that the intervention will benefit the adult and that such benefit cannot reasonably be achieved without the intervention.

Best interests

The Mental Capacity Act 2005 also sets out the steps which must be taken to determine what are in a person's best interests.and lists the factors which are to be taken into account in assessing what are the best interests.

Section 4 states that:

(1) In determining for the purposes of this Act what is in a person's best interests, the person making the determination must consider all the relevant circumstances.

Relevant circumstances are defined as (S.4(11)):

a) of which the person making the decision is aware, and

b) which it would be reasonable to regard as relevant

The steps which the decision maker must take are then identified as including in particular:

*   *Temporary or permanent*
    He must consider:
    a) Whether it is likely that the person will at some time have capacity in relation to the matter in question and
    b) If it appears likely that he will, when that is likely to be

*   *Participation*
    He must, so far as is reasonably practicable, permit and encourage the person to participate, or to improve his ability to participate, as fully as possible in any act done for him and any decision affecting him.

- *Continuation of life*
  He must not, where the determination relates to life-sustaining treatment, be motivated by a desire to bring about his death (or, in particular, any relevant written statement by him when he had capacity). Life-sustaining treatment is defined (S.4(10)) as:
  Treatment which in the view of a person providing healthcare for the person concerned is necessary to sustain life.

- *Wishes and feelings etc.*
  He must consider, so far as is reasonably ascertainable:
  a) the person's past and present wishes and feelings
  b) the beliefs and values that would be likely to influence his decision if he had capacity, and
  c) the other factors that he would be likely to consider if he were able to do so.

- *Views of others*
  He must take into account, if it is practicable and appropriate to consult them, the views of:
  a) anyone named by the person as someone to be consulted on the matter in question or on matters of that kind
  b) anyone engaged in caring for the person or interested in his welfare
  c) any donee of a lasting power of attorney granted by the person, and
  d) any deputy appointed for the person by the court as to what would be in the person's best interests and, in particular, as to the matters mentioned above.

  Any one exercising powers under a lasting power of attorney or any other powers exercised on behalf of a person who is reasonably believed to lack capacity must also obey these duties (S.4(8)).

Compulsion and use of restraint

There is statutory provision for the use of restraint when a person is acting in the best interests of a mentally incapacitated person. Where decisions are made or action taken in connection with the care and treatment of a person, then limitations are imposed under section 6.

Restraint cannot be used unless, in addition to the extra conditions set by section 5, two further conditions are satisfied:

a) that D reasonably believes that it is necessary to do the act in order to prevent harm to P, and

b) the act is a proportionate response to the likelihood of P's suffering harm and the seriousness of that harm.

The definition of restraint for the purpose of the section is if P:

a) uses, or threatens to use, force to secure the doing of an act which P resists, or

b) restricts P's liberty of movement, whether or not P resists.

Codes of Practice have been drawn up giving guidance on the Mental Capacity Act 2005, which came into force in October 2007.

Form 4 of the Department of Health (DH 2009) forms of consent could be used by any health professional providing medication to a person over 16 years who lacks mental capacity.

Covert administration

The UKCC published a position statement in 2001 on the covert administration of medicines disguised in food or drink. It made clear that covert administration would not apply to a patient who had the mental capacity to make his or her own decisions, even in a life-saving situation, and could only be justified where the patient lacked the mental capacity to make his or her own decisions and the administration of medicines in this way was in the best interests of the patient.

The UKCC (2001) stated:

The covert administration of medicines is only likely to be necessary or appropriate in the case of patients or clients who actively refuse medication but who are judged not to have the capacity to understand the consequences of their refusal.

It suggested that the following considerations may apply where covert administration of medicines for a patient is being discussed:

- The best interests of the patient or client must be considered at all times.
- The medication must be considered essential for the patient's or client's health and well being, or for the safety of others.
- The decision to administer a medication covertly should not be considered routine, and should be a contingency measure. Any decision to do so must be reached after assessing the care needs of the patient or client individually. It should be patient - or client - specific in order to avoid the ritualised administration of medicine in this way.

147

- There should be broad and open discussion among the multi-disciplinary clinical team and the supporters of the patient or client, and agreement that this approach is required in the circumstances.

Those involved should include carers, relatives, advocates and the multi-disciplinary team (especially the pharmacist). Family involvement in the care process should be positively encouraged.

- The method of administration should be agreed with the pharmacist.
- The decision and action taken, including the names of all parties concerned, should be documented in the care plan and reviewed at appropriate intervals.
- Regular attempts should be made to encourage the patient or client to take their medication. This might best be achieved by giving regular information, explanation and encouragement, preferably by the team member who has the best rapport with the individual.
- There should be a written local policy, taking into account these professional practice guidelines.

Applying the law to the scenario of Box 14.1

It would appear from the facts that Agnes may not have the necessary mental capacity to make her own decisions. A clear decision must be made on this point, if necessary bringing in a health professional with the necessary expertise to determine her capacity. If the decision is made that she lacks the necessary capacity then the provisions of the Mental Capacity Act 2005 would apply and action would be taken in her best interests. If necessary an application could be made to the Court of Protection (which since October 2007 has jurisdiction over matters covering personal care and treatment as well as property and finance) in respect of any serious medical intervention or withholding of care. Codes of Practice have been prepared on the Mental Capacity Act and also on the DoLS and are available on the Ministry of Justice website (www.justice.gov.uk). In the absence of informal carers independent advocacy services to speak on behalf of Agnes are available to ensure that her best interests are identified and protected. Alternatively it may be that Agnes requires treatment for mental disorder which should be provided under the Mental Health Act 1983. This is considered in Chapter 16.

Conclusions

The implementation of the Mental Capacity Act 2005 was a much awaited statutory provision and now provides considerable assistance in the decision-making on behalf of the many million of mentally incapacitated adults. The Codes of Practice in particular provide detailed guidance on appropriate action. Children under 16 years are excluded from the provisions of the Mental Capacity Act 2005 but would come under the Children Act 1989. Children and young persons under 18 years may or may not be capable of giving consent to medication and it is to this topic which we turn in the next chapter.

Key points

- The presumption in law that an adult has the requisite mental capacity to make a specific decision can be rebutted if there is evidence to the contrary.
- There is a duty to act in the best interests of a mentally incapacitated adult.
- The Mental Capacity Act 2005 replaces the common law principle of acting out of necessity in the best interests of a mentally incapacitated adult.
- Covert administration of medicines should be exceptional and UKCC guidance followed.

References

Department of Health (2009) *Good practice in consent implementation guide*. London

Law Commission (1995) *Mental Incapacity Report No* 231, HMSO. London

Lord Chancellor (1999) *Making Decisions*, Lord Chancellor's Office, The Stationery Office, London

UKCC (2001) position statement on the *Covert administration of medicines – disguising medicine in food and drink*. London

Websites

bailii website www.bailii.org

Department of Health website www.dh.gov.uk

Ministry of Justice website www.justice.gov.uk

CHAPTER 15

Consent to medicines and children

Box 15.1 Situation

Laura is 14 years old and suffering from leukaemia. She has recently lost remission and her prospects for survival are uncertain. She has started refusing treatment and says that she is not prepared to undergo a further course of chemotherapy. Her parents are anxious for everything to be done to ensure her survival and wish chemotherapy to be undertaken. What is the law and would it be different if Laura was 16 or 18 years old?

Introduction

This chapter looks at the law relating to young persons of 16 and 17 years and those below 16 years in relation to consent to medicines.

Statutory right to give consent

A young person of 16 and 17 years has a statutory right to give consent under Section 8(1) of the Family Law Reform Act 1969:

The consent of a minor who has attained the age of 16 years, to any surgical, medical or dental treatment, which in the absence of consent, would constitute a trespass to the person, shall be as effective as it would be if he were of full age; and where a minor has by virtue of this section given an effective consent to any treatment it shall not be necessary to obtain any consent for it from his parent or guardian.

Section 8(1) makes it clear that the consent of the young person is effective in its own right; consent does not also have to be obtained from the parent or guardian. Under the Mental Capacity Act 2005 there is a presumption that a 16 or 17 year old has the necessary capacity, but this can be rebutted if there is evidence to the contrary, as, for example, in the case of a 16-year-old with learning difficulties.

Consent to what?

Section 8(2) explains:

In this section 'surgical, medical or dental treatment' includes any procedure undertaken for the purposes of diagnosis and this section applies to any procedures (including, in particular, the administration of an anaesthetic) which is ancillary to any treatment as it applies to that treatment.

This is a comprehensive definition and covers most care and treatment provided in hospital and the community provided by all health professionals. It does not specifically refer to complementary or alternative therapies, but if these are provided under the aegis of a registered health professional there is no reason why the young person could not give a valid consent for them. It does not cover consent to research, which would be in a different category, unless the research was part of the young person's treatment (this is considered in Chapter 26).

Parental consent and the young person

Section 8(3) makes it clear that the fact that a young person of 16 and 17 years now has a statutory right to give consent does not invalidate any other consent, which would have been valid before 1969.

Nothing in the section shall be construed as making ineffective any consent which would have been effective if this section had not been enacted.

In other words, before 1969, a parent or guardian could give consent on behalf of a child and young person until he or she became an adult (i.e. 21 years before the 1969 Act, 18 years after the 1969 Act). This power of the parent or guardian to give consent, therefore, still continues and a health professional can rely on the consent of either the young person or his or her parent as a defence against an action for trespass to the person.

Overruling a child's consent to treatment

Where a young person has given consent to medication which is in her or his best interests and which is recommended by the health professional, there is no power for the parent to overrule that consent.

Refusal to consent by young person

In the case of Re W (a minor) (medical treatment) [1992] 4 ALL ER 627 where a girl of 16 years was refusing treatment for her anorexia, the Court of Appeal held that the Family Law Reform Act 1969 section 8 did not prevent consent being given by parents or the court. While the girl had a right to give consent under the Act, she could not refuse treatment which was necessary to save her life. Her refusal was therefore overruled.

The courts would not lightly overrule the refusal of a young person. There would have to be strong evidence that it was a life-saving matter. There is a clear difference between a parent acting on behalf of a mentally incapacitated young person in his or her best interests and a parent wishing to overrule the explicit wishes of a youngster. In the latter case, referral to the courts under the Children Act 1989 or under its inherent jurisdiction to consider cases involving children would be necessary. If parents disagree over the action which should be taken in relation to a young person of 16 or 17 years, the case can be brought to court under the Children Act 1989. Where possible the court would wish to give effect to the wishes of a mentally capacitated child. As a result of the decision in Re W and other cases and the view that in a life-saving situation the refusal of a young person could be overruled by the court, it is clear that young persons of 16 and 17 years are not treated as adults and do not have the same rights that a mentally competent adult would have to refuse life-saving treatment.

It has been suggested that competence is defined more strictly in the case of young people than in the case of adults to protect them from the worst effects of their decision (BMA 2001). In other words, a certain paternalism lawfully exists in relation to decision making by and on behalf of young people. As yet there has not been a case where a young person has challenged such an attitude under the Human Rights Act 1998, arguing that article 3 (the right not to be subjected to inhuman or degrading treatment or punishment) together with article 14 (the right not to be discriminated against) are infringed when a young person's wishes are overruled.

The child under 16 years

Children under 16 years do not have a statutory right to give consent. They do, however, have a right recognised at common law to give consent, as a result of the House of Lords decision in the case of Mrs Gillick. The House of Lords held that in exceptional circumstances a girl under 16 could give consent to contraceptive advice and treatment without parental consent. The exceptional circumstances listed by Lord Fraser were that:

- The girl would, although under 16, understand the doctor's advice.
- The doctor could not persuade her to inform her parents or allow him or her to inform the parents that she was seeking contraceptive advice.
- She was very likely to have sexual intercourse with or without contraceptive treatment.
- Unless she received contraceptive advice or treatment her physical and/ or mental health were likely to suffer.
- Her best interests required him to give her contraceptive advice, treatment, or both, without parental consent.

The wider interpretation of the House of Lords decision is that a Gillick-competent (see below) boy or girl could give a valid consent to treatment which was in his or her best interests without the involvement of parents.

The Gillick-competent or competent according to Lord Fraser's guidelines child

The expression 'Gillick-competent' child has now come into regular use. It refers to a child of any age who has achieved sufficient understanding and intelligence to enable him or her to understand fully what is proposed. The level of understanding must, of course, relate to the nature of the decision to be made. (The term 'Gillick-competent' is now sometimes replaced by the phrase 'a child who is competent according to Lord Fraser's guidelines').

Where a child is not able to give consent to treatment and his parents are not with him, emergency treatment could be given to him under the common law power to act out of necessity, recognised in the case of F v West Berkshire HA & Another; F(re) (a mental patient: sterilisation) [1989] 2 ALL ER 545; [1990] 2 AC 1. Health professionals also have power, under the Children Act 1989, to act in the interests of the child, as section 3(5) shows:

A person who

(a) does not have parental responsibility for a particular child, but

(b) has care of the child,

may (subject to the provision of this Act) do what is reasonable in all the circumstances of the case for the purpose of safeguarding or promoting the child's welfare.

This would appear to include giving consent to necessary emergency treatment in the absence of those with parental responsibility.

Health professionals often find that children who suffer from chronic conditions and who receive regular hospitalisation often develop a maturity above their physical years and an understanding of the proposed treatment. They should be given as much information as is reasonable to develop their understanding of the treatments (and this includes medicines) proposed.

The High Court applied the ruling of the House of Lords in the Gillick case where a mother was not informed that her daughter was to have an abortion. The daughter had been assessed as having the requisite competence and the mother had no legal right to be informed or to give her consent (R (On the application of Axon) v. Secretary of State [2006] EWHC 37 admin).

Parental rights

In addition to the right of the Gillick-competent child to give consent to necessary treatment, the parents also have the right to give consent. However, their rights must be exercised in the best interests of the child. There are examples where the parents' refusal to arrange for the necessary treatment has been overruled, and there are examples where treatment arranged by the parents has been stopped as not being in the child's best interests. In every case, the paramount consideration is the welfare of the child. All the principles about information giving which are discussed in Chapter 13 apply to ensuring that parents have the necessary information about the care and treatment of their children. In the Kennedy Report (Kennedy 2001) recommendation 15 states that:

Parents of those too young to take decisions for themselves should receive a copy of any letter written by one healthcare professional to another about their child's treatment or care.

The NSF working groups which have established National Service Frameworks for children's healthcare also considered proposals for research into how this recommendation for copying the professionals' letters can be implemented and have made specific proposals for copying these letters to the patients or parents.

Evidence that consent has been given

The forms set out in the Department of Health's *Good practice in consent implementation guide* can be used for evidencing that consent has been given by the parent or child (where competent) or both (DH 2009). Form 2 is used by a child and parent of a child where it is anticipated that the child will lose consciousness, and Form 3 is used for treatment where the patient will remain conscious. In practice, some trusts are finding that Form 2 is suitable for all procedures to be carried out on children.

Medicines and children

In 2004 the DH gave information about a new initiative to develop medicines designed specifically for use in children. This was welcomed by the British National Formulary (BNF), which responded to the idea of a BNF for children, the first version to be devoted entirely to the needs of children. There are online updates and a new edition is published every year thereafter (www.bnf.org). In 2004, the editor of the BNF, Ian Costello stated:

> The use of medicines in children is particularly complex. Because many medicines are not licensed for use in children, healthcare professionals currently have to rely on a variety of non-standard information resources. Selecting the right medicine and calculating the right dose for a child can be particularly problematic and make treatment more difficult. Healthcare professionals need clear, reliable and up-to-date information to inform prescribing decisions. The BNF for children is a crucial step towards helping them make the best decisions for their younger patients.

(See also the BNF for children website www.bnfc.org)

The safety of children is protected by regulations relating to the packaging and colouring of certain medicinal products (Medicines (Child Safety) Regulations 2003 No 2317 amended by SI 2004/1771 and by SI 2005/1520).

Application of the law in Box 15.1

In this tragic situation, the most important determining consideration of the action which should be taken is the medical prognosis for Laura. If there is a reasonable chance that further chemotherapy would be in the best interests of

Laura, then the parents' consent for this can be given, even though Laura herself is unwilling to receive it. The Re W case, discussed above, is an example where the Court of Appeal overruled the refusal of a 16-year-old girl to have treatment for her anorexia, since it was life-saving and in her best interests. If Laura was 16, therefore, her refusal to have treatment which was in her best interests could be overruled. However, if she were an adult of 18 years, and provided that she had the necessary mental capacity, she could refuse even life-saving treatment. On the other hand, if the medical prognosis was bad, and further chemotherapy was unlikely to be successful or in her best interests, Laura's refusal to have medication could be supported by the health professionals and the parents' desire for the treatment to proceed overruled. It may be necessary to obtain the court's declaration that it was in Laura's best interests to withhold any further chemotherapy or other medication. In a case involving a heart transplant, where a girl of 15 years was refusing to give consent, the mother was prepared to give consent on her behalf, but the NHS trust applied to the court for a declaration. The court held that it was in the best interests of the girl to have the heart transplant (M(re) (medical treatment: consent) [1999] 2 FLR 1097).

Conclusions

It is only recently that the rights of children and young persons have been given weight; some would argue that they are still treated with excessive paternalism. The British Medical Association (BMA) has advocated that greater information should be given to the child and young person and they should have greater involvement in their own care, treatment and decision making (BMA 2001).

Key points

- A young person of 16 or 17 has a statutory right to give consent, but a refusal can be overruled if it is in his or her best interests.
- A child is able to give consent at common law if the treatment is in his or her best interests.
- DH forms for consent should be used.
- A BNF of medicines for children is published.

References

British Medical Association (2001) *Consent, Rights and Choices in Health Care for Children and Young*. BMA, London.

British National Formulary (2004) *Extra: News* 17 August 2004; http://www.bnf.org/.

Department of Health (2009) *Good practice in consent implementation guide*. London

Kennedy (2001) *Learning from Bristol: the report of the public inquiry into children's heart surgery at the Bristol Royal Infirmary 1984–1995*. Command paper CM 5207, Stationery Office, London.

CHAPTER 16

Consent and the mentally disordered detained patient

> ## Box 16.1 Compulsory treatment of a detained patient
>
> *Mavis has been detained under section 2 of the Mental Health Act 1983 for assessment. Her responsible medical officer prescribes for her an antidepressant. She refuses to take it. What is the law?*

Introduction

It does not follow that because a person is mentally ill or suffers from learning disabilities that he or she is therefore incapable of making his or her own decisions. As the case of Re C shows, where a patient in Broadmoor hospital was refusing to have his leg amputated, using the criteria laid down by Judge Thorpe, he was deemed to be mentally capable and an injunction was issued that the amputation should not take place without his consent (C (re) (adult: refusal of medical treatment) [1994] 1 WLR 290). (This situation would now be covered by the Mental Capacity Act 2005) (see Chapter 14). However, there are situations where, when a patient has been detained under the Mental Health Act 1983, he or she may be compelled to have treatment, provided that certain safeguards or conditions are complied with. This chapter looks at the law on the detained patient and treatment by way of medication including the changes effected by the Mental Health Act 2007 to the Mental Health Act 1983. The Mental Health Act 2007 followed a White Paper on the Mental Health laws (DH 2000) and a draft Bill (DH 2003).

Detained patients

Under the Mental Health Act 1983 not all detained patients come under the consent to treatment provisions of Part IV of the Act. Those patients who come under the short stay detention sections such as section 4 (for up to 72 hours); section 5(2) (for up to 72 hours), section 5(4) (for up to 6 hours), and sections 135 and 136 (for up to 72 hours) are not subject to Part IV provisions and therefore cannot be given treatment compulsorily under the Act. In exceptional circumstances, they may be given treatment in their best interests under Mental Capacity Act 2005 which replaced the common law powers which were recognised in the Re F case. (F v West Berkshire HA & Another F(re) (a mental patient: sterilisation) [1989] 2 ALL ER 545 [1990] 2 AC 1.) (See Chapter 14.)

Provisions of Part IV of the Mental Health Act 1983

Patients who are detained under the longer term sections (section 2 (up to 28 days); section 3 (up to six months initially, but can be renewed), section 37 (up to six months but can be renewed)) come under the provisions of Part IV, see Box 16.2.

Box 16.2 Provisions under Part IV of the Mental Health Act 1983 on consent to treatment (sections 57, 58 and 63) as amended by the Mental Health Act 2007

1. Treatments involving brain surgery or hormonal implants can only be given with the patient's consent which must be certified and only after independent certification of the consent and of the fact that the treatment should proceed (section 57).

2. Treatments involving electroconvulsive therapy, or medication where three months or more have elapsed since medication was first given during that period of detention: can only be given either (a) with the consent of the patient and it is certified by the patient's own registered medical practitioner or another registered medical practitioner appointed specifically for that purpose that he is capable of understanding its nature, purpose and likely effects, or (b) the registered medical practitioner appointed specifically certifies that the patient has refused or is incapable of consenting but agrees that the treatment should proceed (section 58).(Subject to a new section 58A shown in Box 16.3)

3. All other treatments: these can be given without the consent of the patient provided they are for mental disorder and are given by or under the direction of the responsible medical officer (section 63).

Box 16.3 Section 58A Mental Health Act 1983 added by the Mental Health Act 2007

58A Electro-convulsive therapy (ECT) etc.

(1) This section applies to the following forms of medical treatment for mental disorder:

    (a) ECT; and

    (b) such other forms of treatment as may be specified for the purposes of this section by regulations made by the appropriate national authority.

(2) Subject to section 62 below, a patient shall be not be given any form of treatment to which this section applies unless he falls within subsection (3), (4) or (5) below.

(3) A patient falls within this subsection if:

    (a) he has attained the age of 18 years;

    (b) he has consented to the treatment in question; and

    (c) either the approved clinician in charge of it or a registered medical practitioner appointed as mentioned in section 58(3) above has certified in writing that the patient is capable of understanding the nature, purpose and likely effects of the treatment and has consented to it.

(4) A patient falls within this subsection if:

    (a) he has not attained the age of 18 years; but

    (b) he has consented to the treatment in question; and

    (c) a registered medical practitioner appointed as aforesaid (not being the approved clinician in charge of the treatment) has certified in writing:

    (i) that the patient is capable of understanding the nature, purpose and likely effects of the treatment and has consented to it; and

    (ii) that it is appropriate for the treatment to be given.

(5) A patient falls within this subsection if a registered medical practitioner appointed as aforesaid (not being the responsible clinician (if there is one) or the approved clinician in charge of the treatment in question) has certified in writing:

    (a) that the patient is not capable of understanding the nature, purpose and likely effects of the treatment; but

    (b) that it is appropriate for the treatment to be given; and

    (c) that giving him the treatment would not conflict with:

    (i) an advance decision which the registered medical practitioner concerned is satisfied is valid and applicable; or

    (ii) a decision made by a donee or deputy or by the Court of Protection.

BOX 16.3 Section 58A Mental Health Act 1983 added by the Mental Health Act 2007 (continued)

(6) Before giving a certificate under subsection (5) above the registered medical practitioner concerned shall consult two other persons who have been professionally concerned with the patient's medical treatment but, of those persons:

> (a) one shall be a nurse and the other shall be neither a nurse nor a registered medical practitioner; and
> (b) neither shall be the responsible clinician (if there is one) or the approved clinician in charge of the treatment in question.

(7) This section shall not by itself confer sufficient authority for a patient who falls within section 56(5) above to be given a form of treatment to which this section applies if he is not capable of understanding the nature, purpose and likely effects of the treatment (and cannot therefore consent to it).

(8) Before making any regulations for the purposes of this section, the appropriate national authority shall consult such bodies as appear to it to be concerned.

Medicinal products come under section 63 or section 58.

Section 63

It can be seen from Box 16.2 that those treatments which do not come under sections 57 or 58 come under section 63 and can be given without the consent of the patient provided that the treatment is for mental disorder and is given by or under the direction of the responsible medical officer. In the case of B. v. Croydon HA [1995] 1 All ER 683 the Court of Appeal held that treatment for mental disorder could include treatment to relieve the symptoms of the mental disorder as well as treatment ancillary to the core treatment. It could therefore cover compulsory feeding of a patient suffering from anorexia. (Force-feeding of anorexia patients was also permitted under section 63 in two other cases:

Riverside Mental Health NHS Trust v. Fox [1994] 1 F.L.R. 6614. and Re KB (1994) 19 B.M.L.R.144).

The definition of treatment for mental disorder was given an extended meaning in the case of Tameside and Glossop Acute Services Trust v. CH (A patient) [1996] 1 F.L.R. 762, where the court held that a patient detained under the Mental Health Act could be given a Caesarean section as treatment for her mental disorder.

From these decisions it is clear that all medicinal products could come under section 63 unless they were hormonal implants for the purposes of reducing male sex drive, in which case they would under section 57 and the consent of the patient and other provisions of section 57 would have to be satisfied, or they had been specified under section 58A when the provisions of Box 16.3 would apply.

Section 58

Medication can only be given for up to three months under section 63. Where three months or more have elapsed since medication was first given during that period of detention, then medication can only be given in one of two circumstances outlined below.

The patient gives consent

Where the patient consents to receiving the medication (after three months or more have elapsed since medication was first given) and the patient's own registered medical practitioner or another registered medical practitioner appointed specifically for that purpose certifies that the patient is capable of understanding its nature, purpose and likely effects, then medication can be given under section 58. The registered medical practitioner signs the statutory form (Form 38) which describes the medication that is to be given and the fact that the patient has consented.

The patient refuses to give consent or is incapable of giving consent

Where the patient refuses to give consent or is incapable of giving consent, then the patient's own registered medical practitioner or the registered medical practitioner appointed specifically certifies that the patient has refused or is incapable of consenting. The doctor agrees that the treatment should proceed. The statutory form 39 is signed by the Second Opinion Appointed Doctor (SOAD). The court has ruled that where the patient is refusing to give consent, then the SOAD should give reasons why the patient's refusal should be overruled (R. v. Broadmoor Hospital (and others) [2002] Lloyd's reports Medical 41). The doctors who provide a second opinion are appointed by the Mental Health Act Commission.

Section 58A

The provisions of section 58 A are shown in Box 16.3 and prevent ECT and other specified treatments being given to a patient unless they give a valid consent, confirmed by an independent doctor or unless they lack the requisite mental capacity. Only subsection 5 enables ECT or other specified treatments to be given without consent, but only where the patient lacks the capacity to give consent and has not drawn up an advance decision which is valid and applicable to the treatment, and where the independent doctor considers that it is appropriate for the treatment to be given.

Urgent treatment for longer term detained patients

In an emergency or where the patient has withdrawn his consent to treatment under section 58, the provisions of sections 57 and 58 do not apply, and section 62 applies. (See Box 16.4)

Box 16.4 Section 62 Mental Health Act 1983

a) Any treatment which is immediately necessary to save the patient's life.

b) Treatment which is not irreversible if it is immediately necessary to prevent serious deterioration.

c) Treatment which is not irreversible or hazardous if it is immediately necessary to alleviate serious suffering.

d) Treatment which is not irreversible or hazardous if it is immediately necessary and represents the minimum interference necessary to prevent the patient from behaving violently or being a danger to himself or others.

Section 62 enables different treatments to be given according to the degree of urgency and whether they are irreversible or hazardous. Box 16.4 illustrates the provisions. Section 58A treatments (i.e ECT and other specified treatments) do not come under a) or b) above.

Irreversible is defined as 'if it has unfavourable irreversible physical or psychological consequences' and *hazardous* is defined as 'if it entails significant physical hazard'.

The significance of section 62 for giving medication is that if an emergency situation arose and the patient had been given medication under section 63 for three months, and needed to have more or different medicine, and there was not time to obtain a second opinion appointed doctor to examine the patient, then medication could be given under section 62 according to the degree of urgency and the conditions laid down in terms of irreversible or hazardous treatment. In one sense all medicine is irreversible, but the act defines irreversible in terms of *unfavourable* physical or psychological consequences.

Implications for nurses administering medication

It will be clear from the law set out above that it is essential for those who are administering medication to be aware of the legal status of the detained patient in terms of Part IV of the Mental Health Act 1983 provisions. If the patient has given consent under section 58, then it is the right of the patient to withdraw consent, and this can be done at any time. If therefore a patient has agreed under section 58 to take medication, but changes his or her mind when the nurse comes to administer it, the nurse cannot compel the patient to take it. Only if section 62 then applies could the patient be compelled to take the medication under one of the provisions of section 62. On the other hand, if Form 39 has been completed in respect of a patient who refuses to give consent or who is incapable of giving consent, then compulsion can be used for the patient in having the medication (unless the treatment is one specified under section 58A). If section 63 applies and the first three months of being given medication have not elapsed then the consent of the patient is not required, provided the medication is given under the directions of the registered medical practitioner and is for the treatment of mental disorder. Whilst, in law, compulsory treatment of the patient is permitted, good practice guidelines would ensure that all reasonable and professional methods are used to persuade the patient to take the medication voluntarily before any forms of compulsion are used.

Treatment in the community

There are no statutory powers to compel a patient to have treatment for mental disorder unless the patient is detained under one of the long-term sections as outlined above. It follows therefore that a patient who is in the community cannot be compelled to have treatment. The Mental Health Act 2007 introduced new community treatment order (CTO) under which a patient on discharge can be subject to supervision and control. The CTO replaces the after care under supervision arrangements of the Mental Health (Patients in the Community) Act 1995 Section 17A to 17G are added to the Mental Health Act 1983 to provide for the recall of a patient who fails to comply with the specified conditions. The CTO does not enable a health professional to force an unwilling patient to accept treatment in the community. If a patient refuses the treatment then he or she can be required to return to hospital.

The responsible clinician may recall a community patient to hospital if in his opinion:

(a) the patient requires medical treatment in hospital for his mental disorder; and

(b) there would be a risk of harm to the health or safety of the patient or to other persons if the patient were not recalled to hospital for that purpose.

The responsible clinician may also recall a community patient to hospital if the patient fails to comply with a condition specified under section 17B(3). These conditions include provision to ensure that the patient receives medical treatment.

If a patient is on leave of absence from hospital under section 17, then refusal by the patient to take medication could lead to a withdrawal of that leave of absence in writing by the registered medical practitioner of the patient and a return to the original hospital.

Criticisms of the Community Treatment Orders

Dr Tony Zigmond of the Royal College of Psychiatrists stated that the use of CTOs is trapping some patients in drug programmes they may not want. (Lister 2011). In 2009/10 the Care Quality Commission (CQC) report found that 4,000 patients were made subject to a CTO more that ten times the number which had been predicted by the DH. The CQC had found in 2010 that 30% of patients who were placed on CTOs did not have a history of refusing to take their medication or cooperate with community services.

Informal patients

Those patients who are admitted without detention to psychiatric hospitals are known as 'informal patients'. Patients who are not detained under the Mental Health Act 1983 or who are detained under the short-term sections (4, 5(2), 5(4), 135, 136 etc.) cannot be given compulsory treatment under the Mental Health Act 1983. If they are considered to have the necessary mental capacity then they can refuse any medication even if it is life saving (see Chapter 12). If they lack mental capacity then the statutory provisions of the Mental Capacity Act 2005 which are discussed in Chapter 14 should be followed.as well as the Deprivation of Liberty Safeguards (DoLS) which were enacted following the decision of the European Court of Justice in the Bournewood case which overruled the decision of the House of Lords. The House of Lords had ruled that it was lawful for an informal person to be treated for mental disorder without their consent under the doctrine of necessity recognised by the common law. The European Court of Human Rights held that such a detention is an infringement of Article 5.1 and Article 5.4 of the European Convention on Human Rights.12. (See Chapter 14 for a detailed discussion of the case.)

The Mental Health Act 2007

An expert committee was set up by the Government in 1998 under the chairmanship of Professor Richardson to review the Mental Health Act 1983. Its terms of reference included the degree to which the current legislation needed updating and to ensure that there is a proper balance between safety (both of individuals and the wider community) and the rights of individual patients. It was required to advise the Government on how mental health legislation should be shaped to reflect contemporary patterns of care and treatment and to support its policy as set out in the paper *Modernising Health Services* (DH 1998). The Expert Committee presented its preliminary proposals which set out the principles on which any future legislation should be based in April 1999 and its full report was published in November 1999. The Government presented its proposals for reform in 1999 with a final date for response by 31 March 2000 (DH 1999b). The DH published a White Paper in December 2000 setting out its proposals for reform. Unusually a draft mental health bill was published in 2002 prior to its introduction into Parliament for debate together with a consultation document and explanatory notes (DH 2002). (Normally following a White paper, the next anticipated stage would have been a Bill introduced into Parliament.) As a result of considerable hostility to the draft Bill, a new draft Bill was published in 2004 and was subjected to pre-parliamentary scrutiny prior to its introduction into Parliament which considered it to be fundamentally flawed. Eventually the Mental Health Act 2007 was enacted which was a very diluted version of the Richardson review and amended the 1983 Act rather than introduced a new mental health statute. During it's passage through Parliament the DoLS were debated and these led to amendments to the Mental Capacity Act 2005 and are discussed in Chapter 14. Under the 2007 Act the Secretary of State is required to set out the principles which should be included in the code of practice to be followed in the care of those with mental disorder. They are shown in Box 16.5.

Box 16.5 Principles to be followed

In preparing the statement of principles the Secretary of State shall, in particular, ensure that each of the following matters is addressed:

(a) respect for patients' past and present wishes and feelings,
(b) respect for diversity generally including, in particular, diversity of religion, culture and sexual orientation (within the meaning of section 35 of the Equality Act 2006),
(c) minimising restrictions on liberty,
(d) involvement of patients in planning, developing and delivering care and treatment appropriate to them,
(e) avoidance of unlawful discrimination,
(f) effectiveness of treatment,
(g) views of carers and other interested parties,
(h) patient wellbeing and safety, and
(i) public safety.

(2C) The Secretary of State shall also have regard to the desirability of ensuring:

(a) the efficient use of resources, and
(b) the equitable distribution of services.

Department of Health guidance

A good practice guide was issued in March 2005 by the National Prescribing Centre, the National Institute for Mental Health in England and the DH (DH 2005). This explores the opportunities for mental health nurses to expand their role in prescribing and supplying medication and improve services for people with mental health problems. The DH published guidance in 2008 on *Medicines management for patients, carers and professionals in the mental health services* (DH 2008a). The leaflet on *Medicines Management: Everybody's business: A guide for service users, carers and health and social care practitioners* is intended to empower service users and carers to ask the relevant questions about the medication and to help health and social care practitioners (HSCPs) to improve their person centred approach in the area of medicines management (DH 2008b). It sets out the standard which patients and carers should expect; what HSCPs should provide; gives advice to service users on taking medication and to HSCPs on prescribing medication; lists questions which service users could ask and advises on reporting adverse side effects.

Application of the law to the situation in Box 16.1

Mavis is detained under section 2 which could last for up to 28 days and be followed, if appropriate, by an application by an approved mental health professional based on two medical recommendations (one of which must be a doctor approved for the purposes of the Mental Health Act) for admission for treatment under section 3. Although section 2 is for assessment, Part IV of the Act enables treatment to be given compulsorily to patients on section 2. Section 63 would apply to Mavis's situation, which means that she can be required to take medication which is a treatment for mental disorder and which is recommended by her responsible medical officer. This means that she could be given this compulsorily, though clearly professional efforts would be made to ensure that she understood the reasons why the medication was recommended and to answer her specific concerns about it. Were she to be subsequently detained under Section 3, after three months from the time medication was first administered she would have the right to insist upon a second opinion doctor visiting her and deciding whether or not to support her doctor's choice of treatment.

Conclusions

The amendments to the Mental Health Act 1983 made by the 2007 Act do not constitute the radical changes recommended by the Richardson Expert Committee but together with the Human Rights legislation, the DoLS and the CTO should make radical changes to the care of the mentally disordered. The replacement of the approved social worker by the approved mental health professional and the introduction of the approved clinician widens the categories of health professionals who can take on the statutory roles and who may be involved in prescribing medication for those suffering from mental disorder.

Key points

■ Mental disorder and mental incapacity are different concepts and may or may not overlap.

■ Statutory provisions exist for persons suffering from mental disorder who are detained under certain sections of the Mental Health Act 1983 to be given compulsory treatment without their consent.

■ Safeguards are specified to protect the patient including the appointment of an independent doctor to provide a second opinion for certain specified treatments and for medication after the first three months.

■ The 2007 Act made significant changes to the statutory provisions of the 1983 Act

References

Care Quality Commission (2010) *Monitoring the Use of the Mental Health Act*

Department of Health (1998) *Modernising Mental Health Services*. London

Department of Health (1999a) *Review of the Mental Health Act 1983: Report of Expert Committee November 1999*. London

Department of Health (1999b) *Reform of the Mental Health Act 1983 – Proposals for Consultation Cm 4480* Stationery Office. London

Department of Health (2000) *White Paper Reforming the Mental Health Act Cm 5016*. London

Department of Health (2002) *Draft Mental Health Bill Cm 5538-1; Explanatory notes (Cm 5538-11) and a consultation document (Cm 5338-111)*. London

Department of Health (2005) *Improving mental health services by extending the role of nurses in prescribing and supplying medication: good practice guide.* London

Department of Health (2008a) *Medicines management for patients, carers and professionals in the mental health services.* London

Department of Health (2008b) *Medicines Management: Everybody's business: A guide for service users, carers and health and social care practitioners.* London

Lister, S (2011) Mental patients 'trapped' by abuse of forced drugs regime *The Times* 2 February 2011

CHAPTER 17

The older person

> ## Box 17.1 Intermittent competence
>
> *Iris was in the early stages of Alzheimer's and on occasions appeared to be completely rational, and then suddenly at other times appeared to lack competence. She had to be admitted to hospital for an ulcerated hiatus hernia, but was refusing to take any medication, even though she was clearly in severe pain. Could she be compelled to have treatment?*

Introduction

There are no clear common features or characteristics in the elderly, other than that they are over a particular age, but this has little significance. An older person of 90 years may be physically and mentally fitter, more mobile, more outgoing than one of 65 years. The same laws of consent, confidentiality, negligence and the duty of care apply to all adult patients, whatever their age. The existence or absence of mental capacity determines what action healthcare practitioners can take and whether or not compulsory treatment can be given. However, because of problems relating to the determination of competence and difficulties arising from intermittent competence, it was considered justified in dealing with this client group in a separate chapter.

Basic principles

As discussed in Chapter 12, if an adult has the requisite mental capacity, he or she is entitled to refuse any treatment, even life-saving treatment, for a good reason, a bad reason or no reason. Capacity is determined in the light of an evaluation of the patient's ability to understand the information given, retain it, and make a decision on the basis of that information. Once capacity to make a particular decision is considered to be present, the fact that the patient wants to make a ridiculous decision, which a typical person would probably not make, is irrelevant. Having determined the fact that the patient has the necessary mental capacity, then the health professional must allow the patient to make his or her decisions. On the other hand, if the health professional determines that the patient lacks the capacity, decisions must be made in the best interests of the patient.

Intermittent competence

The law is black and white:

mental capacity = self-determination
mental incapacity = others acting in the best interests of that person

In practice of course, patients do not fit neatly into one category, and may during the course of a serious illness be classified as mentally competent on some occasions and lacking capacity on others. If at a given moment a patient appears to be mentally capable and is refusing treatment, the fact that they lacked capacity a short time before is irrelevant. That patient is entitled to refuse the recommended treatment.

If, on the other hand, a patient who was once mentally capable, now, at the time treatment is being offered, appears to lack capacity, then medication could be given to the mentally incapable person in his or her best interests. A qualification on this, however, is if the patient when mentally competent had drawn up a living will (known as an advance decision) which covered a time when they might lose capacity and in which the treatments now being recommended are specifically refused. For example, a patient, when mentally capacitated, might draw up a living will, and have it witnessed, that in the event of the patient suffering from Alzheimer's, he or she would not want to be treated with antibiotics. If a situation then arose in which the patient is now suffering with Alzheimer's and had developed a chest condition, the living will refusing antibiotics would be binding upon health professionals. If, however, there are no such advance directions, and the patient lacks mental capacity, health professions have no option other than to fulfil their duty of care to the patient and act in the best interests of the patient which would mean prescribing and administering the appropriate medication. Advance decisions have been put on a statutory basis by the Mental Capacity Act 2005 replacing the common law position.

The passive accepting patient

Some elderly patients may passively accept treatment, even though they do not appear to have the necessary mental capacity. When treatment is given to such patients, there is no consent to the treatment. Health professionals are acting in the best interests of the patient under the Mental Capacity Act 2007 which replaced the common law powers recognised by the House of Lords in the case of F v West Berkshire HA & Another, F (Re) (a mental patient: sterilisation) [1989] 2 ALL ER 545 [1990] 2 AC 1. Unfortunately, it is often a feature of staff/patient relationships in psychiatric hospitals or residential/nursing homes for the elderly, that if the patient does not refuse treatment or care their capacity to consent is assumed to exist; on the other hand, if they refuse any intervention their mental capacity is then questioned. In fact, the passive accepting patient may well not have the mental capacity to give consent, and health professionals are acting in his or her best interests in giving treatment and care.

Relatives

Relatives are required to act in the best interests of a person who lacks the requisite mental capacity under the provisions of the Mental Capacity Act 2005. Where decisions relate to serious medical treatment, then the involvement of a health professional in determining what is in the best interests of the patient would be required. Form 4 of the Department of Health's (DH) practical implementation guide shows clearly the role of the relatives in the consent process (DH 2009a). The relatives should be involved in informing the health professional of the views the patient would have expressed had he or she had the requisite mental capacity. The relatives sign Form 4 to show that they understand that the patient lacks the necessary mental capacity and the reasons for that assessment, and that they understand that the proposed treatment is being given in the best interests of the patient.

Covert administration

If the patient lacks the mental capacity to give consent, if the patient needs treatment in his or her best interests and if health professionals know that the patient would resist being given that treatment, then it is tempting to consider administering the treatment by covert means, without the patient's knowledge, thus avoiding the patient becoming distressed, and yet at the same time ensuring that the patient benefits from the recommended treatment. The issue of covert administration is considered in Chapter 14 where the UKCC paper on covert administration is discussed. Clearly any covert administration should be an exceptional situation and should be closely monitored.

Medication management of the elderly

Even though the elderly do not necessarily share any common characteristics other than age, they are possibly more likely than any other age group to be receiving many different medications for a variety of different conditions. A useful article was published by Ian Peate in the *British Journal of Nursing* which covers the principles of good practice in medicines for the older person (Peate 2003). Guidance for nursing staff is also provided by Rosemount Pharmaceuticals. The booklet and a video on best practice in medication management of the elderly are both available free from Rosemount Pharmaceuticals (FREEPHONE 0800 919 312).

The DH issued National Service Guidance in March 2000 and later published the National Service Framework (NSF) for Older People document in 2001 as well as a booklet on medicines and older people to ensure that older people gain maximum benefit from medication and do not suffer unnecessarily from illness caused by excessive, inappropriate or inadequate consumption of medicines. This booklet is available online from the NSF website (www.doh.gov.uk/NSF/olderpeople).

There is evidence of gross abuse of medicines and the older person. For example a review carried out for the DH in November 2009 found that over 144,000 patients suffering from dementia are being given anti-psychotic drugs unnecessarily (DH 2009b). As a consequence of this report the Care Services Minister undertook to appoint a national clinical director for dementia to conduct an audit of GP's and hospital doctors' prescribing of anti-psychotic drugs. It was believed that the use of anti-psychotic drugs could be reduced by two thirds. The DH published a strategy for dementia in February 2009 which is available on its website (www.dh.gov.uk).

Polypharmacy

Polypharmacy is a specialty of growing importance and expert professional knowledge may be necessary to ensure that all the different preparations are compatible and there are no known unwanted interactive effects. If a health professional failed to take reasonable care when administering medicines to an older person to ensure that there was no contra-indication when several different medicines had been prescribed and as a consequence the patient suffered harm, then there could be vicarious liability of the employer concerned for those staff who had been negligent: these may include the prescribing doctor, the administering nurse and the pharmacist. Most hospitals would have regular ward checks by the pharmacists to ensure that patients were being given appropriate medicines and that the various combinations of medicines were safe. If such a check was not in place, and ward nursing staff were not sure about different medications being prescribed and/or administered together, they should ask for a pharmacist to check. In the community the community nurse may have to check with the GP if she were concerned about the patient's medication and the possibility of dangerous combinations.

Application of law to the situation in Box 17.1

It is essential that there should be an assessment of Iris's mental capacity at the time the medication is to be administered. If she appears to be mentally capable, then she has the right to refuse the medication, even medication for pain relief. However, it is essential that time should be given so that the nurse can explain to her the reason for the medication and the benefits which she would receive. If, on the other hand, an assessment shows that Iris is incapable of understanding why the medication is being offered and she is incapable of giving her consent, then action can be taken in her best interests. Clearly any force required should be reasonable and proportional to the desired outcome. It may be possible to delay the administration until such a time as she is receptive to receiving it. The health professional administering the treatment could use Form 4 from the DH's guidance as evidence that the correct procedure is followed (DH 2009).

Where long-term treatment is proposed and the patient appears to be suffering from mental disorder, then detention under the Mental Health Act 1983 should be considered in order to ensure that the rights of the patient are protected.

Conclusions

The Mental Capacity Act 2005 has filled the vacuum in statute law in relation to decision making on behalf of the mentally incapacitated adult. In Scotland, there is statutory provision for decision making on behalf of mentally incapacitated adults (Adults with Incapacity (Scotland) Act 2000). In Chapter 14 can be found the history of the draft legislation drawn up by the Law Commission in 1995 and the further consultation paper from the Lord Chancellor's Department (1997) followed by a White paper in 1999. The Mental Capacity Act 2005 came into force in 2007 following the publication of Codes of Practice and covers England, Wales and Northern Ireland. (For further details see Chapter 14.)

Key points

- Older people all share only one characteristic, and that is their age.
- Some older persons may suffer from intermittent competence.
- Competence should be determined at the time medication is administered.
- A mentally capable person can refuse even life-saving treatment; a mentally incapacitated person can be given treatment without his or her consent, provided it is in their best interests.
- Where several medicines are being administered, health professionals have a duty of care to ensure that any reasonably foreseeable risks of unfavourable interactions are prevented.
- The Mental Capacity Act which provides for decision making on behalf of the mentally incapacitated adult came into force in 2007.

References

Department of Health (2001) *National Service Framework for Older People*. http://www.doh.gov.uk/NSF/olderpeopleexec.htm (for executive summary). London

Department of Health (2001) SC 2001/007; LAC(2001)12 *National Service Framework for Older People*. London

Department of Health (2009a) *Good practice in consent implementation guide*. London

Department of Health (2009b) *Banerjee Sub Report on the prescribing of anti-psychotic drugs to people with dementia* November 2009 London

Greenwall, R. S. (2004) *Medication Management of the Elderly: A Guide for Nursing Staff. Rosemount Pharmaceuticals*.

Law Commission *Mental Incapacity Report* No 231 1995. HMSO, London.

Lord Chancellor's Department (1997) *Who Decides?*

Lord Chancellor's Department (1999) *Making Decisions*.

Peate, I. (2003) Medicines and the older person: principles of good practice. *British Journal of Nursing*, 12(9), 530–5. London

Websites

Department of Health website www.dh.gov.uk

CHAPTER 18

Self-administration of medicines

Box 18.1 Situation

Doris was admitted to hospital for an appendectomy. She came in with a variety of liquids and pills for several different conditions, including heart problems, arthritis, indigestion, glaucoma, back pain and several others. The admitting nurse said that they would all have to be taken away from her during her stay in hospital, but that she could obtain replacement medicines from the hospital pharmacy and these would be prescribed by the doctor. Doris protested, since she thought this a total waste of money and they were her medicines and should not be removed from her. She also stated that she was perfectly capable of giving herself the medicines, since she did that at home and could save the nurses time. What is the law?

Introduction

Self-administration by patients of their own medicines is the ideal to be aimed at. If the patient understands why medication is in their best interests, how it should be taken and is in control of the process, then such a system promotes the autonomy of the patient. In the home situation, of course, most adults and many older children are responsible for their medication. However, in the hospital setting, not all wards have a policy of self-administration of drugs by patients. The medicines that patients bring in with them are either confiscated until the patient's discharge or removed to be controlled by nursing staff. Medicines newly prescribed are kept under the control of nursing staff, who administer them, and the patient does not acquire during the in-patient stay the skills to deal with them. Such practices encourage a learned helplessness and an institutionalisation of patients so that skills and capabilities that the patient possessed on admission are lost during the in-patient stay. Two separate procedures are relevant here:

- The self-administration of medicines by the patient, including medicines which were brought in by the patient.
- The use of the medication which the patient brings into hospital, but its administration by ward staff.

Self-administration policy

It is advisable that a policy on the self-administration of medicines should be drawn up by a multi-disciplinary team, including pharmacists, doctors and nurses, and that this should cover the following topics:

- Procedure on admission of patient.
- Determination of the competence of patient to self-administer.
- Contraindications to self-administration.
- Storage and security.
- Documentation to be kept by the patient and by the ward staff.
- Risks to and from other patients.
- Polypharmacy and use of complementary therapies: homoeopathic medicines and herbalism.
- Procedure on discharge of patient.

The multi-disciplinary team, including the patient's representative and any other interested health professionals, should be established to draft the policy and review the resources necessary to enable its implementation, initially on a pilot basis. Once in place, the implementation of a self-administration policy should be regularly monitored and amended in the light of any defects.

Guidelines from the Nursing and Midwifery Council

The Nursing and Midwifery Council (NMC) in its *Standards for medicines management* (2007) has welcomed and supported the self-administration of medicines (See standard 5). Standard 9 defines three levels of self-administration and sets out the standards to be followed. The guidance on standard 9 states the factors which should be remembered when the patient agrees to be responsible for the storage and to self-administer medicines in hospital, including the right of the patient to change their mind and the information which should be provided to the patient before they take over the self-administration. Standard 10 covers the principles which apply when children or young people agree to self-administer (or their parents on their behalf). Annexe 4 sets out the exclusion criteria for self-administration of medicines. These include a confused patient who should not be given custody of the medicines but may administer at level 1 or 2.

Guidance from the Royal Pharmaceutical Society of Great Britain

In its guidance on the administration and control of medicine in care homes and children's services, the Royal Pharmaceutical Society of Great Britain (RPSGP) stated the following of service users taking their own medicines:

The National Minimum Standards for Older people and Adults 18–65 (England and Wales) and the National Care Standards (Scotland) place great emphasis on the right of a service user to take responsibility for his/her own medication when possible. This will preserve independence and prepare those in short term care for their return to the community, where they will need to look after their own medicines.

The RPSGB stated that there may be limited situations when a service user is able to take complete control of his/her medicines. A service user can exercise control over his/her medicine provided that the home's staff can assist the service user in taking them for example:

- A service user who has suffered a stroke and is unable to manipulate containers may choose to retain custody of medicines and ask care staff to assist at the time he/she chooses to take the medication.
- A service user may be able to safely manage the application of external creams but may elect to have care staff administer tablets and other prescribed medicine.
- A service user who has limited understanding and awareness may be given prescribed medicines for 24 hours in a compliance aid.

  The responsibility of the carer for each service user should be defined.

This guidance from the RPSGB could also be adapted to apply to patients within hospital or intermediate care, where it is essential to ensure that the patient's ability to return to independence in the community is supported if at all possible.

Many hospitals have their own policy on self-administration of medicines by patients, and the health professional should consult these. Some of these local policies have been put on the internet and it is possible for anyone involved drawing up a local policy to access these. For example East London and the City Mental Health NHS Trust has put on the web its guidelines for the implementation of patient self-administration (www.eastlondon.nhs.uk). As part of the guidelines it includes appendices with forms which are used including assessment and consent forms, monitoring forms and information sheets.

Use of medication brought in by the patient

There should be a presumption in favour of the continued use of medicinal products brought in by the patient, subject to the approval of the patient's doctor and by the pharmacist. However, it would not be appropriate to permit use of the medicines brought in by the patient if any of the following factors was present:

- Expiry date reached
- Poor condition of preparation
- Mixed drugs in one container
- Unsuitable packaging and storage container, e.g. envelopes
- Inappropriate labelling
- Inability to identify label
- Medication changed on admission or prior to discharge.

Each NHS trust should have a policy relating to the use or discarding of medicines brought in by the patient. Where appropriate the discarding should take place with the consent of the patient. (Illegal substances are considered in Chapter 28.)

Application of law to the situation in Box 18.1

There are no statutory provisions which cover the circumstances of Doris, but there are cases at common law which require the health professionals to fulfil their duty of care to Doris and other patients, so that they are not caused reasonably foreseeable harm as a result of any acts or omissions on their part. There are two aspects of the situation:

1. Could Doris continue to use the medicines she has brought from home? and
2. Should she be allowed to administer the medication to herself?

In answer to the first question, it would indeed be a waste of resources if new medicines were to be prescribed and dispensed in place of her existing ones, which were then destroyed. However, before Doris can be allowed to continue to have the medicines she has brought from home, there should be two checks. Firstly a doctor should examine Doris and decide whether she needed new medications; which, if any, of her existing medications were still required; and whether there was any incompatibility between the new and the old. Secondly a pharmacist should check her existing medicines to ensure that they are of a good quality, valid in terms of time and safe.

Whether Doris should be allowed to administer these medicines herself will then depend upon all the issues which have been discussed above. What is Doris's competence? What are the storage facilities for medicines being self-administered? What are the reasonably foreseeable risks to other patients on the ward? If Doris has the requisite mental capacity and arrangements can be made so that Doris can safely administer the medicines herself, there are no legal reasons why this should not take place. Clearly there are advantages if a policy has been agreed across the NHS Trust by all the relevant health professionals and its implementation systematically monitored.

Conclusions

Self-administration of medicines by patients should be part of a concerted policy to promote the autonomy, independence and self-sufficiency of the patient. There are many patient groups where self-administration would be a positive benefit to their after-care when they have to take responsibility themselves for their administration. Thus the elderly, the chronically sick and those who are likely to be on long-term medication at home would benefit from being encouraged to take responsibility whilst in hospital. However, it is essential that progress towards greater acceptance of self-administration proceeds slowly and safely, that proper arrangements are made for the safe custody and storage of the medicines, that policies are regularly revised and monitored and that the safety of the patient is paramount at all times.

Key points

- Self-administration of medicines should be distinguished from the use of medicines brought from the patient's home.
- Self administration of medicines enables a patient's independence to be maintained.

- A self-administration policy is essential to ensure that risks and benefits are evaluated.
- Standards have been set by the NMC and guidance provided by the RPSGB.

References

Nursing and Midwifery Council (2007) *Standards for medicines management*. London

Royal Pharmaceutical Society of Great Britain (2003) *The administration and control of medicine in care homes and children's services*.

Websites

East London and the City Mental Health NHS Trust website www.eastlondon.nhs.uk

CHAPTER 19

Accountability and medicines 1: Criminal law

Box 19.1 Epidural not intravenous

A patient was suffering from leukaemia and was receiving chemotherapy by intravenous transfusion. Unfortunately a junior doctor, in error, administered the drug by epidural. The patient subsequently died.

Introduction

The death of the patient from an error in prescribing or administration can lead to many different court hearings. In this chapter we consider the possible criminal consequences of such an event; in subsequent chapters we look at the consequences in the civil law, disciplinary proceedings and professional conduct proceedings.

Coroner's jurisdiction

In the case in Box 19.1 the death would have been reported to the coroner. Under section 1 of the Coroners and Justice Act 2009, the senior coroner, who is made aware that the body of a deceased is within his area has a duty to conduct an investigation into the death if the following applies:

a) the deceased died a violent or unnatural death,

b) the cause of death is unknown, or

c) the deceased died while in custody or otherwise in state detention.

Until the coroner has formally notified the doctor of his decision in relation to the deceased, the body remains under the control of the coroner, i.e. under his or her jurisdiction. The coroner has the right to request a post mortem and there can be no action taken in respect of the body without the coroner's consent. Once the death is reported the coroner will then decide whether a post mortem is required. If he or she gives instructions for a post mortem to take place, the relatives have no right to refuse. This is so even when the religious views of the deceased would be against a post mortem (R. v. Westminster City Coroner, ex parte Rainer (1968) 112). The relatives are, however, entitled to be notified when the coroner's investigations have been completed and their consent would be required to any withholding of body parts after the coroner's investigations. In the light of the post mortem findings the coroner would decide whether or not to hold an inquest and whether a jury for the inquest should be summoned.

The purpose of the inquest is to ascertain:
- Who the deceased was.
- How, when and where the deceased came by his or her death.
- The particulars (if any) required by the 1953 Mental Health Act to be registered concerning the death Coroners and Justice Act 2009 section 5(1).

Possible verdicts are:
- Natural causes
- Unlawful killing
- Killed lawfully
- Killed him- or herself (whilst the balance of mind was disturbed)
- Accidental death
- Misadventure
- Dependence upon a drug
- Non-dependent abuse of drugs
- Industrial disease
- Neglect
- Want of attention at birth
- Attempted/self-induced abortion
- Open verdict.

An open verdict indicates that there is insufficient evidence to determine the nature of the death, i.e. the evidence did not further or fully disclose the means whereby the cause of death arose.

There can also be a narrative verdict where the death is explained in full, as when one of two Siamese twins died in an operation to separate them.

The coroner's court

A practitioner might be required to give evidence at an inquest on the events which preceded death. It is essential that she obtains assistance from a senior manager or lawyer on the preparation of a statement which the coroner's office will require from her. If she is subsequently asked to attend the inquest she should have assistance in preparation for giving evidence. It should be noted that the coroner's court is known as an inquisitorial one. This means that the coroner determines the witnesses who will give evidence and the course of the proceedings, and will disallow any question which in his opinion is not relevant or otherwise not a proper one. He can himself examine the witnesses, often asking leading questions where information is not disputed to speed up the hearing – hence the words 'inquisitorial' and 'inquest'. In contrast, in the Magistrates, Crown and civil courts an action is brought by one person or organisation against another and the judge controls the proceedings. This is known as 'adversarial' or 'accusatorial'.

Where the death has been reported to the coroner, no certificate can be issued or registration take place until he or she has made his or her decision.

The coroner can not make any finding on the criminal conduct of any person. He or she can, however, at any time adjourn the proceedings, passing information to the police and Crown Prosecution Service for criminal proceedings to be investigated. Once criminal proceedings are completed or a decision is made that they are not to be brought, the inquest can be resumed.

Following a death in 2001 the Coroner made a recommendation that urgent measures should be introduced to make it impossible to inject patients with the wrong drugs during routine surgery. The facts of the case are shown in Box 19.2.

Under Rule 43 of the Coroners' Rules 1984 (as amended by the Coroners (Amendment) Rules 2008 SI 2008 No. 1652) the coroner can send a report to any relevant person or organization if he/she feels that the death could have been prevented and the recipient is required to send a written response.

Criminal proceedings

Once they had been notified of the unexpected death the police would commence an investigation into the circumstances surrounding it. Statements would be taken from any staff involved and a decision would then be made as to whether anyone should be charged with causing the death of the patient and the nature of the offence.

> ## Box 19.2 Error in administration
>
> A 74-year-old man, who was undergoing an operation to repair an aortic aneurysm, died when the consultant anaesthetist wrongly injected a painkiller into his vein. He attached a bag of Bupivacaine, a powerful painkiller, to an intravenous drip which led to a cardiac catastrophe. The drug should have been given only via an epidural catheter inserted into the spine. Recommendations for significant changes to the coroner's jurisdiction and to the procedure for certifi cation of death were made by the Inquiry which followed the convictions of Dr Harold Shipman, some of which have been enacted by the Coroners and Justice Act 2009 (DH 2003).

Murder

The definition of murder derives from a 17th century case:

> *Murder is when a man of sound memory, and of the age of discretion, unlawfully killeth within any country of the realm any reasonable creature in rerum natura under the king's peace, with malice aforethought, either expressed by the party or implied by law, so as the party wounded, or hurt, etc die of the wound or hurt etc. (Coke)*

The original definition set a time limit of a year and a day in which the person must die of the wound or hurt. This limitation of time was removed in 1996. In certain circumstances, what would have been a crime of murder may be reduced to manslaughter.

Manslaughter

Manslaughter is divided into two categories: voluntary and involuntary.

Voluntary covers the situation where there is the mental intention to kill or complete disregard as to the possibility that death could arise from one's actions (i.e. there is the mental requirement (*mens rea*), but there are extenuating factors, such as provocation or death in pursuance of a suicide pact or diminished responsibility. The effect of these extenuating facts is that a murder verdict could not be obtained, but the defendant could be guilty of voluntary manslaughter.

Involuntary manslaughter exists when the mental intention (*mens rea*) for murder is absent. Such circumstances would include gross negligence or recklessness. A conviction for manslaughter may be obtained.

The Coroners and Justice Act 2009 amended the law relating to manslaughter: changing the definition of diminished responsibility and abolishing the common law defence of provocation replacing it with a defence of loss of control.

Where the accused is convicted of manslaughter the judge has complete discretion over sentencing (subject to sentencing guidelines). In contrast, where there is a murder conviction, at present the sentence is a mandatory one of life imprisonment (the judge recommends the length of sentence to be served).

Gross negligence in professional practice may amount to the crime of manslaughter. For example, an anaesthetist failed to realise that during an operation a tube had become disconnected as a result of which the patient died. He was prosecuted in the criminal courts and convicted of manslaughter (R v Adomako [1995] 1 AC 171; [1994] 3 All ER 79). To obtain a conviction for manslaughter the prosecution has to establish beyond reasonable doubt that the gross negligence by the accused caused the death of the patient. In a Crown Court case heard in Cardiff concerning two surgeons in Llanelli who had removed the wrong kidney from the patient, the Home Office pathologist was not able to confirm that the removal of the wrong kidney had actually caused the death of the patient, so the judge ordered the jury to acquit the defendants. If criminal proceedings for manslaughter are brought the jury must be satisfied beyond reasonable doubt that the actions of the defendant amounted to gross negligence and caused the death of the victim.

A manslaughter conviction was upheld by the Court of Appeal in a case where the defendant gave a syringe of heroin to a person ready for immediate self-injection which resulted in that person's death (R. v. Kennedy Court of Appeal, [2005] EWCA Crim 685. (See Chapter 28).

A criminal conviction of a registrant will usually be followed by a fitness to practise proceedings before the Conduct and Competence committeee of the relevant registration body. Their proceedings and considered in Chapter 22.

National Patient Safety Agency and epidurals

There is evidence that within the NHS similar untoward events are repeated and the lessons are not learnt across the service. A report called *An Organisation with a Memory*, written by an expert group chaired by Professor Liam Donaldson,

Chief Medical Officer, Department of Health (DH 2000), put forward radical recommendations to prevent the same errors and incidents occurring across the NHS. It also recommended that the DH should examine the feasibility of setting specific targets for the NHS to achieve in reducing the levels of frequently reported incidents. One of these targets was that by 2001 the number of patients dying or being paralysed by wrongly administered spinal injections should be reduced to zero. Another target was that by 2005 the number of serious errors in the use of prescribed drugs (these currently account for 20% of all clinical negligence litigation) should be reduced by 40%. The targets published in *An Organisation With a Memory* were adopted by the National Patient Safety Agency (NPSA), which was set up in July 2001 as an independent body to receive notification of adverse incidents and to ensure that the lessons are learnt across the NHS. (See Chapter 3 for further discussion on the NPSA.) The first patient safety alert of the NPSA was issued on 23 July 2002 and was about preventing accidental overdose with intravenous potassium. The alert notice refers to the possible risks from treatment with concentrated potassium and the need for additional safety precautions in the way potassium solutions are stored and prepared in hospital.

On 18 March 2005 a nurse was cleared of manslaughter in Liverpool Crown Court. She had accidentally given an 18-month-old boy an injection of Vecuronium, a paralysing agent. She picked up the wrong syringe accidentally giving him Vecuronium which caused his heart to stop instead of the sedative Midazolam.

Application of the law to the situation in Box 19.1

The facts set out in Box 19.1 are similar to an incident in Nottingham where a young man suffering from leukaemia died following an epidural injection of a chemotherapy drug instead of intravenous administration. The doctor concerned pleaded guilty to manslaughter and was sentenced to imprisonment.

Conclusions

Gross negligence in the professional practice of prescribing or administering of medicines, can, if it leads to the death of a patient, result in a manslaughter conviction of the health professional concerned. It will also probably lead to a civil claim for compensation and it is to this topic that we turn in the next chapter.

Key points

- Gross negligence in the prescribing or administering of medicines which leads to the death of a patient can be followed by criminal proceedings.
- A report of an unexpected death would normally be made to the coroner, who then has jurisdiction of the body and decides whether or not an inquest should be held.
- The prosecution have the burden of proving beyond reasonable doubt that there was an act of gross negligence which caused the death of the patient.
- The NPSA has been set up to ensure that the NHS learns from adverse incidents and sets targets in specified areas such as injection errors.

References

Department of Health (2003) *Shipman Inquiry Third Report Death and Cremation Certification*, published 14 July 2003; http://www.the-shipman-inquiry.org.uk/ reports. asp.

Department of Health (2000) *An Organisation with a Memory* chaired by Professor Liam Donaldson Chief Medical Officer; www.doh.gov.uk.

CHAPTER 20

Accountability and medicines 2: Civil law

Box 20.1 Situation

Lyndsey Bohanna, 23 years, had mild depression and had been prescribed Prozac by doctors to combat insomnia and fatigue in September 1999. Two months later during a routine check-up a junior doctor changed her prescription. He gave her an anti-depressant called dothiepin, which is for severe depression and should not be used with Prozac. It is also an anti-depressant, with one of the highest chances of overdose. Nine days later Lyndsey was found dead. An independent review found a host of errors during her treatment at the hospital. The junior doctor had not asked the consultant for advice. Nor did he explain to the patient the risks associated with her new medication. He also failed to inform her GP of how many tablets should be given. What is the law?
(Reported in The Times, 5 December 2002, p. 6.)

Introduction

Where a patient has suffered harm as a result of negligence by the person prescribing or administering a medicinal product or as a result of a defect in the manufacture or dispensing of the medication, then he or she (or the executors or next of kin, in the event of the patient dying) can bring an action in negligence in order to claim compensation for the harm. In addition, where it is alleged that the product is defective then an action could be brought under the Consumer Protection Act 1987, where it need only be established that there was a defect which caused harm. It is not necessary to prove that the manufacturer or supplier was negligent in an action under the Consumer Protection Act.

Negligence

To succeed in the action, the claimant has to show the following elements:
1. That the defendant owed to the person harmed a duty of care.
2. That the defendant was in breach of that duty.
3. That the breach of duty caused reasonably foreseeable.
4. Harm to the claimant.

These four elements – duty, breach, causation and harm – are discussed below.

Duty of care

The law recognises that a duty of care will exist where one person can reasonably foresee that his or her actions and omissions could cause reasonably foreseeable harm to another person. A duty of care will always exist between the health professional and the patient. Clearly, where a nurse is administering or prescribing medicines to a patient, she owes a duty of care in the law of negligence to that person.

Breach of the duty of care

Determining the standard of care

In order to determine whether there has been a breach of the duty of care, it will first be necessary to establish the required standard. The courts have used what has become known as the Bolam Test to determine the standard of care required by a professional. In the case from which the test took its name, the Bolemt Test (Bolam v. Friern Hospital Management Committee [1957] 1 WLR 582), the court laid down the following principle to determine the standard of care which should be followed:

> The standard of care expected is 'the standard of the ordinary skilled man exercising and professing to have that special skill'.
> (Judge McNair)

The Bolam Test was applied by the House of Lords in a case where negligence by an obstetrician in delivering a child by forceps was alleged (Whitehouse v. Jordan [1981] 1 All ER 267):

When you get a situation which involves the use of some special skill or competence, then the test as to whether there has been negligence or not... is the standard of the ordinary skilled man exercising and professing to have that special skill. If a surgeon failed to measure up to that in any respect (clinical judgement or otherwise) he had been negligent and should be so adjudged .

The House of Lords found that the surgeon was not liable in negligence and held that an error of judgement may or may not be negligence. It depends upon the circumstances.

Where medicines are being administered or prescribed, the courts would expect the reasonable standard of professional practice to have been followed. If therefore a nurse is carrying out activities such as prescribing which would usually have been performed by a doctor, the nurse, if she were negligent, could not say in her defence that she was only a nurse, not a doctor. The standard of the reasonable doctor following the accepted approved standard of care should have been followed by the nurse. If she could not meet that standard she should have refused to undertake that activity since it was outside her competence.

Expert witnesses would give evidence to the court on the standard of care they would expect to have found. Lawyers would look to the relevant leading organisations of different professional groups (such as the Royal Pharmaceutical Society (RPS), the Royal College of Physicians (RCP) and the Nursing and Midwifery Council (NMC)) to obtain recommended names of potential experts.

Following the Woolf Reforms (see below) parties to personal injury litigation are expected to agree upon an expert witness, though this is proving difficult in claims relating to clinical negligence. The National Institute of Health and Clinical Excellence (NICE) is providing guidance on research based practice, including the appropriateness of certain medicinal products being prescribed in the NHS.

Has there been a breach of the duty of care? Once it has been established in court what the reasonable standard of care in administering or prescribing medication should have been, the next stage is to decide whether what happened was in accordance with the reasonable standard. Gross negligence which resulted in death could be followed by criminal proceedings (see Chapter 19). In the civil courts evidence will be given by witnesses of fact as to what actually took place. The judge would decide, in the light of the evidence given by experts and witnesses of fact, whether there had been a breach of the duty of care.

Causation

The claimant must show that not only was there a breach of the duty of care, but that this breach of duty caused actual and reasonably foreseeable harm to the claimant. There must be both factual causation and also it must be established on a balance of probabilities that the type of harm which occurred was reasonably foreseeable. Where it is alleged that harm has been caused by a wrongly prescribed or administered medicinal product, the burden is on the claimant to establish on a balance of probabilities that it was this negligence which caused the patient's harm. This may be difficult to do when there are major health problems suffered by the patient. Expert evidence would again be required to show that there was a causal link between the death of the patient (or any harm suffered by the patient) and the negligence in administering or prescribing medication. The case shown in Box 20.2 illustrates the importance of establishing this causal link.

Box 20.2 The cause of deafness

A child suffering from meningitis was given 300,000 units of penicillin instead of 10,000 units. The mistake was discovered and remedial action taken. The health authority admitted liability and made an offer to the parents for the additional pain and suffering that the negligence caused the boy. However, the parents argued that the overdose had caused the boy to become deaf and they rejected the board's offer, claiming instead many thousands of pounds more because they held the health authority liable for the deafness.

The House of Lords decided that the parents had not made out the factual causation between the overdose and the deafness and thus that the boy was not entitled to the larger amount. It is a well-known fact that meningitis itself can cause deafness.

(Kay v. Ayrshire and Arran Health Board [1987] 2 All ER 417)

Harm

Even if there is a breach of the duty of care, compensation will not be payable unless the claimant is able to establish that harm occurred. Harm includes:

personal injury, death, loss or damage to property. Nervous shock (where an identifiable medical condition exists) (now known as post traumatic stress syndrome) is also recognised as the subject of compensation within strict limits of liability using the test of proximity which has been set by the House of Lords. In the situation in Box 20.3 there is a clear breach of the duty of care, but no compensation is payable since the patient has suffered minimal distress. However, Rose could face disciplinary proceedings and be reported to the NMC. However, the fact that she took speedy action to admit her mistake and to ensure the patient was not harmed should be taken into account by both her employer and by the Investigating Committee of the NMC.

Box 20.3 The wrong eye

Rose, a staff nurse on the ophthalmic ward, was doing the medicine round, and in her rush to be finished put eye drops in the left eye of a patient instead of the right eye. She immediately realised her mistake and called the pharmacist urgently to the ward. The patient was reassured that there would be no long-term effects from Rose's error. It was clear, however, that the patient intended to make a complaint and possibly sue the NHS Trust.

Vicarious liability

An employer is vicariously liable for the actions of a negligent employee, so any claim for compensation as a result of a medicinal error would be brought against the employer. The claimant would have to show that the wrong-doer was an employee and was acting in the course of employment at the time of the negligent act. In contrast, a person who was self-employed would have to accept personal and professional liability for her actions. The employer may challenge whether the actions were performed in the course of employment. For example, a practitioner may have undertaken training in a complementary medicine such as homoeopathy. If she decided to use these new skills whilst at work without the agreement, express or implied, of the employer and through his or her use of the remedies caused harm to the client, the employer might refuse to accept vicarious liability on the grounds that the employee was not acting in the course of employment.

In 2001 a court decision in the House of Lords widened the scope of vicarious liability. It ruled that the owners of a boarding school were vicariously liable for sexual abuse carried out by a warden (Lister and others v Helsey Hall Ltd, TLR 10 May 2001; [2001] 2 WLR 1311 (see page Chapter 21 for further details).

Application of the law to the situation in Box 20.1

The internal inquiry pointed to several errors which led to the death of the patient, but unless the NHS trust concerned admits that negligence by one of its employees caused the death and accepts vicariously liability for that negligence, the burden will still be on the next of kin of the deceased to prove on a balance of probabilities that negligence by the doctor caused the death. The next of kin or personal representative of the deceased will have to establish the facts and show from these facts that there was a failure to follow a reasonable standard of care.

She or he will also have to prove that it was this negligence which caused the death, which may be difficult to establish if there is any evidence of an overdose by the deceased. Cases which may apparently on the surface look as though they indicate negligence causing death and therefore compensation is due, may in fact in a court of law be much more difficult to win.

Woolf Reforms

The Woolf Reforms have attempted to speed up the process of claiming compensation for civil wrong. The Final Woolf Report was published in July 1996 and led to the implementation of a new procedure for civil claims in April 1999. The reforms introduced a new system of case management with the courts rather than the parties taking the main responsibility for the progress of cases. Defended cases are allocated for the purposes of case management by the courts to one of three tracks:
1. Small claims (up to £5,000);
2. A new fast track with limited procedures and reduced costs (up to £10,000); and
3. A new multi-track (for more complex cases over £10,000).

Litigation in the NHS is increasing, with the National Audit Office estimating in 2002 that £4.5 billion had to be paid out in compensation claims and the associated costs (this includes cases going back many years but still to be concluded). The NHS Litigation Authority which handles cases brought against the NHS reported that £787 million was paid in connection with clinical negligence claims during 2009/10, up from £769 million in 2008/09 and there is every sign that the figure continues to grow (see www.nhsla.com). The Department of Health (DH) published a consultation paper in June 2003, recommending an NHS Redress Scheme as an alternative to seeking compensation for clinical negligence through the civil courts. The NHS Redress Act 2006 has not yet been brought into force but if implemented, it could lead to much speedier settlements and reduce the need for lawyers.

Conclusions

At the present time, there appears to be little attempt to bring the NHS Redress Act into force although the Minister of Justice is planning to compel litigants and those involved in divorce proceedings to take part in mediation in an attempt to resolve the dispute. Radical reforms are also in hand to reduce the legal aid bill and to amend the system of no win, no fee.

Key points

- Where a patient has suffered harm as a result of an error with medicines a claim for compensation could be made.
- The claimant must prove on a balance of probabilities that a duty of care was owed to her or him.
- The claimant must prove on a balance of probabilities that there has been a breach of this duty of care.
- The claimant must prove on a balance of probabilities that the breach of duty has caused harm to him or her.
- The NHS Redress Act would, if implemented, set up a new scheme for compensation for clinical negligence but has yet to be brought into force.

References

Department of Health (2003) *Making Amends: A consultation paper setting out proposals for reforming the approach to clinical negligence in the NHS*. CMO London

Lord Woolf Final Report (1996) *Access to Justice* July 1996 HMSO. London

Websites

NHS Litigation Authority website www.nhsla.com

CHAPTER 21

Accountability and medicines 3: Employment

Box 21.1 Situation

Mohammed had been trained in a previous post as an independent nurse prescriber. He wished to continue to use those skills in his new post as clinical nurse specialist. He was notified by the Trust that it was not their policy to introduce independent nurse prescribing.

Can he lawfully refuse to obey these instructions?

Introduction

Where harm has been caused to a patient as a result of failures by a nurse, or the nurse has failed to follow reasonable instructions by the employer (whether or not the patient has been harmed) the employer has the right to take disciplinary action against the employee. This chapter considers the accountability of the employee as a result of the employment contract, unfair dismissal and whistle-blowing provisions, all in relation to medicines.

Employment contract

As a result of the contract of employment both employer and employee have duties and rights. The sources of these terms include: express terms, either agreed by the parties individually or resulting from collective bargaining procedures; implied terms; and terms set by statute. It may be expressly set out in the contract that the employee should follow the policies and procedures set by the employer. However, even if there is no specific provision for this, such a term may be implied into the contract of employment.

Implied terms

The law implies into a contract of employment certain terms which are binding upon both parties, even though such terms were never expressly raised by the parties. Box 21.2 lists the terms which would be implied by law as obligations upon the employer and Box 21.3 lists the terms which would be implied by law as obligations upon the employee.

Box 21.2 Implied terms binding upon the employer

1. A duty to take reasonable care for the health and safety of the employer, including the duty to ensure that the premises, plant and equipment are safe, that there is a safe system of work and that the staff are competent.
2. A duty to cooperate with the employee to enable him to fulfil his contract of employment.
3. To pay the employee.

Box 21.3 Implied terms binding upon the employee

1. A duty to obey the reasonable instructions of the employer.
2. A duty to act with reasonable care and safety.
3. A duty to cooperate with the employer. This would include the duty to account for profits, to disclose misdeeds, and not to compete with the employer.
4. A duty to maintain the confidentiality of information learnt during employment..

The basic principle is that where express terms cover the issue, terms will not have to be implied.

In the case of a junior hospital doctor it was argued that there was an implied term that an employer would take care of his employees and not ask him to work an excessive amount of overtime (Johnstone v. Bloomsbury Health Authority [1991] ICR 269). In this case the junior doctor became ill as a result of the excessive amount of overtime he was asked to work. The Human Rights Act 1998 can apply to the field of employment since in certain circumstances an employee of a public authority or of an organisation exercising public functions may be able to argue that he is being treated in an inhuman or degrading way, contrary to Article 3. In addition, where civil rights and obligations are in dispute, a person is entitled to have a hearing by an independent and impartial tribunal under Article 6.

A case where the employee alleged a breach of an implied term by the employer

The case set out in Box 21.4 illustrates the situation where an employee argued that the employer was in breach of the implied term of mutual trust and confidence.

Box 21.4 Holladay v. East Kent Hospitals NHS Trust 2003

H was employed as a nurse by the Trust and appealed against the dismissal of his claim for damages following his arrest on suspicion of theft and possession of Controlled Drugs. The police had been called to the hospital where H worked, following the discovery of a half tablet of Temazepam in his pocket. H explained that the ward sister had given him the tablet only minutes before and asked him to return it to the drugs cabinet. He was arrested and taken into custody, but later released without charge. H was nevertheless suspended from duty and never returned to work, taking early retirement on grounds of ill health.

The judge held that, in order to succeed in his claim for breach of the implied term of mutual trust and confidence in his contract of employment, H had to show that, but for the conduct of his employer's employees, he would not have been arrested. H contended that the judge had applied the wrong test.

(Holladay v. East Kent Hospitals NHS Trust [2003] EWCA Civ 1696; (2004) 76 BMLR 201)

The Court of Appeal allowed H's appeal. It held that the crucial question was not what might have happened if the Trust's employees had acted differently, but whether a breach of duty by the employer had been a material cause of H's arrest. There was no dispute about the breaches of duty for which the Trust was vicariously liable. The ward sister failed to back up H's explanation to the police, and the general manager failed to check H's explanation and failed to tell the police that the allegation had not been investigated. H had been arrested in the belief that he had committed offences of theft and possession of a controlled substance and, on the facts known to the police, that belief had been reasonable. The judge should have found that it was foreseeable that H would suffer psychiatric injury as a result of his arrest and consequently, it could be held that E's breach of duty had caused H's psychiatric injury.

The dismissal of H's claim would be set aside and the question of how much compensation he should receive should be heard by another judge unless the parties came to an agreement on the amount.

Significance of employer's policies and procedures relating to medicines

An NHS Trust or Primary Care Trust (PCT) would be entitled to draft policies and procedures relating to medicines and could reasonably expect an employee to follow these procedures. The registered practitioner would have an obligation to notify the employer if there appeared to be a conflict between these policies and their professional code of conduct.

For example, an NHS Trust might draw up a policy relating to patient group directions, but if this policy failed to follow the legal requirements on Patient Group Directions (PGD) (see Chapter 8) the registered practitioner would be entitled to draw this discrepancy to the notice of the employer and to regard the policy as defective. A request by the employer for the employee to obey the policy would be an unreasonable instruction.

The employer has an implied duty to take reasonable care of the employee and this includes the provision of safe equipment and premises, a safe system of work and competent staff. For example, where a nurse is expected to administer drugs which are carcinogenic, she is entitled to have the necessary equipment and protective clothing which would keep her reasonably safe. Failure by the employer to provide her with the facilities to enable her to be reasonably safe could be seen as a breach of contract by the employer. In the event of a fundamental breach of contract by the employer, the employee is entitled to see the contract as ended and see him or herself as constructively dismissed.

Where the employee is at fault in failing to obey reasonable instructions in relation to medications, then it is the employer which has the right of disciplining the employee and this could be anything from a counselling session, to an oral warning, to a first written warning or dismissal, depending on the circumstances. Where the employee is dismissed there may be a right (depending upon length of continuous service or other circumstances) for the employee to apply to an employment tribunal and claim that the dismissal is unfair. In the situation in Box 21.5 (which is taken from the last chapter on civil accountability) for example even though there would be no liability in the civil courts, the employer could still take action against Rose. It is hoped that any disciplinary proceedings would take account of the facts that Rose had immediately admitted her mistake and took action to ensure that the patient was not harmed.

Box 21.5 The wrong eye

Rose, a staff nurse on the ophthalmic ward, was doing the medicine round, and in her rush to be finished put eye drops in the left eye of a patient instead of the right eye. She immediately realised her mistake and called the pharmacist urgently to the ward. The patient was reassured that there would be no long-term effects from Rose's error. It was clear however that the patient intended to make a complaint and possibly sue the NHS Trust.

If Rose were to be dismissed as a result of her mistake, she could apply to an internal appeal hearing. If the result of this hearing was that her dismissal was upheld, she could then apply to an employment tribunal. The time limit for making such an application is three months from the date of dismissal. Provisions governing a statutory dispute resolution were set out in Schedule 2 to the Employment Act 2002 establishing two forms: a standard three-step procedure and a modified two-step procedure. However these were repealed and replaced by the Code of Practice for Discipline and Grievance Procedures 2008, from the Advisory, Conciliation and Arbitration Service (ACAS) which employers should follow. ACAS has a major role to play in attempting to conciliate between the parties, so that a hearing of the case is unnecessary. Failure by any employer to follow the ACAS guidelines will not make the employer liable to proceedings, but this information could be used against the employer in evidence before an employment tribunal. Statutory rights which became effective on 4 September 2000, state the employee has a right to be accompanied at a disciplinary and grievance hearing (ss10–15 Employment Relations Act 1999 Commencement No 7 Order 2000).

Failure by the employer to allow the worker to be accompanied or to rearrange a hearing (for up to five days) may lead to compensation payable by the employer of up to two weeks' pay.

In defending the application for unfair dismissal, the employer must show the reason for the dismissal and the fact that the reason is recognised in law as capable of being a reason for dismissal. The employer must also provide evidence that he acted reasonably in treating this statutory reason as justifying the dismissal.

Whistle blowing

This is the term which refers to a person (usually an employee) who draws attention to concerns which have health and safety implications.

Under the Public Interest Disclosure Act which came into force on 2 July 1999 and amends the Employment Rights Act 1996, workers are protected if they disclose information of a specified nature from being dismissed or penalised by their employers as a result. Guidance has been issued by the Department of Health (DH Public Interest Disclosure Act HSC(99)198) which requires every NHS Trust and Health Authority to have in place local policies and procedures which comply with the provisions of the Act. If a registered practitioner became aware that a colleague was misusing medicines, or failing to prescribe or administer them correctly, that registered practitioner would have a professional duty to report these concerns to the manager. If the manager failed to act appropriately then this may result in a whistle-blowing situation. If the registered practitioner follows the whistle-blowing procedure closely, he or she should be protected against any victimisation. A duty of candour is recommended as part of the new NHS Redress Scheme (DH 2003) and was also recommended by the Bristol Inquiry (Kennedy 2001) in the hope that there would be a climate of honesty and respect in the NHS. However this duty was not incorporated into the NHS Redress Act which is still to be implemented. (See Chapter 20).

Employers and medicinal products

The final Crown Report (DH 1999) (discussed in Chapter 10) recommended that employers and managers in all sectors who are responsible for staff who supervise or undertake the administration of any medicines should ensure that those staff have the right training and skills to do so safely and regular opportunities for updating their knowledge.

Every NHS trust employer should therefore have in place clear policies relating to patient group directions, independent nurse prescribing and supplementary prescribing. These policies should make provision for the training of staff and supervised practice.

Reasonable instruction

The DH guidance on the implementation of *Extending Independent Nurse Prescribing in the NHS* (DH 2002) suggests (Paragraph 17) that:

No nurse shall be required to undertake training unless he/she wishes to do so.

This was the policy under the now defunct concept of the extended role of the nurse: i.e. a nurse could refuse to accept training for an extended role. However, it is doubtful if this accords with the right of an employer to ask an employee to undertake reasonable instructions. It may, for example, be agreed at an interview that an essential requirement of a particular post is that the employee should be able to undertake independent nurse prescribing (for example an Accident and Emergency (A&E) Clinical Nurse Specialist) and that any person appointed to the post would be expected to undergo the necessary training. Similar requests may be reasonably made of existing staff in the A&E department.

The DH also in its implementation guide of extending independent nurse prescribing sees as one of the criteria for eligibility for a practitioner to be trained:

The support of their employer to confirm that:

- *Their post is one in which they will have the need and opportunity to prescribe from the Nurse Prescribers' Extended Formulary (NPEF) (No longer contained in the British National Formulary (see Chapter 4).*
- *For nurses in primary care, they will have access to a prescribing budget on completion of the course.*
- *They will have access to continuing professional development (CPD) opportunities on completion of the course.*

Responsibility of employer in relation to nurse prescribing

The DH guidance on the implementation of *Extending Independent Nurse Prescribing in the NHS* also suggests that to enable pharmacists to check whether a nurse prescription handed in for dispensing is *bona fide*, all NHS employers should keep a list of all nurse prescribers employed by them and the items that the nurse can prescribe (DH 2002). It is also recommended that a copy of the nurse's or midwife's signature is held by the employing authority and individuals should be prepared to provide specimen signatures to pharmacists should that be required.

Indemnity insurance

The DH in its implementation guidance on independent nurse prescribing suggests that:

> All nurse and midwife prescribers should ensure that they have professional indemnity insurance, for instance by means of membership of a professional organisation or trade union.

This requirement is surprising in view of the fact that the employer is vicariously liable for the negligence of an employee, but there is no stipulation that the DH suggestion only applies to self-employed practitioners. The NMC, following its consultation paper on indemnity cover, has added a new clause to the Code of Professional Conduct on indemnity cover. This clause was revised in the 2008 version of the NMC code and is as follows:

Information about indemnity insurance

> The NMC recommends that a registered nurse, midwife or specialist community public health nurse, in advising, treating and caring for patients/clients, has professional indemnity insurance. This is in the interests of clients, patients and registrants in the event of claims of professional negligence.

> Whilst employers have vicarious liability for the negligent acts and/or omissions of their employees, such cover does not normally extend to activities undertaken outside the registrant's employment. Independent practice would not be covered by vicarious liability. It is the individual registrant's responsibility to establish their insurance status and take appropriate action.

> In situations where an employer does not have vicarious liability, the NMC recommends that registrants obtain adequate professional indemnity insurance.

If unable to secure professional indemnity insurance, a registrant will need to demonstrate that all their clients/patients are fully informed of this fact and the implications this might have in the event of a claim for professional negligence.

Whether or not the employer is vicariously liable for the actions of an employee is a matter of law and it was pointed out in Chapter 20 that a decision of the House of Lords had widened the scope of the meaning of 'in the course of employment'. In the case of Lister and Others v. Hesley Hall Ltd Times Law Reports May 10 2001; [2001] 2 WLR 1311 HL, the House of Lords held that a school was liable to the pupils for the suffering caused to them by sexual acts of the warden. The House of Lords stated that the approach which was best when determining whether a wrongful act was to be deemed to be done by the employee in the course of his employment, was to concentrate on the relative closeness of the connection between the nature of the employment and the particular wrongdoing. The defendant undertook to care for the claimants through the services of a warden, so there was a very close connection between the torts (civil wrongs) of the warden and the defendant. The torts were also committed at a time and place when the warden was busy caring for the claimants. The warden was carrying out his duties, though, in an unauthorised and improper mode.

Application of law to the situation in Box 21.1

As part of the implied terms of the contract of employment, an employer is entitled to give reasonable instructions to the employee and it is the implied duty of the employer to obey these reasonable instructions.

The question that arises therefore in this scenario is whether the instructions to Mohammad are reasonable. No information is given as to whether this topic was discussed at an interview and whether any promises were made to Mohammad about prescribing. If there were none, then it may be that the Trust is entitled to refuse to allow Mohammad to prescribe, and clearly if Mohammad does not wish to lose these skills he may wish to seek work with another employer. In the absence of any broken promises to him, there would be no evidence of constructive dismissal.

Conclusions

The employer has an important role in ensuring that legislative requirements and guidelines from the DH and other authorities on medicinal products are obeyed and implemented. The employer can only work through its employees and therefore has the right to discipline those staff who fail to obey reasonable instructions and fail to work with care and skill. The employer has concomitant responsibilities to make sure that the employee is trained and competent and given support in performing legal and professional responsibilities and that reasonable precautions are taken for the health and safety of the employee.

Key points

■ There is an implied duty in the contract of employment that employees must act with reasonable care and skill and obey the reasonable instructions of their employer.

■ The employer has an implied duty in the contract of employment to take reasonable care of the health and safety of the employee. This would include providing the employee with the appropriate equipment and clothing for the administration of carcinogenic medicines.

■ The employer should ensure that policies and procedures are drawn up in accordance with DH guidelines in respect of administering and prescribing of medication

■ The employer should also ensure that the appropriate training is given to those members of staff who are to take on extended prescribing roles.

References

Department of Health (1999) R*eview of Prescribing, Supply and Administration of Medicines Final Report (Crown Report)*. London.

Department of Health (2002) *Extending independent nurse prescribing within the NHS in England: A guide for implementation*. London.

Department of Health (2003) *Making Amends: A consultation paper setting out proposals for reforming the approach to clinical negligence in the NHS*. CMO, June. London.

Kennedy (2001) *Learning from Bristol: the report of the public inquiry into children's heart surgery at the Bristol Royal Infirmary 1984–1995*. Command paper CM 5207, Stationery Office, London.

Nursing and Midwifery Council (2008) *The Code: standards of conduct, performance and ethics for nurses and midwives*. London.

CHAPTER 22

Accountability and medicines 4: Professional

Box 22.1 Top up epidural

A woman was prescribed a top up epidural following a hysterectomy. The junior doctor had difficulty reading the prescription and discussed the dose with the staff nurse, Mary Brown. They mistook a dose of 3 ml of diamorphine for 30 ml. The woman collapsed following its administration and died a few days later. The staff nurse, Mary Brown, was subsequently reported to the Nursing and Midwifery Council (NMC).

Introduction

Where a registered practitioner fails to follow the code of professional conduct, then, whether or not a patient has been harmed, she could find that she is reported to the NMC, the General Medical Council (GMC) or the Health Professional Council (HPC) (or other registration body) and is then subject to their investigatory processes.

In August 2004, the NMC (Fitness to Practise) Rules Order of Council 2004 Satutory Instrument (SI) I No 1761, and NMC circular 16/2004 was introduced under the provisions of the Nursing and Midwifery Order (2001 SI 2002 No. 253). The HPC has also had similar new proceedings for conduct and competence. This chapter seeks to explore the disciplinary machinery of the NMC in the light of an incident about the administration or prescribing of medication by a registered practitioner.

Allegations

Once information has been received in the form required by Council about allegations of Mary Brown's unfitness to practise, she would be informed of the allegation and invited to make written representations. An allegation could be related to the fact that:

[Her] fitness to practice is impaired by reason of:

i. misconduct

ii. lack of competence

iii. a conviction or caution in the UK for a criminal offence; or a conviction elsewhere for an offence, which if committed in England and Wales, would constitute a criminal offence

iv. [her] physical or mental health, or

v. a determination by a body in the UK responsible under any enactment for the regulation of a health or social care profession to the effect that [her] fitness to practise is impaired, or a determination by a licensing body elsewhere to the same effect.

The Investigating Committee

The Investigating Committee is one of three Practice Committees appointed by the NMC (the others are the Health Committee and the Conduct and Competence Committee (CCC); see below). Following the referral about Mary Brown it is required to:

- Notify without delay the person against whom the allegation is made (i.e. Mary Brown) and invite her to submit written representations within a prescribed period.
- Where it sees fit, notify the person making the allegations of these representations and invite him to deal within a specified period with any points raised by the Committee in respect of those representations.
- Take such other steps as are reasonably practicable to obtain as much information as possible about the case.
- Consider in the light of the information which it has been able to obtain and any representations or other observations, whether in its opinion there is a case to answer or an entry has been fraudulently procured or incorrectly made.

The NMC has the power to draw up rules to make provision for the procedure to be followed by the Investigating Committee. The Council has the power to require disclosure of documents by any person who is believed to be able to supply information or produce any document which appears relevant to the discharge of any functions of the Practice Committee. No person can be required to disclose information which is prohibited by or under any other enactment.

The Investigating Committee would hear the allegations and consider whether any interim suspension or interim conditions of practice are justified. This latter is a new power, which would enable the general public to be protected, but allow the registered practitioner to remain on the register.

Mary Brown would have the opportunity to respond to representations against her. In the light of her response and all the information before it, the Investigating Committee can decide if Mary Brown has a case to answer in relation to the allegation of unfitness to practise. If they decide that there is no case to answer, then the case is closed. Mary will remain on the register and there is no further action taken. On the other hand, where the Investigating Committee reaches a decision that there is a case to answer, it shall notify in writing both the registered professional concerned and the person making the allegation of the decision, giving its reasons. The case could then be referred to the CCC. (If the allegation related to ill health, then the referral would be to the Health Committee.) Alternatively, screeners could be asked to mediate or investigate the allegations.

Screeners

The NMC may provide for the appointment of screeners to whom allegations may be referred.A screener may be a member of Council, and of any of its committees except a Practice Committee. Employees of Council are prohibited from being screeners. There must be a panel of at least two screeners considering an allegation; one of the panel must be a lay person and one must be a registrant from the same field as the person concerned. The number of registrants on the panel cannot exceed the number of lay persons. The functions of the screeners include the following:

a) Considering the allegation and establishing whether, in their opinion, power is given by the Order to deal with it if it proves to be well founded.

b) If the power is given, of referring the matter together with a report of the results of their consideration to such Practice Committee as they see fit.

c) If the power is not given, of closing the case – where there are two screeners, the lay person agrees (i.e with closing the case), or – where there are more than two screeners, it is the decision of the majority. If either of these conditions is not satisfied, the screeners may refer the matter to the Practice Committee.

d) Where requested to do so by a Practice Committee, to mediate in any case with the aim of dealing with the allegation without it being necessary for the Health Committee or the CCC (as the case may be) to reach the stage at which it would arrange a hearing.

e) In the event that mediation fails, the matter is referred back to the Practice Committee which referred it to the screeners.

No person may act as a screener or sit on a Practice Committee in respect of a particular case if he or she has been involved in that case in any other capacity.

Legal assessors

The Council is required to appoint legal assessors to advise the screeners, the Practice Committees or the Registrar on questions of law, and to perform other functions which the Council confers on them by its rules. There are stipulations relating to who is eligible to be a legal assessor.

Medical assessors

Medical assessors are to be appointed by the Council to give advice to the same persons as the legal assessors, and there are similar provisions relating to eligibility or non-eligibility.

Conduct and Competence Committee

The CCC has the responsibility of hearing any allegation referred to it by the Council, screeners, Investigating Committee or Health Committee, and also any application for restoration to the Registrar referred to it by the Registrar. If the Investigating Committee refers Mary Brown's case to the CCC, it will have a hearing following which it can decide that the allegation is not well founded, in which case the case is closed.

Alternatively, if it decides that the allegation of unfitness to practise is well founded it could do the following:

- Refer the matter to screeners for mediation or itself undertake mediation.
- Decide that it is not appropriate to take further action.
- Issue a striking off order.
- Issue a suspension order (lasting up to one year).
- Issue a conditions of practice order (lasting up to three years).
- Issue a caution order (lasting up to five years).

In making its decision, the principal concern of the CCC is the protection of the public from persons who are unfit to practise.

An interim suspension order can be made if the Committee is satisfied that it is necessary for the protection of members of the public or is otherwise in the public interest, or is in the interests of the registered professional concerned, for the registration of that person to be suspended or to be made subject to conditions.

In addition to hearing cases of alleged unfitness to practise, the CCC also has the responsibility of advising the Council (having consulted the other Practice Committees as it thinks appropriate) on:

- The performance of the Council's functions in relation to standards of conduct, performance and ethics expected of registrants and prospective registrants.
- Requirements as to good character and good health to be met by registrants and prospective registrants.

Where a registrant is convicted in the criminal courts (see Chapter 19) this information will be passed on to the appropriate registrant organisation. For example the case of Bernadette Gerard, a registered nurse, who had been convicted of manslaughter and sentenced to six months prison suspended for 12 months following the death of a resident in a care home as a result of an epileptic fit, came before the CCC of the NMC on 17 May 2010. (Details can be seen on the NMC website www.nmc-uk.org). The CCC accepted the findings of the judge that the absence of the necessary medication to deal with the patient's epileptic fit (a diazepam pessary) was not the responsibility of the registrant; that she had not been trained to deal with an epileptic fit and the resident had been inappropriately placed in the care home. The NMC took into account many mitigating circumstances and placed her under a caution order for five years.

Health Committee

If the Investigating Committee or the screeners consider that the unfitness to practise relates to the ill health of the registered practitioner, then a referral would be made to the Health Committee. The functions of the Health Committee are to consider:

- Any allegations referred to it by the Council, screeners, Investigating Committee or CCC, and
- Any application for restoration referred to it by the Registrar.
  It has similar powers to the CCC.
  The Health Committee would seek advice from medical assessors appointed by the Council (see above).

Publication of decisions

The Council is required to publish without delay particulars of any orders and decisions made by a Practice Committee and of its reasons for them. The Council may also disclose to any person any information relating to a person's fitness to practise which it considers it to be in the public interest to disclose. The information is available on the NMC website (www.nmc-uk.org).

Appeals

If the person concerned appeals, or where new evidence becomes available, then there are powers, depending upon the order and the Committee concerned, to confirm the order, extend the period for which the order has effect (subject to the maximums indicated above), reduce the period, revoke the order, vary any condition, or replace the order with another.

Council for the Regulation of Healthcare Professionals (Subsequently known as the Council for Healthcare Regulatory Excellence)

Section 25 of the National Health Service Reform and Health Care Professions Act 2002 provided for the establishment of a body corporate known as the Council for the Regulation of Health Care Professionals (CRHP). Set up in the wake of the Kennedy Report into children's heart surgery at Bristol Royal Infirmary, its remit covers nine regulatory bodies, including the NMC (Kennedy 2003). It is an independent body which reports annually to Parliament. Its functions are set out under section 25(2) of the Act and shown below:

- To promote the interests of patients and other members of the public in relation to the performance of their functions by the GMC, GDC, NMC, HPC and other health professional registration bodies and by their committees and officers.
- To promote best practice in the performance of those functions
- To formulate principles relating to good professional self-regulation, and to encourage regulatory bodies to conform to them and
- To promote cooperation between regulatory bodies; and between them, or any of them, and other bodies performing corresponding functions.

Under Section 29 of the NHS Reform and Health Care Professions Act 2002, if the Council considers that a decision by one of the healthcare professions' regulatory bodies under its jurisdiction (the NMC, GMC etc.) is unduly lenient, and it would be desirable for the protection of members of the public for the Council to take action, it can refer the case to the relevant court (the High Court in England and Wales). The court then has the power to dismiss the appeal, allow the appeal and quash the relevant decision, substitute for the relevant decision any other decision which could have been made by the committee or person concerned, or remit the case to the committee or other person concerned to dispose of the case in accordance with the directions of the court. The referral must be within four weeks, beginning with the last date on which the practitioner concerned has the right to appeal against the decision.

The High Court held on 29 March 2004 that the CRHP had the right to refer cases to court even after an acquittal by the appropriate regulatory body. The GMC had challenged the CRHP's right to refer the case of Dr Ruscillo to the court. This judgment applies to all those health registration bodies under the CRHP, including the NMC (CRPH v General Medical Council and Another [2004 EWHC 527 (Admin).

In another case the High Court held that where a decision of the GMC was referred by the CRPH to the High Court, the question for the court was whether the GMC had been unduly lenient and not whether the decision was wrong (CRPH v General Medical Council and Another *The Times* Law Report 1 September 2004).

In July 2004 the CRHP changed its name to the Council for Healthcare Regulatory Excellence (CHRE) and announced that the Council's corporate identity would be officially launched with publication of its first annual report to Parliament in the Autumn of 2004. The change of name was formally recognised in the Health and Social Care Act 2008 which amended the constitution of the CHRE to make it a smaller more effective body. In the review of Arms' length bodies, (DH 2010) it is proposed that the CHRE should become a self-funding body based on fees from those organisations it regulates and its remit will be extended to other registers maintained by health and social organisations.

Procedure in relation to the circumstances of Box 22.1

Once Mary Brown had been reported to the NMC, a decision would be made over whether the facts should be sent to the Investigating Committee or whether screeners should be appointed. The Investigating Committee has the power to make an interim order at the same time or at any time before referring a case to the Health Committee or CCC. If there is evidence that Mary Brown is unfit to practise because of ill health, the Investigating Committee may refer the case to medical screeners or to the Health Committee. The hearing would take into account the extent to which Mary Brown was responsible in comparison with the responsibilities of the junior doctor.

Reports of fitness to practice proceedings can be found on the NMC website (www.nmc-uk.org). In its series on professional misconduct cases, the *British Journal of Nursing* reported on a case where a matron of a private nursing home was removed from the register for drug administration errors (Castledine 2005).

Standard of proof

In arriving at their decisions, the Practice Committees originally had to be satisfied beyond reasonable doubt of the facts of misconduct, unfitness to practise etc. The NMC consulted upon whether this standard should be changed to the civil standard of proof, i.e. a balance of probabilities. The outcome was that there should be no change in the standard adopted. However subsequently the Health and Social Care Act 2008 section 112 amended the Health Act 1999 by inserting section 60A which states that the standard of proof applicable to any proceedings to which this subsection applies is that applicable to civil proceedings. The proceedings of the NMC are covered by this change.

General Medical Council

The GMC has similar conduct and competence proceedings to those of the other Registration bodies. Box 22.2 sets out the facts of a case where a doctor appealed against the decision of the Professional Conduct Committee of the GMC that he was guilty of serious professional misconduct in prescribing addictive painkilling drugs.

Box 22.2 Seyedi v. General Medical Council [2003]

Dr Seyedi appealed against the decision of the GMC Professional Conduct Committee that he was guilty of serious professional misconduct. He had prescribed addictive painkilling drugs to a patient who subsequently died as a result of an overdose of those drugs. He argued that there was no evidence to prove that he had prescribed inappropriate medication and the findings that his actions were inappropriate, irresponsible and not in the best interests of the patient were therefore unfounded; that the finding of serious professional misconduct was not justified and the condition that he should not prescribe Controlled Drugs (CD) for a period of 12 months was disproportionate and oppressive given that the conduct related to one patient who was a liar. Dr Seyedi lost his appeal to the Privy Council, which held that there was evidence that the drugs prescribed were highly addictive and had been excessively prescribed. There was no explanation as to why he had prescribed the drugs in such quantities. He had breached all three basic rules relating to the prescribing of addictive drugs:

1. Had failed to carefully consider whether to prescribe the drugs.
2. Had failed to monitor the development of dependency, and
3. Had failed to avoid becoming the unwitting supplier of addictive drugs.

He had also failed to keep adequate records of consultations with the patient and on the basis of his admissions and the expert evidence, a finding of serious professional misconduct was inevitable. The Privy Council also held that the condition that he could not prescribe CD for 12 months was sensible and by no means oppressive.

(Seyedi v. General Medical Council [2003] UKPC 67; (2004) BMLR 173)

Council for the Regulation of Healthcare Professionals

If the CCC decided that Mary Brown could stay on the register, then the person who made the allegations of misconduct and unfitness to practise could apply to the Council for the Regulation of Healthcare Professionals for a review of the case (see above).

Conclusions

New procedures for the NMC and its Practice Committees came into force on 1 August 2004 designed to protect the public from registrants who are unfit to practice. The CHRE has developed its role of ensuring that the Registration Bodies are not unduly lenient in dealing with cases of professional misconduct. At the time of writing the Health and Social Care Bill is being considered in Parliament with radical provisions for a re-organisation of the structure of the NHS which if enacted will have significant consequences for health professionals whether they work within the NHS or outside. The Bill would also substitute the name of the Professional Standards Authority for Health and Social Care for that of the Council for Healthcare Regulatory Excellence, extend its remit to include social workers and make it a self-funding body from receipts from the registration bodies it oversees.

Key points

- Following negligence in relation to the administration or prescribing of medicines, allegations about the fitness to practise of a registered practitioner can be made to the NMC.
- These allegations could be considered by screeners, an Investigating Committee, or a Conduct and Competence or Health Committee.
- The sanctions available to the Practice Committees are greater under the NMC.
- The remit of the CHRE has been extended and strengthened and it is likely to become a self-funding body.

References

Castledine, G. (2005) Matron who continued to make numerous drug administration errors. *British Journal of Nursing*, 14(5) 264. London

Department of Health (2010) *Liberating the NHS: Report of the Arm's Length Bodies*. Crown London.

Kennedy (2001) *Learning from Bristol: the report of the public inquiry into children's heart surgery at the Bristol Royal Infirmary 1984–1995*. Command paper CM 5207, Stationery Office, London.

Websites

NMC website www.nmc-uk.org

CHAPTER 23

Storage, destruction of drugs and management of pharmaceutical services

---

Box 23.1 Situation: checking stocks

Mavis, a staff nurse, queries the fact that the Controlled Drugs (CD) stock is not checked at the end of each shift as it was in her last job. What is the law?

Storage of medicinal products

Ward stocks

Recommendations were given in the Aitken Report (DHSS 1958) and in the Roxburgh Report (Scottish Home and Health Department 1972) on ward stocks that the pharmacist should agree with the ward or department a list of medicines which it could hold as a standard stock list in addition to a specialist list of medicines appropriate to the ward specialty. The original system was for ward stocks to be ordered by the person in charge of the ward or department from the pharmacy on a printed requisition form. A more recent system adopted in some hospitals is for the pharmacist to take responsibility for requisitioning ward stocks and to make sure that stocks are kept up to the standard agreed list.

The Aitken Report and the Roxburgh Report recommended that storage cupboards should be lockable and the keys should be kept by the sister in charge of the ward. The reports also cover the siting of the cupboards and refrigerated storage.

The Gillie Report (DH 1970) recommended, in addition to cupboards, the use of ward trolleys, subject to suitable safety precautions when they were not in use.

Controlled drugs

The Aitken Report recommended that the person in charge of a ward or department should keep a register of CD, and this is supported by guidance from the Department of Health (DH) and Nursing and Midwifery Council (NMC).

Safe custody of controlled drugs in NHS hospitals

The Regulations on safe custody of CD (SI 1973 No 798 as amended) do not apply to NHS hospitals apart from the requirement that they must be kept in a locked receptacle to which the person entitled to be lawfully in possession (usually the ward sister) has the key. Other rules relating to the nature of the container may be laid down in Trust policies or other official guidance.

Safe custody of controlled drugs outside NHS hospitals

The Regulations on safe custody apply to all CD except drugs listed in Schedules 4 and 5; liquid preparations, apart from injections which contain specified products; and other specified products such as cathine. The safe custody rules apply to the following premises:

- Any premises occupied by a retail dealer for the purposes of his or her business.
- Any nursing home under the Public Health Act 1936 or Scottish equivalent.
- Any residential or other establishment under Scottish legislation.
- Any mental nursing home under the Mental Health Act 1983.
- Any private hospital within the meaning of the Mental Health (Scotland) Act 1960.

Under these regulations, the occupier and every person concerned with the management of any of these premises must ensure that all CD (except those mentioned above) are, so far as circumstances permit, kept in a locked safe, cabinet or room which is so constructed and maintained as to prevent unauthorised access to the drugs.

In addition, any person having possession of any CD to which the safe custody regulations apply must ensure that, as far as circumstances permit, it is kept in a locked receptacle which can be opened only by him or her or by a person authorised by him or her.

This latter regulation does not apply to a carrier in the course of his business or the Post Office or to a person to whom the drug has been supplied on the prescription of a practitioner for his or her own treatment or that of another person or animal.

Destruction of controlled drugs

Any person who has in their possession a Schedule 2, 3, 4 or 5 drug which has been supplied by or on prescription of a practitioner for the treatment of that person, may supply that drug to any doctor, dentist or pharmacist for the purpose of destruction (regulation 6(2) Misuse of Drug Regulations SI 2001 No 3998).

Destruction of ward stocks of CD can be carried out in the ward by the sister in charge or charge nurse. It is advisable that such destruction is witnessed, preferably by a pharmacist. Under regulation 27 of the 2001 Misuse of Drug Regulations:

No person who is required by any provision of, or by any term or condition of a licence to keep records with respect to a drug specified in Schedule 1, 2, 3, or 4 shall destroy such a drug or cause such a drug to be destroyed except in the presence of and in accordance with any directions given by a person authorised (whether personally or as a member of a class) for the purposes of this paragraph by the Secretary of State.

An authorised person may, for the purposes of analysis, take a sample of a drug specified in Schedule 1, 2, 3, or 4 which is to be destroyed.

Where a Schedule 1, 2, 3, or 4 drug is destroyed, the records must include particulars of the date of destruction and the quantity destroyed and shall be signed by the authorised person in whose presence the drug is destroyed.

These provisions do not apply to the destruction of a drug which has been supplied to a practitioner or pharmacist for destruction under Regulation 6(2) and (3).

Policies, procedures and guidance from employers

Frequently NHS trusts and other employers prepare policies and practices for the safe handling, administration and storage of drugs which go beyond the specific statutory requirements for the legislation.

It is the duty of the employee to obey all reasonable instructions of the employer (see Chapter 21), so unless these policies and procedures are in conflict with legal provisions or any policies issued by the health registration body, they should be obeyed by the health practitioner. Often they provide added safety for patients and staff. The result, however, is that there are varying practices across the NHS.

Application of the law to the situation in Box 23.1

It is not a legal requirement that the CD stocks are checked at the end of a shift, but there are very sound reasons why this could be seen as good practice. It is reasonable for employees to carry out this policy and where policies are not so strict, individual practitioners could recommend revised policies to the employer. As a consequence of the Shipman Fourth Report (DH 2004), there have been major changes to our laws relating to CD. Amongst the many recommendations was the following:

Inspection arrangements:

a controlled drugs inspectorate should be created, comprising small multi-disciplinary inspection teams, operating regionally but co-ordinated nationally. The inspection team would inspect the arrangements in pharmacies, dispensaries and surgeries as to both safe keeping of stocks of controlled drugs, and the maintenance of controlled drugs registers (CDR) and other records. The team would also monitor the prescribing of controlled drugs by examining the data of the prescribing analysis and cost. Other responsibilities for the team such as the issue of special controlled drugs prescription pads and the assumption of some of the inspection functions of the Home Office drugs inspectors could also be considered.

The Controlled Drugs (Supervision of Management and Use) Regulations 2006

The Controlled Drugs (Supervision of Management and Use) Regulations (SI

2006/3148) which came into force in January 2007 in England and in March 2007 for Scotland implemented some of the recommendations of the Shipman Inquiry (DH 2004). Under these regulations, health service organisations such as primary care trusts, NHS trusts and Foundation trusts are required to appoint an accountable officer who has specified functions in relation to the management and use of controlled drugs. Under Regulation 8 the accountable officer is required to have regard to best practice in relation to the management and use of controlled drugs and under Regulation 9 to secure the safe management and use of controlled drugs. He must ensure that there is in place adequate and up-to-date standard operating procedures. These procedures must cover the following matters:
a)   who has access to the CD;
b)   where the CD are stored;
c)   security in relation to the storage and transportation of CD as required by misuse of drugs legislation;
d)   disposal and destruction of CD;
e)   who is to be alerted if complications arise; and
f)   record keeping, including
     (i) maintaining relevant CD registers under misuse of drugs legislation, and
     (ii) maintaining a record of the CD specified in Schedule 2 to the Misuse of Drugs Regulations 2001 that have been returned by patients.

The accountable officer is also responsible for ensuring that there are adequate destruction and disposal arrangements for CD. There must be arrangements in place for monitoring and the audit of the management and use of the CD. The accountable officer who works for a PCT can require general practitioners to provide information about CD. He is required to investigate any concerns and keep records relating to these concerns and take appropriate action if these concerns are well-founded. Information is to be shared between accountable officers.

Part 3 of the regulations covers powers relating to the entry and inspection of premises.

Part 4 covers co-operation between health bodies and other organisations. Where information has been disclosed under regulations 25, 26, 29 or 30 then provided the informant acted in good faith civil proceedings do not lie against a person in respect of loss, damage or injury of any kind suffered by another person (Regulation 31).

Medicines management in NHS trusts

The first wave of the Medicines Management Framework provided trusts with an opportunity to review their medicines management systems and put remedial action plans into place ahead of the Audit Commission's *Value for Money* audits in 2001/2. The weakest area shown up in the Audit Commission's survey was senior management involvement in and awareness of medicines management issues. Only 22% of Trusts had a strategy for medicines management that had been approved at board level. The DH published a *Vision for Pharmacy in the New NHS* (2003a) which referred to the launch of a second edition of the hospital medicines management framework. Trusts were required to carry out self assessments on their medicines management performance. The Medicines Management Framework has two key components:

1. Clinical and cost-effectiveness.
2. Safe and secure handling of medicines.

Standards are set in the Framework to cover:

*   Senior management involvement.
*   Information, finance and business planning.
*   Medicines policy.
*   Procurement of medicines.
*   Designing services around patients.
*   Influencing prescribers and training.
*   Managing risk.

The Audit Commission has considered the management of medicines in the NHS in two separate reports. The first, *A Spoonful of Sugar*, was published in 2001 and emphasised that medicines management was central to the quality of healthcare and underpinned many of the specific objectives set out in the NHS Plan (DH 2000) and in the *Pharmacy in the Future* report (DH 2002). They identified some of the main obstacles to progress as including:

*   The current low status of some hospital pharmacy services.
*   Staff recruitment and retention problems.
*   The need to introduce computer technology.

Its recommendations included:

*   Dissemination of the DH *Medicines Management Framework* (DH 2003b).
*   Local audits to ensure implementation within clinical governance.
*   The National Patient Safety Agency (NPSA) should give priority to medication errors and near misses in medication.

- A standard national system for coding medicines and barcodes should be introduced across the NHS.
- The NHS Purchasing Supply Agency should consider establishing a national contract for the supply of patients' medicines lockers.
- NHS trusts should introduce risk management arrangements for reporting near misses.
- Arrangements should be introduced for the use of patients' own medicines in hospitals.

The second report by the Audit Commission on *Acute Hospital Portfolio: Medicines Management* published in 2002 noted that many trusts were working towards implementing effective medicines management arrangements and pharmacy services were playing an important multi-faceted role in managing medicines effectively and in redesigning services around patients' needs. Expenditure on medicines was rising and continued to put pressure on budgets. Managing medicines expenditure across the whole health economy was the key to controlling costs. It noted that only a minority of trusts had implemented the recommendation in *A Spoonful of Sugar* for original pack dispensing to be introduced.

Nearly 40% of trusts break down medicines from larger packs for routine dispensing, a process that is both time-consuming and involves greater risk of errors, with increased risk for patients. The second report also noted that a failure to obtain agreement with primary care on how to make the best use of funding for medicines across the local health economies remained a key obstacle to change. Shortages of pharmacists was also causing problems and their importance in influencing and improving cost-effective prescribing could not be overemphasised. The Audit Commission recommended that:

- medicines management should be part of the annual process of monitoring performance;
- be an integral part of the ongoing performance management role of strategic health authorities; and
- be reflected in clinical governance reviews undertaken by CHI (now replaced by CQC).

Further details of the *Medicines Management Framework* are available from the DH (www.dh.gov.uk).

Further developments in the relationship of the NHS to the Pharmaceutical Industry are likely to take place as a result of a House of Commons Report (2004) on the influence of the pharmaceutical industry.

The role of pharmacists working in the community is considered in Chapter 29.

Key points

■ Regulations apply to the safe custody of CD.

■ Hospital policies cover the storage and security of drugs.

■ The destruction of CD must comply with the regulations.

■ An accountable officer must be appointed with specified functions in relation to the management and use of CD.

■ Medicines management in NHS Trusts is crucial to clinical cost effectiveness and secure and safe handling.

References

Audit Commission (2001) *A Spoonful of Sugar – Medicines Management in NHS Hospitals.*

Audit Commission (2001/2) *Value for Money audits in 2001/2*

Audit Commission (2002) *Acute Hospital Portfolio: Medicines Management.*

Department of Health (1970) Joint Sub-Committee of the Standing Medical, Nursing and Pharmaceutical Advisory Committees (Gillie Report) *Measures for Controlled Drugs on the Wards.* London.

Department of Health (2000) *The NHS Plan: A Plan for Investment, A Plan for Reform.* HMSO London.

Department of Health (2001) *Pharmacy in the Future.* The Stationery Office. London.

Department of Health (2003a) *Vision for Pharmacy in the New.* London.

Department of Health (2003b) *Medicines Management in NHS Trusts.* London.

Department of Health (2004) *Shipman Inquiry Fourth Report: The Regulation of Controlled Drugs in the Community*, 15 July 2004 Cm 6249 Stationery Office; http://www.the-shipman-inquiry.org.uk/reports.asp.

DHSS (1958) Joint Sub-Committee of the Standing Medical Nursing and Pharmaceutical Advisory Committees (Aitken Report 1958) *Control of Dangerous Drugs and Poisons in Hospitals.* London.

House of Commons (2005) 4th Report 2004–5 *Influence of the Pharmaceutical Industry* HC 42

Scottish Home and Health Department (the Roxburgh Report) 1972 and 1979(GEN)11 A Report on *Control of Medicines in Hospital Wards and Departments.*

CHAPTER 24

Homoeopathy and herbal medicines

Box 24.1 Situation

The parents in a particular case are firm believers in homoeopathic medicine and learn that there is a treatment for diabetes. They decide not to give their daughter insulin, but instead to use alternative therapies. The daughter dies. What is the law?

Introduction

There is no doubt about the growing popularity in recent years of complementary or alternative therapies. Increasingly, such treatments are available within the NHS, a process which was accelerated during the years of fundholding practices. The registered practitioner might be affected by these developments in two ways. On the one hand she may herself have developed an interest in a specific complementary therapy and received training in it and become a member of a society. Alternatively, she may find that she is caring for patients who are receiving complementary or alternative treatments and she must be aware of any contra-indications between the use of these treatments and those proposed through conventional medicine. In exploring the laws relating to both these aspects we shall consider homoeopathy and herbal medicines in separate sections of this chapter.

Homoeopathy

Definitions

'Homoeopathic medicinal products' means any medicinal product (which may contain a number of principles) prepared from products, substances or compositions called homoeopathic stocks in accordance with a homoeopathic manufacturing procedure described by the *European Pharmacopoeia* or, in the absence thereof, by any pharmacopoeia used officially in a member state (Council Directive 92/73/EEC). Homoeopathic medicines for human-use must be licensed, but a simplified system of certification is permitted under the regulations. Under this system a certificate of registration may be granted in respect of a homoeopathic medicinal substance for human use under the Medicines (Homoeopathic Medicinal Products for Human Use) Regulations 1994 SI 1994 No 105 as amended) if the following conditions are satisfied:

- They are administered orally or externally.
- No specific therapeutic indication appears on the label of the product or in any information relating thereto.
- There is a significant degree of dilution to guarantee the safety of the product; in particular, the product may not contain either more than one part per 10,000 of the mother tincture or more than 1/100th of the smallest dose used in allopathy with regard to active principles whose presence in an allopathic product would result in it requiring a doctor's prescription.

To register a homoeopathic medicinal product, the application must be in writing and contain the particulars required by the Council Directive 92/73/EEC.

The Nursing and Midwifery Council

The NMC has provided guidance for registered midwives on the administration of homoeopathic and herbal substances in the midwives' code of practice (NMC 2004). The guidance is shown in Box 24.2.

Box 24.2 Administration of homoeopathic and herbal substances

Rule 7 Guidance:

Homoeopathic and herbal medicines are subject to the licensing provisions of the Medicines Act 1968. A number of these, however, have product licences but have not been evaluated for their efficacy, safety or quality and you should look to the best available evidence to inform women.
A woman has the right to use homoeopathic and herbal medicines. However, if you believe that using the medicines might be counterproductive you should discuss this with the woman.

Standards of medicines management of the Nursing and Midwifery Council

The NMC in its *Standards for medicines management* (2008a) states in Standard 23 that:

Registrants must have successfully undertaken training and be competent to practise the administration of complementary and alternative therapies.

In the guidance on this standard the NMC states that:

Complementary and alternative therapies may interact with other types of medicinal products and laboratory tests. All complementary and alternative medicines should be recorded alongside other medicinal products and prescribed on inpatient prescription charts. You need to ensure that your employer has accepted vicarious liability for any complementary/alternative therapy you may undertake or that you have indemnity insurance to cover your practice.

Application of the law to the situation in Box 24.1

Parents have a duty enforceable in the criminal courts to take reasonable care of their children. If the parents have ignored professional advice that their daughter required insulin and as a consequence of their failure to ensure that she received it she died, then the parents could face criminal charges for manslaughter. In a case reported in 1993 a father was convicted of manslaughter and imprisoned and the mother given a suspended sentence for failing to give their diabetic daughter insulin The couple refused to allow their diabetic daughter to receive modern medicine because of their religious beliefs (*The Times*, 29 October 1993).

Herbal medicines

This section considers herbal remedies, looking at both aspects: the registered practitioner as a provider of herbal remedy treatment and the registered practitioner caring for patients who are taking herbal remedies.

Box 24.3 Situation

A cancer patient who was on medicines to thin her blood was also taking garlic tablets. She had not informed the doctor of this. She suffered an extremely severe haemorrhage and almost died. Her family are threatening to sue for compensation.

Definition

Under Section 132 of the Medicines Act 1968 a herbal remedy is:

a medicinal product consisting of a substance produced by subjecting a plant or plants to drying, crushing or any other process, or of a mixture whose sole ingredients are two or more substances so produced, or of a mixture whose sole ingredients are one or more substances so produced and water or some other inert substance.

Licensing

Herbal remedies are exempt under section 12 of the Medicines Act from the licensing provisions of the Act. No marketing authorisation/licence is required for the sale, supply, manufacture or assembly in the following situations:

1. Any herbal remedy which is manufactured or assembled on premises of which the person carrying on the business is the occupier and which he or she is able to close so as to exclude the public, and the person carrying on the business sells or supplies the remedy for administration to a particular person after being requested by or on behalf of that person and in that person's presence to use his or her own judgment as to the treatment required.

2. Any herbal remedy where the process to which the plant or plants are subjected in producing the remedy consists only of drying, crushing or comminuting, and the remedy is, or is to be, sold or supplied:

    a) under a designation which only specifies the plant or plants and the process and does not apply any other name to the remedy, and

    b) without any written recommendation (whether by means of a labelled container or package or a leaflet or in any other way) as to the use of the remedy.

Under the Herbal Remedies Order SI 1977 No 2130 there is no exemption from the restriction on retail sale or supply for herbal remedies:

- That are not on the General Sales List.
- That are not exempted from licensing as in 2 above.
- That are exempted from licensing as in 2 above but contain one or more of the substances listed in Part 1 or Part 2 of the Schedule to the order.

Further exemptions for herbal practitioners

A herbal remedy which satisfies the following conditions is also exempt from the controls on retail sale or supply:

1. The herbal remedy concerned does not contain:

   a) any substance included in part 1 of the Schedule to the Order SI 1977 No 2130, or

   b) any substance in Part III of the order, except for internal remedies, when sold or supplied in or from containers or packages labelled to show a dosage not exceeding that specified, or for external remedies, when sold or supplied with the strength of the substance not exceeding the percentage specified.

2. The person selling or supplying the herbal remedy (a herbal practitioner):

   a) has been requested by or on behalf of a particular person and in that person's presence to use his or her own judgment as to the treatment required; and

   b) has notified the enforcement authority (the Secretaries of State and the Royal Pharmaceutical Society (RPS)) in writing that he or she is selling or supplying or intends to sell or supply from the premises specified in the notice herbal remedies as in 1, 2 or 3 in the section above on exemptions from controls on retail sale.

Information to enforcement authorities

The enforcement authorities may require the herbal practitioner or the person selling or supplying herbal remedies to furnish a list of the substances contained in those herbal remedies. Failure to furnish the list within the time specified in the notice issued by the enforcement authorities may mean that the exemptions outlined above do not apply.

Schedule to Herbal Order

The Schedule to Herbal Order (SI 1977 No 2130) sets out in three parts the different degrees of control over the retail sale or supply of herbal remedies. The substances listed in Part I may only be sold by retail at registered pharmacies and by, or under, the supervision of a pharmacist. Under Part II the substances listed in Part III may only be sold by retail from registered pharmacies and by or under the supervision of a pharmacist, except when the conditions under Part III are met. Persons (i.e. herbal practitioners) who comply with the specified requirements (see above) can sell or supply by retail herbal remedies containing any of the substances listed in Part III subject to the maximum dosages and strengths indicated. This SI was amended by the Medicines (Traditional Herbal Medicinal Products for Human Use) Regulations 2005 No. 2750 which implemented the European Directive in relation to Traditional Herbal Medicinal Products (see below).

Banned herbal remedies

Legislation prohibits in unlicensed medicine Aristolochia species and a number of other herbal ingredients which can be confused with Aristolochia (The Medicines (Aristolochia and Mu Tong etc) (Prohibition) Order 2001 No 1368). These measures were introduced following reports of serious cases of renal toxicity and evidence of substitution of certain ingredients in traditional Chinese medicines (TCM).

Standards from the Nursing and Midwifery Council

The NMC has set standards for complementary and alternative therapies which would include herbal substances (see above).

European Directive on herbal medicines

In 2003 a proposed European Directive on herbal medicines was defended by the Minister of Health Lord Hunt. The proposed directive on traditional herbal medicines aimed to standardise regulations across Europe.

Lord Hunt stated that:

Whilst there are many responsible producers out there, we have also come across repeated examples in UK and elsewhere, of unsafe or poor quality unlicensed products which contain illegal ingredients, the wrong herb and which also come with poor labelling.

The new Directive set quality standards or safety standards, and require consumer information about safe use of the products and for companies to tell the consumer what the product is for.

The Traditional Herbal Medicines Products Directive

The Traditional Herbal Medicinal Products Directive (2004/24/EC) (THMPD) came into force on 30 April 2004. Under this regulation, all herbal medicinal products are required to obtain an authorisation to market within the EU. Those products marketed before this legislation came into force can continue to market their product until 30 April 2011, under the transitional measures defined in the THMPD. Once this time limit has expired, all herbal medicinal products must have prior authorisation before they can be marketed in the EU. For those herbal medicinal products that were not on the market before 30 April 2004, an authorisation must be obtained prior to marketing. The only herbal medicines that are exempted from the provisions of the THMPD are those unlicensed remedies that are made up for a patient following a consultation with a herbalist. Herbal medicines must be now manufactured under Good Manufacturing Practice (GMP) to ensure the quality of the finished product and also demonstrate safety. Under the THMPD, a company needs to demonstrate the safety and efficacy of the herbal medicine through traditional use within the EU for at least 30 years or 15 years within the EU and 30 years outside the EU. There is concern that some herbal remedies of 30 years ago, which are no longer in widespread use, could still be sold but that valid new herbs which cannot meet the 30 year rule may require to be withdrawn from sale. The rule could also mean that it may not be possible to license some traditional herbal medicines which were in common use more than 30 years ago, but have since fallen into disuse. There are key eligibility criteria for a herbal medicine to qualify under this legislation:

- Only herbal medicines that are administered orally, externally, or by inhalation are suitable. Any medication that requires intravenous administration will not be authorised.
- Only herbal medicines that are intended to be used without supervision by a medical doctor will be authorised by this scheme. The intended use of a herbal medicines will only be authorised on the basis of its traditional history and/or the recognised pharmacological properties of the herbal ingredient(s).
- Vitamins and minerals may be added to the herbal medicine provided that their use is ancillary to the herbal ingredient(s).

If the competent EU member judges that the herbal medicine fulfills the criteria for a marketing authorisation, then an authorisation under THMPD should be granted.

Herbal medicine products manufactured using isolated active ingredients from plants will not be regarded as herbal medicines and will not receive an authorisation under this scheme.

The THMPD does allow medicinal claims to be made on the label of the final product, although restrictions do apply on the final wording. The 30 April 2011 marks the end of a transitional period during which time the Medicines and Healthcare Products Regulatory Agency (MHRA) could deem a manufactured herbal product to be a medicine and therefore enable it to be distributed without having a medicine registration granted. If the product is not a medicine, it has to comply instead with legislation relating to food, cosmetics or medical devices.

The MHRA (see below) has provided guidance on the traditional herbal medicines registration scheme for retailers, wholesalers, importers and manufacturers which is available on its website. The Traditional Herbal Registration (THR) certification mark is a type of trade mark. It indicates that the herbal medicine has been registered with the MHRA under the THR scheme and meets the required standards relating to its quality, safety, evidence of traditional use and other criteria as set out under the THMPD.

The Health Professions Council (HPC) is establishing a statutory register for practitioners supplying unlicensed herbal medicines. Registration of practitioners will be underpinned by strengthened medicines legislation.

Medicines and Healthcare Products Regulatory Agency

An extensive report on the Safety of Herbal Medicinal Products in July 2002 was published by the Medicines Control Agency (MCA). It recommended that information relating to risks should be systematically collected and analysed. Its successor body, the MHRA, published in 2008 an overview on the *Public Health Risk with Herbal Medicines* which focused on the risks arising with unlicensed herbal medicines and in particular poor practice in the sourcing and supply to patients of such products. It gave examples where serious harm was caused by the use of herbal medicines. For example in Belgium women attending a slimming clinic were given the wrong herbal medicine a herbal medicine containing the wrong, toxic, herb Aristolochia species. Over 100 women developed kidney failure and many subsequently went on to develop cancer. The MHRA overview sets out the risks which could arise including:

- Delay in effective treatment for serious condition
- Interference with vital treatment
- Exploitation of vulnerable groups such as children and the seriously ill
- Overloading patient with multiple medications
- Unexpected rare but serious liver toxicity of plants

- Toxic plants used
- Side effects
- Interactions with other medicines
- Wrong, toxic, plant used
- Adulteration with pharmaceutical substances
- Addition of analogues of pharmaceutical substances.
- Addition of heavy metals/toxic elements as ingredients
- Contamination
- Confusion over standards
- Weak or missing information
- Failures in communications.

Inaccurate labelling has led to a warning about the safety of St John's Wort (Lister 2004). Inaccurate labelling could lead to inaccurate doses being taken. Research at the Royal Marsden Hospital found that in a sample of more than 300 patients more than half took some form of complementary medicine (NMC News, 21 January 2004). Dr Werneke said that some doctors do not have the knowledge or the time in routine appointments to advise patients of all the potential dangers and therefore need to advise them to be cautious.

Examples of some of the dangers include:

- Garlic and cod liver oil are anticoagulants and may exaggerate the effect of blood-thinning drugs taken by some cancer patients.
- St John's Wort can interfere with the action of hormones, antibiotics and chemotherapy.

Further information

Barnes, Anderson and Phillipson (2007) wrote a book on herbal medicines covering herbs commonly used in complementary and alternative medicines. It also includes an overview of the uses, efficacy and safety of herbal medicines, and data on legislation applicable to the use of herbal substances in medicines. Detailed structured monographs on 148 of the most commonly used herbs are included.

Consultation by Medicines Health Products Regulatory Agency

In 2010 the MHRA consulted on revoking the exemption from licensing requirements for unlicensed herbal remedies supplied under section 12(2) of the medicines act 1968. The Consultation ended on 17 Janury 2011. No further developments n MHRA website have been reported.

Department of Health Regulatory Working Group on Herbal Medicines

A working group set up by the DH to consider the possibility of regulating practitioners involved with herbal medicines put forward proposals that herbalists should register with a new governing body to be eligible to practice, and that some herbal treatments should only be available from licensed practitioners..As a consequence of the recommendations of this working group (and a working group on acupuncture), in March 2004 the DH put forward proposals for the establishment of a Complementaryand Alternative Medicine Council. This would have similar powers to the General Medical Council (GMC) or NMC, would assess qualifications in herbal medicine and acupuncture, and would require possession of a registration certificate to practise in these fields. Following the consultation, the DH announced considerable support for a new council and a draft order for the new council was to be published (DH 2005).

However in 2006 the DH established a herbal medicine regulatory working group to prepare the ground for the regulation of practitioners of acupuncture, herbal medicine, TGM and other traditional medicine systems practised in the UK. The Steering Group report (DH 2008) recommended that the groups should be registered under the Health Professions Council (HPC). It also recommended that section 12(1) of the Medicines Act 1968 (which exempts the sale or supply of herbal remedies from the provisions of the Medicines Act if certain conditions are satisfied) should be restricted to healthcare professionals who come under state regulation.

The document consists of the main report that makes specific recommendations for regulation. This is followed by a series of Annexes that explain the nature of herbal/traditional medicine, acupuncture and TCM and provide further detailed information that should be useful to members of the public and other health professionals as well as to the DH and the future statutory regulatory body. Other Annexes provide information on the development of a research and evidence base for these sectors, on existing training provision and accreditation arrangements as well as the criteria used by the Steering Group to assess the potential of professional practitioner associations to qualify for direct transfer to the chosen regulatory body.

Complementary and Natural Healthcare Council

In 2009 the Complementary and Natural Healthcare Council (CNHC) was established to register health related professions with four main functions:

- To establish and maintain a voluntary register of complementary healthcare practitioners in the UK who meet its standards of competence and practice.
- To make the Register of practitioners available to the general public and to educate them about the CNHC quality mark as a quality standard.
- To operate a robust process for handling complaints about registered practitioners.
- To work with professional bodies in the complementary healthcare field to further develop and improve standards of professional practice.

At the time of writing the CNHC registers practitioners of Alexander Technique teaching; aromatherapy, bowen therapy, massage therapy, nutritional therapy, reflexology, shiatsu, sports and remedial therapy, yoga therapy, craniosacral therapy, healing, hypnotherapy, microsystems, acupuncture, naturopathy and reiki. Further information is available on its website at www.cnhc.org.uk.

A strategy to develop research capacity in complementary and alternative medicine was put forward in 2002 (Pighills and Bailey 2002) and the DH invited Higher Education Institutions (HEIs) to register their interest in hosting research into this field.

Application of law to the situation in Box 24.3

Research has shown that many patients are taking complementary therapies alongside traditional medicines and often the doctor does not inquire of the patient whether this is so. Reasonable medical practice would probably require the doctor caring for the patient to ascertain from the patient whether she is taking other products and preparations and warn the patient of any contra-indications. If the doctor had asked the patient, who had then denied that she was taking any alternative medicines or supplements, then it would appear that the doctor had done enough to fulfil his duty of care to the patient. On the other hand, if the doctor failed to make the relevant enquiries and give the appropriate warnings of contra-indications, then the doctor might be found to be in breach of his duty of care. If the warnings would have prevented the patient's haemorrhaging then there may be liability. However, it may be difficult to establish that the failure to warn the patient resulted in this harm or that the garlic contributed to the haemorrhage. The patient might have suffered a haemorrhage anyway.

The Court of Justice of the European Communities held in July 2005 that EC Directive 2002/46/EC regulating the manufacture and trade in food supplements was valid (R (Alliance for Natural Health) and Another v. Secretary of State for Health, Cases C-154/04 and C-155/04).

In 2011 it was reported that Boots, the Retailer Chemists, was facing an inquiry into health claims it makes for alternative remedies that are not backed by scientific evidence, following complaints being made to the Advertising Standards Authority (Henderson 2011).

Conclusions

This is a developing field, and as a result of EC directives more restrictions and controls in this area have come into place. The further increase in the popularity which complementary and alternative medicines have enjoyed over recent years, and in particular their use within the NHS, will depend upon the extent to which randomly controlled trials prove the efficacy of such products over conventional medicines. It remains to be seen how effective the CNHC is in setting and achieving high standards of those who are registered with it.

Key points

■ The use of complementary and alternative medicines is growing in popularity.

■ Homoeopathic medicine is regulated and subject to guidance by the NMC.

■ Herbal medicines may be exempt from the Medicines Act if certain conditions are satisfied.

■ The EC has strengthened controls over the standards and marketing of herbal remedies.

■ The CNHC has been established to register complementary and alternative therapists.

References

Barnes, J., Anderson, L. A. and Phillipson, J. D. (2007) *Herbal Medicines,* 3rd edn. The Pharmaceutical Press, London.

Department of Health. (2002) *Developing Research Capacity in Complementary and Alternative Medicine: a strategy for Action.* by Pighills, A. and Bailey, C. London

Department of Health press release 2003/0023: *New Herbal Directive will protect consumers*, 20 January 2003. London

Department of Health (2005) *Backing for crackdown on bogus alternative medical practitioners*, 14 February 2005. London

Department of Health (2006) Steering Group on the *Statutory Regulation of Practitioners of Acupuncture, Herbal Medicine, Traditional Chinese Medicine and Other Traditional Medicine Systems Practised in the UK).* London

Henderson M (2011) Boots faces challenge on new ads for alternative medicine *The Times* 5 February 2011

Lister, S. (2004) Labelling errors create St John's Wort risk. *The Times*, 9 February.

Medicines Control Agency (2002) *Safety of Herbal Medicinal Produc*ts.

Medicines Health Products Regulatory Agents (2008) *An overview on the Public Health Risk with Herbal Medicines*

Nursing and Midwifery Council (2004) *Midwives' Rules and Standards.* London

Nursing and Midwifery Council (2008a) *Standards for medicine management.* London

Nursing and Midwifery Council (2008b) *Code of professional conduct: standards for conduct performance and ethics.* London

Nursing and Midwifery (2004) *NMC Council News*, 21 January 2004. London

Wright, O. Johnston, C. and Bennett, R. (2003) Clampdown on alternative medicines. *The Times*, 20 September.

Websites

Complementary and Natural Healthcare Council website www.cnhc.org.uk.

CHAPTER 25

Documentation and confidentiality

Box 25.1 Situation

Rose, a staff nurse on the medical ward, was under considerable pressure because of a staffing shortage and was rushing doing the evening medicines round before she went off duty. In her haste, she failed to record the medicines which she had administered to Maud. Subsequently, when Rose had gone off duty, Joy, the night nurse, asked Maud if she had had her sleeping tablets. Maud said that she had not and Joy checked with her prescription sheet and found that there was no evidence that she had had her medication and gave her a further dose. Maud went into a deep coma and the amount of medication which she had had was queried.

Introduction

This chapter considers two related topics: documentation relating to medicinal products and confidentiality.

Documentation

All nurses are required to keep contemporaneous records which are unambiguous and legible. The Nursing and Midwifery Council (NMC) has published guidelines for records and record keeping (NMC 2009). The Department of Health (DH) has provided advice in its guidance on the implementation of independent nurse prescribing on the standards for prescription writing (DH 2004).

Paras 86–88 state that:

86: All nurses are required to keep contemporaneous records which are unambiguous and legible. The UKCC (now NMC) Standards of Record and Record Keeping outline the requirements of nurse's records. The record of the nurse's or midwife's prescription should be entered into the nursing patient record (where a separate nursing record exists e.g. in hospitals) at the time of writing. The prescription, together with other details of the consultation with the patient, should be entered into the general (GP or hospital) patient record as soon as possible and preferably contemporaneously. It should be marked to indicate that it is a nurse or midwife prescription and should include the name of the prescriber. The maximum time to be allowed between writing the prescription and entering the details into the general records is for local negotiation, but best practice suggests that this should be immediately.

Only in exceptional circumstances should this period exceed 48 hours from writing the prescription. Arrangements for the sharing of all relevant patient records can be put into locally agreed statements of good practice.

87: It is recommended that the record clearly indicates the date, the name of the prescriber, the name of the item prescribed and the quantity prescribed (or dose, frequency and treatment duration). For medicinal preparations, items to be ingested or inserted into the body, it is recommended that the name of the prescribed item, the strength (if any) of the preparation, the dosing schedule and the route of administration is given e.g. 'paracetamol oral suspension 120 mg/5 mls, 5 mls to be taken 4 hourly as required for pain, maximum of 20 mls in 24 hours'. For topical medicinal preparations, the name of the prescribed item, the strength (if any), the quantity to be applied and frequency of application should be indicated. For dressings and appliances, details of how to be applied and how frequently changed are useful. It is also useful, but not mandatory to note advice given in Over The Counter items.

88: In some circumstances, in the clinical judgement of the nurse or midwife prescriber, it may be necessary to advise the GP or consultant immediately of the prescription. This action should be recorded in the nursing records.

In Annex C to its guidance on implementation, the DH has provided a policy statement on record keeping. It states that:

All records created and maintained by health professionals should provide legible, accurate, current, comprehensive and concise information concerning the condition treatment and care of the patient/client and associated observations.

The DH suggests that properly made and maintained records must meet the following requirements:

- They must be entered within 48 hours of the events to which they relate.
- If the date of entry does not coincide with the date of the contact with the patient then the date of the entry, actual time of visit and the date of contact must be recorded.
- They must be written legibly and indelibly. Each entry must be signed with a full signature and dated.
- They must be clear and unambiguous.
- They must be accurate in each entry as to date and time.
- Alterations must be made by scoring out with a single line. **OTHER FORMS OF ERASURE OR DELETION – SUCH AS THE USE OF CORRECTION FLUID – MUST NEVER BE USED.** The correct entry should then be initialled, dated and timed.
- Additions to existing entries must be individually dated, timed and signed.
- All professionally held records must be stored in a secure manner in a locked file, drawer or cupboard.
- Systems for storing and record keeping will exclude unauthorised access and breaches of confidentiality.
- Meaningless phrases and offensive subjective statements unrelated to patient care must not be used.
- Abbreviations are only acceptable from the previously agreed list.
  The policy statement also suggests that:
- The record of the nurse's prescription must be entered into the patient's records as close as possible to the time of writing the prescription.
- Where more than one record exists (e.g. a trust nursing home or Walk-in Centre record and the hospital or GP record) information must be entered into each record as soon as possible.
- The record should clearly indicate the date, the name of the prescriber, the name of the item prescribed, the strength (if any) and the quantity prescribed. In hospitals the date and time of the last dose to be given may be used in place of a quantity to be dispensed. For preparations to be given or taken at a fixed dose or interval, the duration(s) of treatment can be recorded in place of prescribed quantity.

For medicinal preparations (items to be ingested or inserted into the body), the dosage schedule and the route of administration must be stated.

For topical medicine preparations, the quantity to be applied and frequency of application must be included.

- In some circumstances, in the clinical judgement of the nurse prescriber, it may be necessary to advise the patient's doctor immediately of the prescription.

Controlled drugs register and records

The Misuse of Drugs Act 1971 identifies in Schedule 2 certain medicinal products known as Controlled Drugs (CD) to which special controls and offences apply. The Misuse of Drug Regulations 2001No 3998 has five schedules which set out the CD in order of their seriousness and the penalties relating to their misuse. These rules were considered in Chapter 2.

The Regulations require a register of CD to be kept and an entry to be made in respect of every quantity of any drug listed in Schedules 1 and 2 which is obtained or supplied (whether by administration or otherwise). This requirement does not apply to:

- A sister or acting sister for the time being in charge of a ward, theatre or other department in a hospital or nursing home.
- A person licensed to supply by the Secretary of State if the licence does not require a register to be kept (Reg.19).
- A pharmacist or practitioner handling any prescribed drug returned to him or her for destruction.

The records to be kept by midwives were discussed in Chapter 11 relating to midwives and medicinal products.

Drugs listed in Schedules 3 and 4 are subject to Regulations 22, 23, 26 and 27. These cover rules in relation to:

- Reg. 22: Record keeping requirements in respect of drugs in Schedules 3 and 4
- Reg. 23: Preservation of registers, book and other documents
- Reg. 26: Furnishing of information with respect to controlled drugs
- Reg. 27: Destruction of controlled drugs

Under Regulations which came into force in 2007 an accountable officer must be appointed to oversee the management and use of CD in each health service organisation. His responsibilities are considered in Chapter 23. In 2007 (updated February 2008) the DH published guidance on the *Safer Management of Controlled Drugs* and the changes to record keeping requirements. This states (DH 2008):

10. From 1st February 2008, it will no longer be a legal requirement to maintain a CDR in a prescribed format. The regulations will specify only the headings/ fields to be used in the CDR. The CDR may set out "entries to be made in case of obtaining" and "entries to be made in cases of supply" on the same or separate pages. Two separate pages will no longer be required. This supports the increasing use of electronic registers and maintenance of running balances. Separate pages (in paper) or sections for each strength and form of an individual drug will be required. Each page must specify the strength and form of the drug at the head of the page, together with the name of the drug to which the entries on the page of the CDR relate. In the case of electronic registers, they must be capable of printing or displaying the name, form and strength of the drug in such a way that the details appear at the top of each display or printout.

11. From 1st February 2008, the regulations require the following information to be recorded in the CDR, under the following specified headings, when CDs are obtained:

- *Date supply obtained.*
- *Name and address from whom obtained (e.g. wholesaler, pharmacy).*
- *Quantity obtained.*

12. When CD are supplied to patients (in response to prescriptions) or to practitioners (in response to requisitions), the regulations require information to be recorded in the CDR, under the following specified headings:

- *Date supplied.*
- *Name and address of person or firm supplied.*
- *Detail of authority to possess – prescriber or licence holder's details.*
- *Quantity and form in which supplied.*

In addition from the 1st February 2008 additional information must be recorded as follows:

Information in relation to the identity of the person collecting a Schedule 2 CD supplied on prescription:

- *whether the person who collected the drug was the patient, the patient's representative or a healthcare professional acting on behalf of the patient and;*
- *if the person who collected the drug was a healthcare professional acting on behalf of the patient, that person's name and address;*
- *if the person who collected the drug was the patient or their representative and whether evidence of identity was requested (annotated in the yes/no columns). (As a matter of good practice a note as to why the dispenser did not ask may be included but this is not mandatory)*

- and whether evidence of identity was provided by the person collecting the drug.

Preservation of records

All registers and midwives' record books relating to CD must be preserved for two years from the date on which the entry is made therein. Every requisition, order or prescription (other than a health prescription) on which a CD is supplied must be preserved for two years from the date on which the last delivery is made (Reg. 23).

Application of the law to the scenario in Box 25.1

Rose would clearly be personally and professionally accountable for her failure to document the medications which she had administered. Whilst she personally would probably not have to pay any compensation to Maud, since her employers would be vicariously liable for her negligence (see Chapter 20), she could be disciplined by her employers. In addition, the incident would be reported to the NMC which would hold a preliminary investigation into the events to determine whether a fitness to practice hearing should take place before the Conduct and Competence Committee (CCC).

Conclusions on record keeping

Good standards of record keeping are an essential prerequisite in the prescribing, supply and administration of medicines. The legislation requirements are supplemented by additional guidance from the DH, NMC and other health registration bodies. In addition individual employers have prepared policies and guidelines providing additional safeguards which health professionals are obliged to implement. Any uncertainties about the documentation required can be clarified with the pharmacists or GPs.

Confidentiality

Box 25.2 Should the police be called?

On admission, Jim Brown is found to be carrying a large package, which the ward sister suspects may contain Schedule I drugs. She calls the pharmacist to the ward and the pharmacist confirms that it is cannabis. The pharmacist says that he will arrange to take it to the pharmacy department and for it to be destroyed, but discusses with the ward sister whether the police should be notified. Should they inform the police?

All health professionals are required in law to respect the right of the patient to have information about his condition, history, prognosis etc. kept confidential. The duty arises from a variety of sources, including a duty laid down in the code of professional conduct and ethics by the relevant registration body or professional association; a duty arising from the trust relationship between patient and healthcare professional; a duty arising from an implied (or sometimes express) term in the contract of employment; and a duty specified in many Acts of Parliament including the Data Protection Act 1998 and the Human Fertilisation and Embryology Act 1990 (as amended by the 2008 Act). Failure by a health professional to observe this duty of confidentiality in the absence of lawful justification could lead to fitness to practice hearings by the registration body, disciplinary proceedings by the employer, civil action for compensation by the patient or an action for an injunction to prevent publication or even criminal proceedings. Further details can be found in *Legal Aspects of Patient Confidentiality 2nd Edition* (Dimond 2010)

Lawful justifications for disclosing confidential information

The law recognises that there are circumstances where it would be justified in law, and there may even be a duty in law, to disclose what is considered to be confidential information.

Consent by the patient

Where the patient has agreed to the disclosure of information, this would be a complete defence to any action for breach of confidentiality. However, if this consent is not evidenced in writing, it may be one person's word against another.

Disclosure in the best interests of the patient

This would include disclosure between health professionals necessary to ensure that the patient is protected. For example, it would be vital for a nurse to ensure that a doctor was aware of a patient's allergy to particular medicines before a prescription was drawn up.

Disclosure ordered by the court

The court has the power to order disclosure of information relevant to an issue arising in a court hearing and no health professional can refuse to answer questions in court unless it is on grounds of self incrimination. Refusal to answer allowable questions could lead to imprisonment for contempt of court.

Disclosure required by Act of Parliament

Certain statutes require confidential information to be made available. For example, the Prevention of Terrorism Acts make it a criminal offence to fail to pass on to the police information about possible acts of terrorism. The Human Fertilisation and Embryology Act 1990 makes it a criminal offence to disclose confidential information about fertility treatment without the consent of the patient; the 1992 Act amended the consent requirements and these were incorporated in the 2008 Act. The Notification of Infectious Diseases legislation stipulates such information being passed on to the appropriate authorities. Under the Medicines Health Act 1968, section 118 prohibits the disclosure by inspectors of information obtained under the provisions of this Act unless the disclosure was made in the performance of his duty.

Disclosure in the public interest

All health professional regulatory bodies recognise that there are circumstances when the public interest requires that a health professional passes on confidential information in the health and safety interests of the patient or of other people. The most obvious example would be that of child protection. If there were reasonable fears that a child might be in danger then any health professional would be justified in ensuring that the appropriate child protection services were notified. In one case, where an independent psychiatrist provided a report at the request of a patient, the Court of Appeal held that it was in the public interest for that psychiatrist to notify the mental health review tribunal and the Home Secretary of the dangers which he believed the patient presented (W. v. Egdell [1989] 1 All ER 1089 HC, [1990] 1 All ER 835 CA).

Guidance

Most health professional regulatory bodies have provided guidance for their registrants on confidentiality. For example, the General Medical Council (GMC) published guidance in 2009 and the Royal Pharmaceutical Society of Great Britain (RPSGB 2004a) published a fact sheet on *Confidentiality, the Data Protection Act 1998 and the Disclosure of Information*.

In 1997 a report by a committee chaired by Dame Fiona Caldicott recommended that there should be a person appointed at trust board level to be responsible for ensuring confidentiality throughout the organisation. This person became known as the Caldicott Guardian (NHS 1999). Guidance was provided by the DH on how he or she should function. Community pharmacists are also expected to implement the Caldicott principles and the Caldicott Guardian would usually be the pharmacist owner of the business (if owned personally) or the superintendent pharmacist (if owned by a corporate body).

In 2003 the DH issued a Code of Practice on confidentiality which it is intended to be regularly updated. In 2007 the DH published an *NHS Information Governance* document providing guidance on the legal and professional obligations in relation to information. This best practice guidance outlines the likely impact of legal provisions primarily on NHS information but also includes some social care information. It recommends that where necessary organisations should obtain professional legal advice. The document lists the relevant legal and professional obligations generally in alphabetical order preceded by common law requirements and details at the end of each sub-section the information governance considerations, to assist those that work in this area.

Data Protection Act 1998

Information on medicines and prescription sheets etc. comes within the provisions of the Data Protection Act 1998 and the eight principles set out in that Act apply. The Act, unlike its 1984 predecessor, applies not just to computerised records but also to most manual records. The Act also restricts access to personalised information. Statutory instruments (SI) permit patient access subject to specific restrictions, which include:

- Where serious harm is feared to the physical or mental health or condition of the patient or another person or
- Where the identity of a third person (who has not agreed to the disclosure) would be disclosed.

  For further information on confidentiality and access see Dimond (2009).

Application of the law to the scenario in Box 25.2

There is at present no specific statutory requirement that the police should be notified when it is discovered that a person is carrying illegal substances. The Misuse of Drugs Regulations allow for the pharmacist or ward sister to take possession of CD for the purpose of destruction and for the purpose of handing it over to a police officer, and this could be done without notifying the police of the name of the patient. It is probable that in these circumstances, if there was only a small quantity of the CD, the confidentiality of the patient would be respected, but if there was a large quantity the exception of disclosure in the public interest may apply (RSPGB 2004b). Much may depend upon the cooperation of the patient in handing over the drugs (see Chapter 28 on illegal drugs). In no circumstances could Schedule 1 drugs, once removed from the patient, be returned to the patient.

Conclusions

Where it is alleged that confidential information has been disclosed unlawfully, the onus is on the health professional to justify that disclosure. It is essential therefore that advice on the disclosure is taken and that a clear record is kept of the reasons for the disclosure in case of a subsequent challenge to that disclosure.

Key points

■ Guidance is provided by the DH and NMC on documentation of medicines.
■ The Misuse of Drugs Regulations 2001 set out the records to be kept of CD.
■ Patient confidentiality must be respected.
■ The exceptions to the duty of confidentiality cover consent of the patient, disclosure to court and disclosure in the public interest.
■ A record must be kept giving reasons for any disclosure of confidential information.

References

Department of Health (2003) *The NHS Confidentiality Code of Practice*. Available at www.doh.gov.uk/ipu/confi den/protect/ (superseding HSG(96) 18 LASSL (96)5). London

Department of Health (2004) 2nd Edition *Extending independent nurse prescribing within the NHS in England: A guide for implementation*. London

Department of Health (2007) *NHS Information Governance*. London

Department of Health (2008) *Safer Management of Controlled Drugs*. London

Dimond, B. C. (2010) *Legal Aspects of Patient Confidentiality*. 2nd edition Quay Books, Dinton, Wiltshire.

General Medical Council (2009) *Confidentiality*.

NHS (1999) NHS Executive HSC 1999/012, Caldicott Guardians.

Nursing and Midwifery Council (2009) *Record keeping: Guidance for nurses and midwives*. London

Royal Pharmaceutical Society of Great Britain (2004a) *Fact sheet 12: Confidentiality, the Data Protection Act 1998 and the Disclosure of information*.

Royal Pharmaceutical Society of Great Britain (2004b) *Fact sheet 2: Controlled Drugs and Hospital Pharmacy*; www.rpharms.com.

CHAPTER 26

Research and medicines

Box 26.1 An unknown research subject

Mary, a staff nurse on a medical ward, was aware that the Senior Registrar was trying out a new treatment for a heart condition, but that he had not told the patients that the treatment was part of a research project. Mary was asked by Beryl, a retired solicitor in her eighties, whether the tablets she was being given were of proven efficacy for her condition. What should Mary say?

Introduction

Registered practitioners may be involved in research into medicinal products in several ways. They may be caring for patients who are involved in a drugs trial and the practitioner may therefore be concerned to ensure that the patient's consent is properly obtained and that the patient is given all the necessary information relating to the trial, including their right to opt out at any time (provided it is clinically safe to do so). Alternatively, the practitioner may herself be involved in a research project which involves a medicinal product. Both these aspects of research will be considered in this chapter. In addition, of course, it is the duty of every registered practitioner, for which she may be held personally and professionally accountable, that she keeps up to date and maintains her competence and this will include ensuring that she has up-to-date knowledge about the efficacy and dangers of any medicinal product that she may be administering to the patient or prescribing and that she acts on any warnings issued by relevant authorities.

Research into medicinal products

The safety of our medicines comes under the jurisdiction of the Commission on Human Medicines (CHM), and its committees advise the UK Licensing Authority to ensure that medicines meet the standards of quality, efficacy and safety that the public and health professions would expect.

The Commission came into being on 30 October 2005 (SI 2005/1094) and has the following duties which are set out in Section 3 of the Medicines Act 1968, as amended by the Medicines (Advisory Bodies) Regulations 2005 and include the following:

- To advise ministers on matters relating to human medicinal products (except those that fall under the remit of Advisory Board on the Registration of Homoeopathic Products (ABRH) and Herbal Medicines Advisory Committee (HMAC)).
- To advise the licensing authority (LA) where the LA has a duty to consult the Commission or where the LA chooses to consult the Commission including giving advice in relation to the safety, quality and efficacy of human medicinal products.
- To consider representations made in relation to the Commission's advice (either in writing or at a hearing) by an applicant or by a licence or marketing authorisation holder.
- To promote the collection and investigation of information relating to adverse reactions for human medicines (except for those products that fall within the remit of ABRH or HMAC) for the purposes of enabling such advice to be given.

The Commission is supported in its work by Expert Advisory Groups covering various therapeutic areas of medicine.

Drugs marked in the *British National Formulary* (BNF) or *Nurse Prescriber's Formulary* (NPF) with a black triangle symbol indicate that the Committee on Safety of Medicine (CSM) and Medicines Healthcare Protection Regulatory Agency (MHRA) are monitoring that product. Further information on the Black Triangle scheme can be obtained from the CSM website www.mhra.gov.uk. (The CSM was incorporated into the Commission of Human Medicine on 30 October 2005 which can be accessed on the MHRA website) (see Chapter 3).

Clinical trials

'Clinical trials' is defined in Section 31 of the Medicines Act 1968 as meaning:

An investigation or series of investigations consisting of the administration of one or more medicinal products, where there is evidence that they may be beneficial to a patient or patients, by one or more doctors or dentists for the purpose of ascertaining what effects, beneficial or harmful, the products have.

Under section 35 it is not necessary to have a manufacturer's licence or a marketing authorisation if a medicinal product is manufactured or assembled to be used in a clinical trial. Sections 31 to 39 of 1968 Act as amended lay down further requirements in relation to clinical trials (SI 1995 No 2808 and 2809).

A doctor or dentist wanting to have a product manufactured or imported for use in a clinical trial does not need a certificate if certain conditions are met. The products must have been manufactured or imported specially for the trial and only for administration to the practitioner's own patients. The trial must not have been arranged by, or at the request of, a third party (section 31(5) and (6) SI 1972 No 1200).

Where a practitioner's prescriptions are dispensed in a registered pharmacy, hospital or health centre under the supervision of a pharmacist there is no need for any certificate section 31(7) and 33(4).

International conventions covering research

Nuremberg Code

At the end of the Second World War, military trials were held in Nuremberg where members of the Nazi party, some of the worst perpetrators of crimes against humanity, were prosecuted. In its judgment, the Court set out 10 basic principles which should be observed in order to satisfy moral, ethical and legal concepts. These have become known as the Nuremberg Code. The 10 principles are summarised in Box 26.2.

Box 26.2 Principles for research from Nuremberg Code

- The voluntary consent of the human subject is absolutely essential.
- The experiment should be such as to yield fruitful results for the good of society, unprocurable by other methods.
- The experiment should be based on results of animal experiments and a knowledge of the natural history of the disease or other problem so that the anticipated results should justify the performance of the experiment.
- The experiment should be so conducted as to avoid all unnecessary physical and mental suffering and injury.
- No experiment should be conducted where there is an a priori reason to believe that death or disabling injury will occur; except, perhaps, in those circumstances where the experimental physicians also serve as subjects.
- The degree of risk to be taken should never exceed that determined by the humanitarian importance of the problem to be solved by the experiment.
- Proper preparations should be made and adequate facilities provided to protect the experimental subject against even remote possibilities of injury, disability or death.
- The experiment should be conducted only by a scientifically qualified person. The highest degree of skill and care should be required through all stages of the experiment of those who conduct or engage in the experiment.
- During the course of the experiment the human subject should be at liberty to bring the experiment to an end if he had reached the physical or mental state where continuation of the experiment seems to him to be impossible.
- During the course of the experiment the scientist in charge must be prepared to terminate the experiment at any stage, if he has probable cause to believe, in the exercise of the good faith, superior skill and careful judgment required of him that a continuation of the experiment is likely to result in injury, disability, or death to the experimental subject.

Declaration of Helsinki

The World Medical Association published a *Declaration of Helsinki* in 1964 which set out principles for the carrying out of research on human subjects. Amendments were made in 2000 following a conference in Edinburgh (WMA 2000). In 2008 an amendment to the *Declaration of Helsinki* required that clinical trials should appear on public registers. (A copy is contained in Appendix 1 of the Association of British Pharmaceutical Industry (ABPI 2002) (see below) publication on an introduction to the work of ethics committees.)

European Commission rules relating to clinical trials

The EC Directive 2001/20/EC on the implementation of good clinical practice in the conduct of clinical trials on medicinal products for human use, stipulates the procedures which must be followed by all member states in carrying out clinical trials. The contents of the Directive are shown in Box 26.3.

A copy of the EC Directive is set out in the Association of British Pharmaceutical Industry (ABPI 2002) (see below) publication on an introduction to the work of ethics committees. The EC Directive 2001/20/EC on clinical trials was implemented by means of statutory regulations, which came into force on 1 May 2004. They can be accessed via the Stationery Office website (www.tso.co.uk).

Local Research Ethics Committees

The DH has requested that each health authority ensure that an Local Research Ethics Committees (LREC) is set up to examine research proposals. Any NHS body asked to agree a research proposal falling within its sphere of responsibility should ensure that it has been submitted to the appropriate LREC for research ethics approval. The Centre for Medical Law and Ethics at Kings College London (1997) publishes a manual for research ethics committees provides guidance on every aspect of its work, including the special procedure for multi-centre research. In certain cases, Multi-Centre Research Ethics Committees (MRECs), established by the DH, oversee research which is carried on across several LREC catchment areas. Where fewer than five LRECs are involved, one LREC can act on behalf

Box 26.3 EC Directive on clinical trials

Article 1 Aim of the Directive:
- To establish specific provisions regarding the conduct of clinical trials, including multi-centre trials on human subjects involving medicinal product as defined by Article 1 of Directive 65/66/EEC.
- Good clinical practice to be identified and complied with.
- To adopt and if necessary revise principles of good clinical practice and detailed guidance to be published by the Commission.
- All clinical trials to be designed, conducted and reported in accordance with the principles of good clinic practice.

Article 2 Definitions

Article 3 Protection of clinical trial subjects

Article 4 Clinical trials on minors

Article 5 Clinical trials on incapacitated adults not able to give informed legal consent

Article 6 Ethics Committee

Article 7 Single Opinion

Article 8 Detailed guidance to be published by Commission

Article 9 Commencement of a clinical trial

Article 10 Conduct of a clinical trial

Article 11 Exchange of information

Article 12 Suspension of the trial or infringements

Article 13 Manufacture and import of investigational medicinal products.

Article 14 Labelling

Article 15 Verification of compliance of investigational medicinal products with good clinical and manufacturing practice

Article 16 Notification of adverse events

Article 17 Notification of serious adverse reactions

Article 18 Guidance concerning reports

Article 19 General provisions

Article 20 Adaptation to scientific and technical progress

Article 21 Committee procedure

Article 22 Application

Article 23 Entry into force 4 April 2001

of the others. The role of the LREC is defined as being "to consider the ethics of proposed research projects which will involve human subjects" and to advise the NHS body concerned. It is the NHS body which has the responsibility of deciding whether or not the project should go ahead, taking into account the ethical advice of the LREC. They are not "in any sense management arms of the District Health Authority". The LREC is comprised of multi-disciplinary members including lay persons. The guidelines require the LREC to be consulted for any proposal which involves:

- NHS patients, including those private sector patients treated under contract.
- fetal material and IVF involving NHS patients.
- the recently dead, in NHS premises.
- access to the records of past or present NHS patients.
- the use of, or potential access to, NHS premises or facilities.

The LREC **MUST** be consulted, but the NHS body must also give permission before the project can proceed.

Obtaining the approval of an LREC should ensure that the patient/client is reasonably protected from zealous researchers. However, particular difficulties can arise where the researcher is also the health professional concerned with the treatment of the patient. In such cases, it is not easy to ensure that treatment concerns remain paramount and the patient is assured that he or she can opt out of the research at any time without suffering any sanction from the health professional.

New guidance was issued by the DH in 2001 and the new arrangements came into force in April 2002 (DH 2001a). The Governance statement defines the purpose of a REC in reviewing the proposed study:

...to protect the dignity, rights, safety and well-being of all actual or potential research participants. It shares this role and responsibility with others, as described in the Research Governance Framework for Health and Social Care (DH 2001b) (see below).

Research may not be started until ethical approval has been obtained.

It is the personal responsibility of the person named as principal investigator to apply for approval by the REC and this person retains responsibility for the scientific and ethical conduct of the research.

Section A of the guidance provided by the DH sets out a *Statement of General Standards and Principles* and covers the following topics:

- Role of Research Ethics Committees
- The remit of an NHS REC
- Establishment and support of NHS RECs

- Membership requirements and process
- Composition of an REC
- Working procedures
- Multi-centre research
- The process of ethical review of a research protocol
- Submitting an application
- Glossary.

Section B provides more detailed guidance on operating procedures and the requirements for general support for RECs.

Section C provides a resource for RECs and collates current advice on ethical issues and is to be regularly updated.

Research Governance Framework for Health and Social Care

The DH published its *Research Governance Framework for Health and Social Care* in February 2001 (DH 2001c). A second edition was published in 2005 to take account of legislation passed since 2001, including the Mental Capacity Act 2005 and the Human Tissue Act 2004. The framework sets standards for all research within the responsibility of the Secretary of State for health, including research concerned with the protection and promotion of public health, research undertaken in or by the DH, its non-Departmental bodies and the NHS and research undertaken by or within the social care services that might have an impact on the quality of those services.

The research governance framework covers the following topics:

- Purpose and scope
- Standards:
    - Ethics
    - Science
    - Information
    - Health and safety
    - Finance
    - Quality research culture.
- Responsibilities and accountability
    - General
    - Agreements
    - Specific Responsibilities

- – Responsibilities of participants
- – Responsibilities of researchers
- – Responsibilities of the principal investigator
- – Responsibilities of research investigator
- – Responsibilities of research sponsor
- – Responsibilities of universities and other organisations employing researchers
- – Responsibilities of organisations providing care
- – Responsibilities of care professionals
- – Responsibilities relating to research ethics committees.
- Delivery systems
- Monitoring, inspection and sanctions.

The introduction to the Framework emphasises that proper governance of research is essential to ensure that the public can have confidence in, and benefit from, quality research in health and social care.

The public has a right to expect high scientific, ethical and financial standards, transparent decision-making processes, clear allocation of responsibilities and robust monitoring arrangements. Further information can be obtained from the DH website (www.dh.gov.uk).

National Research Ethics Service

The National Research Ethics Service (NRES) was launched in April 2007. The head quarters of the NRES at the National Patient Safety Agency (NPSA) is implementing measures that will give ethics committees expert support, and help simplify the review of low-risk studies and surveys. The implementation plan *Building on improvement: Implementing the recommendations of the Report of the Ad Hoc Advisory Group on the Operation of NHS Research Ethics Committees* was published in 2006.

Future developments of the research framework

In 2010 the Coalition Government published a White Paper on the NHS (DH 2010a) and also an arms' length review of public bodies (DH 2010b). The latter document envisages the abolition of many organisations with the transfer of functions to the DH or other organisations. In respect of the research framework the DH made the following comments:

> *The Research Governance Framework for health and social care defines the broad principles of good research governance and is key to ensuring that health and social care research is conducted to high scientific and ethical standards. Research governance framework for health and social care.*

The White Paper on Equity and excellence: liberating the NHS (DH 2010a) said:

> *The Government will cut the bureaucracy involved in medical research. We have asked the Academy of Medical Sciences to conduct an independent review of the regulation and governance of medical research. In the light of this review we will consider the legislation affecting medical research, and the bureaucracy that flows from it, and bring forward plans for radical simplification.*
>
> *These plans will include a review of the Research Governance Framework.*

The Academy of Medical Sciences published its report *A new pathway for regulation and governance of health research* on 11 January 2011. At the time of writing the response of the Government has not been announced.

Compensation to the patient

If a patient were to be harmed as a result of participation in a drug trial, there is at present in law no recognition of strict liability in relation to that harm. The Pearson Report in 1978 recommended that both volunteers and patients who take part in medical research and clinical trials and who suffer severe damage as a result should receive compensation on the basis of strict liability (Royal Commission 1978). This recommendation has never been implemented in law, though the ABPI has recommended that such persons should obtain compensation without proof of negligence if harm arose as a result of the research project. In its introduction to the work of ethics committees the ABPI (2002) states that it is a condition of membership of the ABPI that members abide by its Code of Practice, which contains a clause recognising the duty to compensate volunteers on a no-fault basis. Further details can be obtained from appendix 7 of its introduction to the work of ethics committees. Research Ethics Committees are required to establish that there has been an agreement to pay compensation before any research on medicinal products takes place.

The practitioner caring for a patient involved in a clinical trial

Where a practitioner is aware that his or her patient is being asked to take part in a research trial, the practitioner should ensure that the research has been approved by the appropriate ethics committee, that the patient or parent has been given information about the research proposed and that a valid consent has been obtained from the patient or parent before the research proceeds.

Consent of the patient

Child and young person

Under the Family Law Reform Act 1969 a young person of 16 or 17 years does not have a statutory right to give consent to research. Only if the treatment proposed was part of the therapeutic care of the patient but also part of a research project would the treatment come under the definition of treatment under section 8(2) of the Act. (This is considered in Chapter 15.) A child under 16 years may be able to give consent to participation in a research project, but only if it is established that he or she has the mental capacity to understand what is involved. It is probably unlawful for a parent to give consent on behalf of a child's or young person's participation in research where any significant risks arise, unless the research is therapeutic and the child or young person thereby benefits from the research.

Mentally competent adult

Exactly the same principles of law apply to the consent by mentally capacitated adults to participation in research as apply to their receiving treatment. These principles are considered in Chapter 12 and the giving of information is covered in Chapter 13.

Mentally incompetent adult

Under the Mental Capacity Act 2005 statutory provision is made to protect the mentally incapacitated adult in research. Approval has to be obtained from an authorised body such as a local research ethics committee. In addition, the following conditions must be satisfied:

- The research must be connected with a condition which affects P (the person lacking mental capacity), and
- The research is attributable to, or causes or contributes to, the impairment of, or disturbance in the functioning of, the mind or brain.
- There must be reasonable grounds for believing that the research would not be as effective if carried out only on, or only in relation to, persons who have the capacity to consent to taking part in the project.
- The research must have the potential to benefit P without imposing on P a burden that is disproportionate to the potential benefit to P or,
- Be intended to provide knowledge of the causes or treatment of, or of the care of persons affected by, the same or a similar condition.
- There must be reasonable arrangements in place for ensuring that the requirements of sections 32 and 33 (consulting carers etc. and additional safeguards) are in place.

In addition, the researcher 'R' is required to take reasonable steps to identify a person who is not engaged in a professional capacity nor receiving remuneration, but is engaged in caring for P or is interested in P's welfare and is prepared to be consulted by the researcher under section 32. If such a person cannot be identified, then R must in accordance with guidance issued by the Secretary of State nominate a person who is prepared to be consulted by R but has no connection with the project.

R must provide the carer or nominee with information about the project and ask him for advice as to whether P should take part in the project and what, in his opinion, P's wishes and feelings about taking part in the project would be likely to be if P had capacity in relation to the matter. If the person consulted advises R that in his opinion P's wishes and feelings would be likely to lead him to decline to take part in the project (or to wish to withdraw from it), if he had the capacity, then R must ensure that P does not take part, or if he is already taking part, ensure that he is withdrawn from it. If treatment has commenced it is not necessary to discontinue the treatment if R has reasonable grounds for believing that there would be a significant risk to P's health if it were discontinued.

The Mental Capacity Act 2005 came into force by October 2007. The LREC should ensure that the statutory protection is provided for mentally incapacitated adults. The Mental Capacity Act 2005 does not cover research which comes under the Clinical Trials Regulations and these make their own provision for the protection of the mentally incapacitated adult.

Application of the law to the situation in Box 26.1

Clearly Beryl is entitled to know the status of the medicines which she is being prescribed and the staff nurse should try to arrange a meeting between the senior registrar and Beryl in which Beryl can be told about the research and her consent to participation can be requested. She has the right not to take part in the research and her refusal to participate should not prejudice in any way the care she is given. The clinical team would still have a responsibility to treat her with the conventional treatment accepted as reasonable care by a competent body of professional opinion.

Conclusions

It is essential that where treatment is given experimentally to patients the latter should be notified of the research project and the patients' rights to participate or not should be protected. The new stringent rules set out in the EC directive should ensure that the rights of the patient are protected and the provisions of the Mental Capacity Act 2005 in relation to those lacking capacity should provide further protection. At the time of writing the Government's plans for a new Research Framework and a new central body for overseeing health and social care research are awaited.

Key points

- Clinical trials on medicinal products are subject to EC Regulations.
- International codes of practice set standards for the conduct of research.
- Research Ethics Committee approval must be obtained before research commences.
- The NRES facilitates obtaining ethical approval for research.
- Government plans for healthcare research envisage a review of the regulation and governance of medical research and of the research Governance Framework.

References

Academy of Medical Sciences (2011) *A new pathway for regulation and governance of health research*

Association of the British Pharmaceutical Industry (2002) *Introduction to the Work of Research Ethics Committees, 2nd edn.*

Department of Health (2001a) *Governance Arrangements for NHS Research Ethics Committees*; replaces HSG(91)5 (the red book) and HSG(97)23 on multi-centre Research Ethics Committees. London http://www.doh.gov.uk/research/rd1/researchgovernance/corec.htm.

Department of Health (2001b) *Research Governance Framework for England*, 1st edn; draft 2nd edn 2003. London http://www.doh.gov.uk/research/rd3/nhsandd/researchgovernance.htm.

Department of Health (2001c) *Research Governance Framework for Health and Social Care*. London

Department of Health (2006) *Building on improvement: Implementing the recommendations of the Report of the Ad Hoc Advisory Group on the Operation of NHS Research Ethics Committees*. London

Department of Health (2010a) *Equity and Excellence: Liberating the NHS*. Crown London

Department of Health (2010b) *Liberating the NHS: Report of the Arm's Length Bodies*. Crown London

Kings College (1997) Centre for Medical Law and Ethics, *Manual for Research Ethics Committees*. King's College London, 1997.

Royal Commission (1978) Civil Liability and Compensation for Personal Injury. Chaired by Lord Pearson. Cmnd 7054 1978 HMSO. London.

World Medical Assocation (2000) *Revising the Declaration of Helsinki: a fresh start*

Websites

CSM website www.mhra.gov.uk

Department of Health website www.dh.gov.uk.

The Stationery Office website www.tso.co.uk

CHAPTER 27

The right to obtain medicinal products

Box 27.1 Beta Interferon, North Derbyshire case

The North Derbyshire Health Authority decided that it would not enable Beta Interferon to be prescribed for patients in its catchment area, since it was not yet proved to be clinically effective for the treatment of multiple sclerosis. A sufferer from multiple sclerosis challenged this refusal of the Health Authority and succeeded on the grounds that the Health Authority had failed to follow the guidance issued in the NHS Executive Letter: EL (95)97 by the Department of Health (DH). A declaration was granted that the policy adopted by the health authority was unlawful and an order of mandamus was made requiring the defendants to formulate and implement a policy that took full and proper account of national policy as stated in the circular.

(R. v. North Derbyshire Health Authority [1997] 8 Med L R 327)

Introduction

Patients in the NHS do not have an absolute right to access services and have prescribed for them the medicines and other treatments which they consider that they need. The statutory duty placed upon the Secretary of State is to provide a reasonable service, and this is subject to the constraints of limited resources.

Right to obtain NHS services

The Secretary of State has a statutory duty under NHS legislation to provide a comprehensive NHS to meet all reasonable requirements, which covers both prevention and treatment and specifically requires a number of services to be provided. These duties have been considered by the courts in a number of different cases and the general consensus is that the statute does not give an absolute right to obtain services, and that, provided there is no obvious evidence of irrational or unreasonable setting of priorities, then the courts will not be involved in the determination of the allocation of resources.

Thus in the inevitable situation where resources are finite and demand outmatches supply, providers and commissioners of services have to weigh priorities. Examples of when individual patients have sought to enforce the statutory duty to provide services, and the courts have refused to intervene, include:

- Patients who brought an action for breach of statutory duty against the Secretary of State for Health and the Regional and Area Health Authorities on the grounds that they had waited too long for hip operations failed in their claim. In the case of R v Secretary of State for Social Services ex parte Hincks and others. 29 June 1979 (1979) 123, the court held that it could only interfere if the Secretary of State acted so as to frustrate the policy of the Act or as no reasonable minister could have acted.

- In the case of R. v Central Birmingham Health Authority ex parte Walker (1987) 3 BMLR 32, Mrs Walker failed to obtain a declaration that heart surgery should be carried out on her child. The court held that it was not for the court to substitute its own judgement for that of those responsible for the allocation of resources. It would only interfere if there had been a failure to allocate funds in a way which was unreasonable or where there had been breaches of public duties. Mrs Walker's application was refused.

- In the case of R. v. Cambridge HA ex parte B [1995] 2 All ER 129, Jamie Bowen, a child suffering from leukaemia, was refused by the purchasers a course of chemotherapy and a second bone marrow transplant on the grounds that there was only a very small chance of the treatment succeeding and therefore it would not be in her best interests for the treatment to proceed. The Court of Appeal upheld the decision of the health authority. The Court of Appeal was unable to fault the process of reasoning of the authority and allowed its appeal.

The Master of the Rolls (Sir Thomas Bingham) stated that:

while I have every sympathy with B, I feel bound to regard this as an attempt – wholly understandable, but nevertheless misguided – to involve the court in a field of activity where it is not fitted to make any decision favourable to the patient.

An anonymous donor then came forward and paid for further treatment for the child, but she died a year later.

More recently, however, there have been several cases where the courts have upheld the right of an individual patient to access services.

The first was in relation to the failure of a health authority to permit a drug for multiple sclerosis to be prescribed in its catchment area. The facts of the case are set out in Box 27.1.

In the second case (North West Lancashire Health Authority v. A, D, and G [1999]) a health authority refused to fund treatment for three transsexuals who wished to undergo gender reassignment. The health authority refused to fund such treatment on the grounds that it had been assigned a low priority in its lists of procedures considered to be clinically ineffective in terms of health gain. Under this policy, gender reassignment surgery was, amongst other procedures, listed as a procedure for which no treatment, apart from that provided by the Authority's general psychiatric and psychology services, would be commissioned, save in the event of overriding clinical need or exceptional circumstances. The transsexuals sought judicial review of the health authority's refusal and the judge granted an order quashing the authority's decision and the policy on which it was based. The health authority then took the case to the Court of Appeal but lost its appeal.

The Court of Appeal held that:

1. Whilst the precise allocation and weighting of priorities is a matter for the judgment of the Authority and not for the court, it is vital for an Authority:

    a) to assess accurately the nature and seriousness of each type of illness, and

    b) to determine the effectiveness of various forms of treatment for it, and

    c) to give proper effect to that assessment and that determination in the formulation and individual application of its policy.

2. The Authority's policy was flawed in two respects:

    a) it did not treat transsexualism as an illness, but as an attitude of mind which did not warrant medical treatment, and

    b) the ostensible provision that it made for exceptions in individual cases and its manner of considering them amounted to the operation of a 'blanket policy' against funding treatment for the condition because it did not believe in such treatment.

3. The authority were not genuinely applying the policy to the individual exceptions.

4. Article 3 and Article 8 of the European Convention on Human Rights did not give a right to free healthcare and did not apply to this situation, where

the challenge is to a health authority's allocation of finite funds. Nor were the patients victims of discrimination on the grounds of sex.

In spite of the decision of the Court of Appeal in the transsexual case that the Articles of the European Convention of Human Rights did not apply to the allocation of resources, there are undoubtedly likely to be cases in the future where claimants utilise the Human Rights Act 1998 where facilities and services have not been made available and as a consequence a person has been subjected to inhuman or degrading treatment. Such actions will be assisted where the National Institute for Health and Clinical Excellence (NICE), Care Quality Commission (CQC) and National Service Frameworks publish guidance on what they consider are minimal standards of care.

Herceptin

Mrs Rogers appealed against the decision of the High Court which had upheld the refusal of her Primary Care Trust (PCT) to fund the treatment of herceptin for her breast cancer. The Court of Appeal unanimously held that Swindon PCT's policy with respect to Herceptin was irrational and so unlawful. The Court of Appeal ordered that the PCT's decision be quashed (Rogers, R (on the application of) v Swindon NHS Primary Care Trust & Anor [2006] EWCA Civ 392).

National Institute for Health and Clinical Excellence

The NHS Plan envisaged the establishment of a body which would evaluate a wide range of treatments and medicines and issue guidance on their clinical and cost effectiveness (DH 2008a). This statutory body was established on 1 April 1999 with the stated task of abolishing postcode variation in the country, so that there would be national standards for the provision of healthcare treatments including medicines. One of the functions of is to issue clinical guidelines and clinical audit methodologies and information on good practice. The NICE (renamed after it joined with the Health Development Agency) has a major role to play in the setting of standards of practice, by disseminating the results of research of what is proved to be clinically effective, research-based practice.

NICE issues three kinds of guidance:

1. **Technology appraisals** – guidance on the use of new and existing medicines and treatments within the NHS in England and Wales.
2. **Clinical guidelines** – guidance on the appropriate treatment and care of people with specific diseases and conditions within the NHS in England and Wales.
3. **Interventional procedures** – guidance on whether interventional procedures used for diagnosis or treatment are safe enough and work well enough for routine use in England, Wales and Scotland.
   NICE has a user-friendly website which is regularly updated (www.nice.org.uk). Some examples of NICE recommendations are listed below:

- One of its first activities was to recommend to the Secretary of State that the expense of Relenza, a drug developed by Glaxo Welcome for preventing flu did not justify funding through the NHS, since it appeared to have little benefit for those groups most at risk: the elderly and asthma sufferers. NICE's recommendations were accepted by the Secretary of State. Subsequently, following further research, it recommended the use of Relenza in the NHS.
- In May 2000 NICE issued guidance on the use of Taxanes in the treatment of ovarian cancer. It recommended that the drug paclitaxel (Taxol) should be used to treat women who have previously received it and whose cancer had recurred or been resistant to other forms of treatment (NICE 2000).
- On 21 June 2000, it was reported that NICE was about to announce that the drug Beta Interferon does not justify the cost of £10,000 per year for patients suffering from multiple sclerosis. The Association of British Neurologists recommended that the drug should be used for about 10% of the country's 85,000 sufferers.
- It was announced in April 2000 by the DH that NICE was to prepare guidelines advising GPs on when to refer patients with acute lower back pain to specialists.

One of the results of NICE guidance is that those patients who claim that they have suffered as a result of a failure to provide a reasonable standard of care may be able to use evidence of clinical effectiveness and research-based practice to illustrate failings in the care provided to them. It could be argued that failure to follow the recommendations of NICE will be prima facie evidence of a failure to follow a reasonable standard of care according to the Bolam Test (Bolam v. Friern Barnet Hospital Management Committee [1957] 1 WLR 582). It does not follow, however, that failure to follow NICE guidelines will always constitute clinical negligence, since as NICE itself recognises, the guidelines are based on the best available evidence:

- They help healthcare professionals in their work, but they do not replace their knowledge and skills.
- There may, for example, be special circumstances relating to an individual patient which mean that the medicine or practice recommended in the guideline is not appropriate for that particular patient.

In a more recent case (Eisai Ltd v. National Institute for Health and Clinical Excellence (Alzheimer's Society and Shire Pharmaceuticals Ltd Interested parties) [2007] EWHC 1941) the NICE guidance on a drug for Alzheimers was challenged by the manufacturers Eisai Ltd. The judge held that its findings and methods were in general acceptable but it had failed to fulfil its duties under Disability and Race Discrimination legislation by not offering specific advice regarding people with learning disabilities and people who lacked English as a first language in its technology appraisal guidance.

In January 2011 NICE guidance came into force on the use of three drugs for Alzheimer's which it had originally ruled against. Donepenzil (Aricept), galantamine (Reminyl) and rivastigmine (Exelon) should be prescribed for those with early or moderate stage Alzheimer's. In addition it advised that memantine (Ebixa) should be available for severe forms of the disease and some patients with moderate Alzheimer's (Bennett 2011).

Abatacept

Bristol-Myers Squibb Pharmaceuticals Ltd, (BMS) challenged the decision of NICE in refusing to recommend the use of the drug Abatacept (for treatment in connection with rheumatoid arthritis) in the NHS. The High Court distinguished the circumstances from those which pertained in the Esai case (see above) (Bristol-Myers Squibb Pharmaceuticals Ltd, R (on the application of) v National Institute for Health and Clinical Excellence [2009] EWHC 2722 (Admin)).

Protelos

The Court of Appeal allowed an appeal for judicial review of the decision of NICE in relation to Servier's drug strontium ranelate (brand named Protelos) as treatment for the prevention of osteoporotic fractures in post-menopausal women. NICE had recommended strontium ranelate (Protelos) only for a limited group of patients who could not tolerate alendronate, the drug NICE supported. The Court of Appeal held that:

The court must be prepared to analyse the decision making process and the reasoning involved. The central flaw in the decision making progress is the absence of a satisfactory explanation as to why the post-hoc subgroup analysis on which the appellants relied has been rejected.

Servier won it's appeal (Servier Laboratories Ltd v National Institute for Health and Clinical Excellence & Anor [2010] EWCA Civ 346).

In its *Review of Arms' Length Bodies* (DH 2010), the Government proposed to place NICE on a firmer statutory basis and to extend its remit to include preparing quality standards for adult social care. These provisions are included in the Health and Social Care Bill Part 8 clauses 216 to 232 and at the time of writing are being debated in Parliament.

It is likely that in future, where NICE has published clear findings on the efficacy of specific medications for certain conditions, there will be strong pressure on Primary Care and NHS Trusts to make these medicinal products available to those patients who would benefit. If patients are refused effective treatment then they are likely to take legal action using the law of negligence and asserting that there has been a failure to follow the reasonable standard of care. It may also be argued that there is a violation of their rights set out in the European Convention on Human Rights and particularly article 3:

the right not to be subjected to inhuman and degrading treatment or punishment.

Refusal of Recombinant Factor VII

An unsuccessful attempt by a haemophiliac to challenge the refusal of a primary care trust to fund his treatment is set out in Box 27.2.

Box 27.2 Refusal to fund treatment

The claimant had suffered from haemophilia since birth and since May 2000 had refused to be treated with plasma derived from Factor VIII products on the grounds that he believed that there was a risk of an attack by a mutated or new virus that could not be eliminated from human plasma products. On his behalf the Haemophilia Centre requested that the PCT should consider funding treatment of the claimant with recombinant Factor VIII. The PCT refused on the grounds that alternative treatment was available and the claimant did not fit the current or likely future criteria of the DH for recombinant Factor VIII.
(R (on the application of Longstaff) v Newcastle NHS Primary Care Trust 2004 Lloyd's Rep Med 400)

The High Court refused the claimant's application for judicial review.

One of the grounds for its refusal was that the patient's views on the clinical effectiveness and risks of treatment could not be determinative of the question of whether the defendant's decision not to fund specific treatment should be quashed in public law, and the guidance issued by the DH had been followed.

Efficient management of medicines

The NHS is also concerned that medicines should be managed carefully, particularly in terms of patient usage. Stories abound of medicines obtained on prescription and being stockpiled by patient and carers, and every so often there have been amnesties when pharmacists have offered to take back all unused, including out-of-date, medicines on a no-questions-asked basis.

In March 2001 the DH announced that it was investing £1.9 million for medicines management (DH 2001a) (see also Chapter 23). It said that of the £5 billion annually spent on medicines in the NHS, over £100 million are returned unused to pharmacies, and it estimated that perhaps as many as 1 in 9 households have at least one prescribed medicine no longer being used. It intended using the investment to assist health authorities, primary care groups and trusts to collaborate in running a medicines management site. Twenty-five such sites were to be established:

Sites would recruit local facilitators to work closely with GPs, pharmacists and primary healthcare teams to re-shape local services to meet the needs of patients and ensure the money the NHS spends is to the best effect.

It gave as an example of the work of a site, the reorientation of services to help identify a patient's individual pharmaceutical needs. Another example was the more effective coordination of the processes of repeat prescriptions and dispensing. (For further details on this, contact Richard Seal Medicines Management Action team at the National Prescribing Centre, Liverpool.)

In December 2010 AstraZeneca announced that it has started to evaluate new medicines for colorectal cancer, which will be more effective among certain genetic groups. It was collaborating with a genomics company to use a personalised medicine approach at an earlier stage of development than before.

Protecting patients when medicines are discontinued

The DH issued best practice guidelines in May 2001 to protect patient needs when pharmaceutical companies withdraw a medicine from the market (DH 2001b). The guidelines were drawn up by the DH, NHS healthcare professionals and the ABPI. Key features of the guidelines are:

- A central contact point and dedicated e-mailbox in the DH.
- A clear timetable for notification.
- Clarity about the information to be provided.
- A list of contacts to be notified.
- An emphasis on exchanging information at an early stage.

There is a legal obligation on pharmaceutical companies to inform the Medicines and Health Care Products Regulatory Agency (MHRA) where a product is being discontinued on grounds of safety, quality or efficacy.

The DH launched the *Pharmacy in the Future – Implementing the NHS Plan* in September 2000 (DH 2000b). It sets out a comprehensive programme for reshaping pharmacy services (see Chapter 29).

Withdrawal of anti-diabetic drug

Camden NHS trust issued advice on the internet relating to the withdrawal of rosiglitazone. It stated that a Europe-wide review of the risks and benefits of medicines containing rosiglitazone had concluded that the benefits of treatment no longer outweighed the risks. Following the review, it was recommended that rosiglitazone be withdrawn from use. The most recent review was triggered by new studies showing that rosiglitazone was associated with an increased risk of cardiovascular disorders, including heart attacks and heart failure. A few months notice was given of the withdrawal to enable patients taking the drug to consult their doctor to review the medication and discuss alternatives.

The DH is also concerned in ensuring a continuous supply of medicines and in August 2009 tendered for companies to provide buffer stocks:

Wide varieties of medicines are routinely used in primary and secondary care and are key to the treatment of many life-threatening conditions. Treatment of these conditions is reliant on the medicines supply chain supplying the NHS. In the event of a pandemic or other emergency, the medicines supply chain may be at risk of an interruption of supply with a consequential impact on health care.

285

> The Department of Health wishes to strengthen the UK supply chain through
> the purchase of a stock of medicines used routinely in the NHS to increase stock
> volumes, which can be used as a buffer in the supply chain, ready for release into
> the UK market in the event of a pandemic or other emergency.

The MHRA is developing an online information service about medicines for patients. (See Chapter 13.)

Application of the law to the situation in Box 27.1

As can be seen from the case in Box 27.1, any strategic health authority or NHS or PCT that formulates a policy about the availability of medicines for its catchment area must ensure that it follows DH advice in drawing up a policy on access to the specific medicines, and that this policy is transparent and reasonable. It is unlikely that there will ever be the resources to ensure that all patients who would benefit from new treatments are able to access them, and there are therefore likely to be court challenges to the NHS over failures to provide certain services or medicines. In these disputes, the work of NICE in determining, from the basis of research evidence, which treatments should be made available is a vital factor in assisting in the prevention of post code differences developing across the country. However, there is evidence, on the basis of research conducted by *The Times*, that there were considerable variations in the costs of drugs which some patients were having to obtain by private prescriptions because they were not available on the NHS (Lister 2005). Thus the cost of three drugs for Alzheimer's, fertility drugs and a nasal spray varied by as much as 79% across the country. The attempt to ensure equality in access to healthcare treatment is still far from achieved. The problems for doctors when NICE deferred its decision over drugs for Alzheimer's disease is highlighted in a letter to *The Times*, since doctors have a duty to provide a reasonable standard of care (Burns 2005). The possibility that drugs could be individually tailored to the genetic makeup of individuals may eventually have major implications for both the manufacture and prescribing of medications and could herald a new era in medicines management.

Key points

- There is no absolute right to obtain NHS services.
- NICE was established to prevent the postcode lottery for obtaining NHS services.
- NICE guidelines set out information on clinically effective treatments.
- NHS organisations have a duty to take account of these guidelines.

References

Bennett, R (2011) Alzheimer's drugs made available *The Times* 18 January 2011 page 15

Burns, A (2005) Availability of costly drugs. Letter to *The Times*, 21 July.

Department of Health (2000a) *NHS Plan: a Plan for Investment, a Plan for Reform*. CM 4818-1.London

Department of Health (2000b) *Pharmacy in the Future – Implementing the NHS Plan*. London

Department of Health (2001a) Press release 2001/0127: *Improved support nationwide for patients using medicines*. London

Department of Health (2001b) Press release 2001/0211: P*atients to benefit from new guidance on discontinued medicines*. London

Department of Health (2010) *Liberating the NHS: Report of the Arm's Length Bodie*s Crown. London

Lister, S. (2005) Drugs lottery that means some pay twice as much for vital medicines. *The Times*, 5 March, p. 11.

NICE (2000) Healthcare Parliamentary Monitor, Issue no 250, 24 April 2000.

NICE (2000) Healthcare Parliamentary Monitor, Issue No 251, page 5, 15 May 2000; http://www.nice.org.uk/appraisals/taxguide.htm.

CHAPTER 28

Illegal use of drugs

Box 28.1 Situation

Philip, a young man of 20, is admitted to the orthopaedic ward following a road traffic accident. He is prepared for surgery and Angela, the staff nurse, discovers that he appears to be carrying cannabis. He says that he wants to keep it on him: he paid for it and it is his. Angela is not happy allowing him to remain on the ward whilst carrying cannabis and is concerned about who is responsible for it when he is in theatre. What is the law?

Introduction

There are considerable concerns over the use of illegal substances. The statistics on drug use issued by the Department of Health (DH) in 2007 presented the following findings:

- In 2005/06, 10.5% of adults had used one or more illicit drug in the last year, a decrease from 12.1% in 1998.
- 6.3% had used an illicit drug in the last month, a fall from 7.1% in 1998.
- The use of any Class A drug in the last year has increased, from 2.7% in 1998 to 3.4% in 2005/06, mainly due to a rise in the use of cocaine powder.
- Men are more likely to take illicit drugs than women, 13.7% of men compared with 7.4% of women took drugs in the last year.
- People living within the South West Government Office Region reported higher levels of any illicit drug use, compared to the total for England and Wales.
- For Class A drugs, the highest levels were found among those living in London.

- For younger adults aged 16 to 24, drug use in the last year fell between 1998 and 2005/06, from 31.8% to 25.2%, whilst the use of Class A drug use has remained stable.
- European figures show that 38% of 15 and 16 year olds in the UK had tried cannabis – one of the highest rates among 35 European countries.

There are still changing attitudes as to whether so-called 'soft drugs', such as cannabis, should be legalised. The government has issued confusing advice, suggesting that whilst there should be no change in the laws there should be no prosecutions for merely possessing soft drugs, but only prosecution of the dealers. An experiment in Lambeth led to young people who were found in possession of small amounts of having their drugs confiscated and being given an informal warning (Tendler, S. (2002) Children at risk from 'flawed' drug policy. *The Times*, 11 May 2002). The experiment saved 1,350 hours of police work, the equivalent of putting two extra officers on the streets full-time. The experiment also saved another 1,150 hours of civilian work which would have gone into processing cases. Whatever the views of police and enforcement agencies, the laws were changed in January 2004 to reclassify cannabis from a Class B drug to a Class C drug (and subsequently back again) (see below).

Misuse of Drugs Act 1971

The legislation which was considered in Chapter 2 sets out the definition of Controlled Drugs (CD). Schedule 2 (of the Misuse of Drugs Act 1971) is divided into three parts according to the degree of harmfulness of the drugs, and the penalties for offences differ according to the Class of the drug.

- Class A includes morphine, mescaline, pethidine, phenazocine.
- Class B includes codeine and amphetamine.
- Class C includes diazapam and temazepam.

Schedule 4 of the Act is a tabulated summary of offences created by the Misuse of Drugs Act and sets out the penalties for these offences.

Department of Health guidelines

The DH and the associated departments in Wales, Scotland and Northern Ireland published guidelines on the clinical management of drug misuse and dependence in 1999. These cover treatment, assessment, responsibilities and principles of prescribing for drug dependence, management of dependence and withdrawal, dose reduction regimes and preventing relapse.

Drug addicts

In the past there was a requirement that doctors should send to the Home Office particulars of drug addicts. However, this requirement was revoked by the Misuse of Drugs (Supply to Addicts) Regulations 1997 (SI 1997 No 1001) in May 1997. In the regulations the expression 'drug' means a CD specified in the Schedule to the regulations.

The schedule includes the following drugs:
* Cocaine
* Dextromoramide
* Diamorphine
* Hydrocodone
* Hydromorphone
* Levorphanol
* Methadone
* Morphine
* Opium
* Oxycodone
* Pethidine
* Pheazocine
* Piritramide
* Any stereoisomeric form of a substance specified above, not being dextrorphan
* Any ester or ether of a substance specified above, not being a substance for the time being specified in part 11 of Schedule 2 to the Misuse of Drugs Act 1971
* Any salt of a substance specified above
* Any preparation or other product containing a substance or product specified above.

An addict is a person:

If, and only if, he or she had, as a result of repeated administration, become so dependent on a drug that he or she has an overpowering desire for the administration of it to be continued.

Under Regulation 3 a doctor shall not administer or supply to a person who he considers, or has reasonable ground to suspect, is addicted to any drug, or authorise the administration or supply to such a person of, any substance specified in [paragraph 3 below] (cocaine, diamorphine and dipipanone or their salts), or prescribe for any such a person any such substance, except:

a)   for the purpose of treating organic disease or injury; or

b)   under and in accordance with the terms of a licence issued to him, in pursuance of the Regulations.

Regulation 3 does not apply to the administration or supply by a doctor of a substance specified in paragraph 3 if the administration or supply is authorised by another doctor under and in accordance with the terms of a licence issued to him in pursuance of the Regulations.

Doctors are now expected to report on a standard form cases of drug misuse to their local Drug Misuse Database (DMD). Phone numbers are set out in the *British National Formulary* (BNF) (See Chapter 4 for more information). The notification to the DMD should be made when a patient first presents with a drug problem or re-presents after a gap of six months or more. All types of problem drug misuse should be reported, including opioid, benzodiazepine and CNS stimulant. The data held on the databases is anonymised, so it cannot be used to check on multiple prescribing.

Under the Misuse of Drugs (Supply to Addicts) Regulations 1997 only medical practitioners who hold a special licence issued by the Home Secretary may prescribe, administer or supply diamorphine, Diconal or cocaine in the treatment of drug addiction. Other practitioners must refer any addict who requires these drugs to a treatment centre.

Addicts can receive daily supplies of cocaine, heroin, dextromoramide, dipipanone, methadone and pethidine on special prescription forms (FP(10) HP) issued by drug addiction clinics. General medical practitioners can by using special prescription forms (FP(10) MDA) provide Schedule 2 CD for the treatment of addiction.

These are administrative arrangements under the NHS and do not form part of the Misuse of Drugs Regulations.

Provision of information

Under the Misuse of Drugs Act 1971 the Secretary of State can require doctors, pharmacists and persons lawfully conducting retail pharmacy businesses to give particulars of the quantity of any dangerous or otherwise harmful drugs (not necessarily CD) which have been prescribed, administered or supplied over a particular period of time, if it appears that a social problem exists in that area caused by a drug or drugs. Failure to provide this information or to give false information is an offence if notice in writing has been served specifying the information required.

Overdoses and addicts

The National Addiction Centre at the Maudsley Hospital London has carried out a pilot project where 225 drug addicts were given their own supply of, and were trained to inject, naloxone, which is given in the event of an overdose. It was claimed that as a consequence 30 lives were saved (Charter, D. (2001). Addicts should get cure for overdose. The Times, 13 April 2001). It has been recommended that naloxone, which can legally be given only by doctors and paramedics, should be given to drug addicts to keep their own supply. Suggestions that this could lead to abuse were denied by the researchers, who recommended that their project should be repeated on a larger scale.

Advisory Council on Misuse of Drugs

This was established in February 1972 under the Misuse of Drugs Act 1971 (SI 1971 No 2120). Its role is to advise Ministers on the misuse of drugs and keep under review the situation with respect to drugs which are being or likely to be misused.

In particular it must advise on measures:
- To restrict the availability of such drugs and to supervise the arrangements for their supply.
- To enable persons affected by the misuse of such drugs to obtain proper advice, and to secure the provision of proper facilities and services for the treatment, rehabilitation and aftercare of such persons.
- To promote cooperation between the various professional and community services which, in the opinion of the Council, have a part to play in dealing with social problems connected with the misuse of such drugs.
- To educate the public (and in particular the young) in the dangers of abusing such drugs, and to give publicity to those dangers.

- To promote research into, or otherwise to obtain information about, any matter which in the opinion of the Council is of relevance for the purpose of preventing the misuse of such drugs or dealing with any social problem connected with their misuse.
- To advise on any matter relating to drug dependence or misuse of drugs which any of the Ministers may refer to it.

Department of Health's strategy on treatment of drug users

The National Treatment Agency was set up as a special health authority in April 2001 with the remit of expanding the availability and quality of drug treatment. It is responsible for monitoring the use of the pooled drug treatment budget and is accountable to the Secretary of State for Health. In each area a drug action team is established made up of the key local stakeholders: Primary Care Trusts (PCT), local authorities and probation officers. The teams have the responsibility of commissioning drug treatment services to meet the needs of the local population. In 2004 the DH announced that every drug action team would have its budget increased by 55% with an allocation of £219 million extra funds across the country. It was believed that the new money would allow 40,000 extra drug users to be helped by 2008 and would ensure that more people get the treatment they need. The Government also planned to invest £40 million every year to expand drug treatment within prisons to ensure that an estimated 78,000 prisoners receive effective treatment services by 2008. In the review of *Arms' Length Bodies* (DH 2010) the abolition of the National Treatment Agency as an arms' length body is proposed. Its functions are to be transferred to the Secretary of State as part of the new Public Health Service.

Criminal justice system and drug addicts

A drug treatment and testing order has been piloted. The offender, if he or she consents, undergoes treatment for their drug problem with regular testing to monitor compliance. The order can be given on its own or in association with an existing community sentence. Random testing for drugs in schools was proposed by the Government in February 2002 and met with strong opposition from the Secondary Heads Association (Carter 2004).

Change in classification of cannabis

In 2004 cannabis was changed from a Class B to a Class C drug (Misuse of Dug Acts 1971 (Modification) (No 2) Order 2003 SI 2003 No 3201). The effect of the reclassification was that whilst it was still an offence to possess, cultivate or supply cannabis, the maximum sentence for possession fell from five years to two years. Guidelines were published by the Association of Chief Police Officers (2003) explaining the effect of reclassification. The British Medical Association (BMA) criticised the change in classification. It claimed that the reclassification sent out all the wrong messages to people thinking about experimenting with cannabis. The BMA pointed to the new evidence which showed that people who used cannabis in their teens were more likely to develop psychosis, delusional episodes or manic depression (Wright 2004). The BMA view was criticised by Michael Rawlins, the Chair of the Advisory Council on the Misuse of Drugs, who stated that the Council had considered in some depth possible links between cannabis and mental illness and concluded that there is little significant evidence of a causal link, particularly with schizophrenia, although cannabis use can unquestionably worsen a mental illness which already exists (Rawlins, 2004). In a subsequent letter Professor Robin Murray pointed out that his research into the link between cannabis and schizophrenia had not been published at the time the Advisory Council Report was published and since that date there have been five new studies which have implicated heavy cannabis use as a contributory cause of psychosis (Murray 2004).

In 2008 cannabis was reclassified from Class C to Class B (SI 2008 No 3130). There are continuing calls for the decriminalisation of illegal drugs. In 2010 Sir Ian Gilmore, the former president of the Royal College of Physicians, said he agreed that drug laws should be 'reconsidered with a view to decriminalising illicit drugs use'. This recommendation was supported by Drugscope (see Ford R *Sunday Times* 24 August 2010. Further information available from www.drugscope.org.uk). In September 2010 Tim Hollis, Chairman of the Association of Chief Police Officers' drugs committees and Chief Constable of Humberside police, said that he did not want to criminalise people caught with minor amounts of substances such as cannabis. He stated that youngsters caught carrying personal amounts of drugs such as cannabis should 'not be criminalised'. More resources should be dedicated to tackling high-level dealers. Tim Hollis said the criminal justice system could offer only a 'limited' solution to the UK's drug problem, a tacit admission that prohibition has failed. Hollis also backed calls for the current drug classification system into Class A, B and C to be re-examined following concerns that bracketing substances such as heroin and ecstasy in the same class is confusing (News Item *Sunday Times* 19 September 2010).

Use of cannabis in healthcare

Considerable claims have been made for the pain relieving and antiemetic effects of cannabis in the treatment of patients who are receiving chemotherapy or are suffering from multiple sclerosis. The case against a wheelchair bound Orkney woman who was facing charges of supplying cannabis chocolates to fellow multiple sclerosis sufferers was dropped by the Crown Office on medical grounds. She was charged with growing, handling and dealing with cannabis. She admitted that she had created chocolates laced with cannabis and had started using the drug when her MS became unbearable (English 2003).

A trial was set up by the Medical Research Council to look at whether painkillers based on cannabis can be considered a normal form of pain relief. Patients awaiting surgery in 35 hospitals were to be asked if they would like to try cannabis-based medicines to control their post-operative pain (Hawkes 2003). Research using cannabis-based drugs has also been carried out with patients suffering from inflammatory bowel diseases (*The Times*, 1 August 2005, p. 20).

Criminal law and illegal drugs

In addition to the specific laws for being in the possession of or supplying illegal drugs, the criminal laws relating to manslaughter also apply. In 2005 the Court of Appeal held that where the defendant gave a syringe of heroin to a person ready for immediate self-injection which resulted in that person's death he could be found guilty of manslaughter (R. v. Kennedy Court of Appeal, [2005] EWCA Crim 685). The Criminal Cases Review Commission had referred the case to the Court of Appeal because of uncertainties in the criminal law relating to the criminal guilt of a person who handed the drug to another person. The Court of Appeal held that to convict, the jury had to be satisfied that when the heroin was handed to the deceased for immediate injection, he and the deceased were both engaged in the one activity of administering heroin. Those were not necessarily to be regarded as two separate activities. The Court of Appeal compared it to the situation where two nurses were carrying out lawful injections. One nurse might carry out certain preparatory actions, including preparing the syringe, and hand it to a colleague who inserted the needle and administered the injection, after which the other nurse might apply a plaster. In such a situation, both nurses could be regarded as administering the drug. They were working as a team. Both their actions were necessary. They were interlinked but separate parts in the overall process of administering the drug. In those circumstances they could be said to be jointly responsible for carrying out that act. The Court of Appeal held that following the reclassification of cannabis as a Class C drug the defendant was entitled to a reduction of sentence for the offence of cultivating cannabis where the cultivation was for private use (R. v. Herridge CA *The Times* 7 June 2005).

Drugs Act 2005

The Drugs Act 2005 creates a new offence of aggravated supply of a CD, in the vicinity of school premises to a person under 18 years. The Act also extends police powers in relation to drug offence searches, the authorisation of X-rays and ultrasound scans, and testing for the presence of Class A drugs. Persons found to have taken Class A drugs can be required to attend for an initial assessment, and possibly a follow-up assessment. An intervention order can be made if the relevant conditions are satisfied.

Application of the law to the situation in Box 28.1

Cannabis is included in schedule 1 of the Misuse of Drug Regulations 2001 (SI 2001 No 3998 amending and re-enacting the Misuse of Drugs Regulations S I 1985 2066). This means that it can only be produced, possessed or supplied on a licence from the Home Office in the public interest for the purposes of research or other special purposes (see Chapter 2). An occupier of premises is entitled to lay down the conditions on which visitors (and this includes patients) are invited on the premises and Philip can be told that the only condition on which he can stay on the ward is if he surrenders the illegal substance to an authorised person such as a pharmacist. Although he has paid for them he has committed an illegal act in so doing, and there would be no duty on the pharmacist (and it would be a criminal offence) to return the drugs to the patient on discharge. The pharmacist would only be able to hold a Schedule 1 drug under licence, except in two situations:

1. Where he or she takes possession of a CD for the purpose of destruction and
2. Where he or she takes possession for the purpose of handing it over to a police officer.

The pharmacist would not be able to hand the controlled drug back to the patient as he could be guilty of an offence of unlawful supply of a CD.

Conclusions

Dealing with patients who misuse drugs and other substances presents challenges to health professionals who need to be clear as to the legal position and their own responsibilities personally and professionally.

There is a wealth of literature on substance abuse and a book by Philip Robson (1999) provides good background reading covering a variety of substances, together with a useful bibliography to follow up.

Key points

- The Misuse of Drugs Act 1971 creates criminal offences in relation to specified controlled drugs.
- A health professional is protected if lawfully in possession for the purpose of their destruction.
- The Advisory Council on the Misuse of Drugs keeps under review the situation relating to the use of illegal substances.
- Cannabis has changed its classification twice in recent years, but its use remains illegal.

References

Association of Chief Police Officers Guidelines 2003.

Charter, D. (2001) Addicts should get cure for overdose. *The Times*, 13 April 2001.

Charter, D. (2004) Teachers rebuff random tests for drugs in schools. *The Times*, 23 February 2004.

Department of Health (2004) Press Release: *£219 million extra funding for drug treatment*, 28 September 2004. London

Department of Health Scottish Office (2007) *Statistics on Drug Misuse England*.

Department of Health, Welsh Office and Department of Health and Social Services Northern Ireland (1999) *Drug Misuse and Dependence: Guidelines on Clinical Management*.

Department of Health (2010) *Liberating the NHS: Report of the Arm's Length Bodies* Crown London

English, S. (2003) MS sufferer too ill to be tried over cannabis. *The Times*, 3 July 2003.

Ford R *Sunday Times* 24 August 2010.

Hawkes, N. (2003) Cannabis on offer to hospital patients. *The Times*, 21 August 2003.

Murrary, (2004) Letter to the editor, *The Times*, 28 January 2004.

News Item (2010) Go Easy on cannabis says police chief. *Sunday Times* 19 September 2010

Rawlins, (2004) Letter to the editor, *The Times*, 23 January 2004.

Robson, P. (1999*) Forbidden Drugs*, 2nd edn. Oxford University Press, Oxford.

Tendler, S. (2002) Children at risk from 'flawed' drug policy. *The Times,* 11 May.

Wright, O. (2004) BMA condemns plan to downgrade cannabis. *The Times*, 21 January.

Websites

Drugscope website www.drugscope.org.uk

CHAPTER 29

Pharmacists in the community

Box 29.1 Unable to get out

Phyllis Price lived on her own and was unable to get to the shops. She depended upon neighbours and friends to do various errands. She was visited by her district nurse, who prescribed a new ointment for a severe skin condition. The nurse told her that it was contrary to her employer's policy for her to collect medicines for patients from the chemist, and she could lose her job if she helped Phyllis in this way. Phyllis asked if the nurse could take the prescription to a chemist, who could then deliver the medicine to her.

Introduction

Pharmacists may be employed by primary care or community trusts to provide a service for patients and for residents in nursing homes and care homes. Retail pharmacists also have a major role to play in promoting good medicines management and ensuring the safety of the patient. The NHS Plan (DH 2000) envisaged retail pharmacists having a new contract for the provision of community pharmacy services which will enable them to have greater involvement in primary care by providing advice and additional services to patients, and this came into force in April 2005 (see below).

Prescription collection and home delivery

Guidance has been issued by the Royal Pharmaceutical Society of Great Britain (RPSGB 2004a) on prescription collection, home delivery and repeat medication services. The guidance states that the service may be advertised in doctors' surgeries by way of posters or leaflets available for self-selection by patients. They should not be handed out by surgery staff, since this could be misinterpreted by patients as being an endorsement of the services of a particular pharmacy and could give rise to complaints. Service Specification 7 of the RPSGB's code of ethics gives guidance on the provision of prescription collection services.

It recommends that the patient should complete a written consent form to request collection of a prescription from the surgery and dispensing of that prescription.

Home delivery services may be offered by pharmacies in conjunction with prescription collection services. Some pharmacies restrict the home delivery service to patients who are house bound, disabled or elderly. The RPSGB advises that it is not professionally acceptable for medicines to be posted through letterboxes or left unattended in porches or on doorsteps, and cites examples of children and animals having found medicines delivered in these ways. It states:

> It is therefore important that all home delivered medicines are only handed over to the patient or their carer after confirming that the name and address of the patient is correct. A signature to indicate safe receipt of the medicines by the patient or carer is desirable.

The RPSGB has provided a service specification for delivery services in its Code of ethics.

Repeat medication services

Arrangements can be established between patient, prescriber and pharmacist whereby the pharmacist assists in the management of a patient's repeat medication needs and in ordering repeat prescriptions. Both the patient and the prescriber must explicitly agree to the system being initiated. The RPSGB (2004b) recommended that:

> A patient medication record system (PMR) registered with the Data Protection Commission (author's note: now the Information Commissioner) and the existence of a full audit trail are other prerequisites for the provision of the service and therefore back ups of your PMR system should be undertaken regularly. If you offer a repeat medication service the Society's inspector will expect you to be able to produce documentation showing each stage of the process and which is capable of verifying the audit trail. As with all professional services you should regularly monitor the standard of service.

The RPSGB service specification 6 covers the repeat medication services.

Oxygen services

In 1999 the DH asked the Royal College of Physicians to lead a multidisciplinary working party to devise new clinical guidelines for the use of domiciliary oxygen. Following the review, the old system whereby domiciliary oxygen was ordered for patients by general practitioners was replaced by a new model which transferred responsibility for ordering oxygen for long-term oxygen therapy from general practitioners to specialist consultants in hospitals. (GPs can continue to prescribe oxygen for those patients who need small amounts of oxygen.) Specialist contractors will then have the responsibility to ensure that the patients' needs are met in the most appropriate way. Indicative budgets for Primary Care Trusts (PCT) included provision for domiciliary oxygen therapy services, which includes fees payable to pharmacy contractors for delivering and collecting oxygen cylinders and associated professional advice and support, and also a budget for oxygen hardware.

Contracts for community pharmacists

In August 2003 the DH put forward proposals to reform and modernise the community pharmacist services (DH 2003). Contractual arrangements for community pharmacists came into force in April 2005 which widen the scope of pharmacists to use their professional expertise (The NHS (Pharmaceutical Services) Regulations 2005. SI 2005 No 641 amended by SI 2005 No 1015 and SI 2005 No 1501). Their functions are divided into three categories: essential, advanced and enhanced.

1. **Essential** services include dispensing, repeat prescriptions, public health involvement, signposting, support for self care, disposal of unwanted medicines, and clinical governance, including audit and staff development.

2. **Advanced** services include medicines use reviews for patients with long-term conditions and prescription intervention.

3. **Enhanced** services include services which can be commissioned locally, such as minor ailments, smoking cessation, supervised administration of medicines and screening.

The enhanced role of the community pharmacist will continue the emphasis on primary care in the NHS. It will be facilitated by the information technology developments, in particular the electronic transfer of prescriptions (ETP) and by the further developments in pharmacist's prescribing powers and enhanced role in advising patients envisaged in the consultation paper issued in February 2005 (DH 2005a) (see Chapter 10).

Further information on the contract can be found on the DH website (www.dh.gov.uk) and in its press release (DH 2005b).

Health Act 2009

Section 25 to 29 relate to the provision of pharmaceutical services and require the primary care trust to assess the need for pharmaceutical services in its area and publish a statement of its first assessment and any revised assessment.

Regulations must make provision for:
a) information which must be contained in a statement;
b) the extent to which an assessment must take account of likely future needs;
c) specifying the date by which a PCT must publish the statement of its first assessment;
d) as to the circumstances in which a PCT must make a new assessment.

Regulations may in particular make provision:
a) as to the pharmaceutical services to which an assessment must relate;
b) requiring a PCT to consult specified persons about specified matters when making an assessment;
c) as to the manner in which an assessment is to be made;
d) as to matters to which a PCT must have regard when making an assessment.

Section 28 makes provision for notices and penalties for when a pharmacist is in breach of the arrangements which have been made with the PCT.

The Regulations were enacted by Statutory Instrument 2010/914 and can be found on the website (www.opsi.gov.uk). Information for primary care trusts is provided by the DH (2010a) in the document: *Pharmacy in England: Building on strengths – delivering the future –Regulations under the Health Act 2009: Pharmaceutical Needs Assessments*.

Application of the law to the situation in Box 29.1

The district nurse should be familiar with the various services offered by local pharmacies and be able to give the patient such information. In the actual situation it may be that her employer's instructions forbid her collecting medicines from pharmacists for delivery to patients, but do allow her to take the prescription to a pharmacist of the patient's choice, who may have a home delivery service for house bound patients. If so, the nurse could deliver the prescription with a written note from the patient confirming that that was her wish and requesting a home delivery service. Alternatively, if the nurse were not allowed by her terms of service to take the prescription to the pharmacist, the latter may provide a service for the collection of the prescription and the delivery of the medicinal products.

Conclusions

The new contractual arrangements for community pharmacists have led to an enhanced role for community pharmacists to the benefit of patients and doctors. It is clear that they have a central role to play in primary care health services and in liaison with primary care trusts could develop the significant part they already play. The abolition of PCT and strategic health authorities and the transfer of their functions to the NHS Commissioning Board and consortia of General Practitioners as envisaged in the White Paper *Equity and Excellence: Lberating the NHS* (DH 2010b) is likely to further strengthen the role of the community pharmacist within the NHS. These developments are considered in Chapter 31.

Key points

- ■ Guidance has been issued by the RPSGP on prescription collection and home delivery of medicines.
- ■ Special contractors now provide oxygen services for PCTs.
- ■ A new contract for community phramacists came into force in April 2005.
- ■ Each PCT is required to carry out a Pharmaceutical Needs Assessment.
- ■ Significant changes are envisaged as a result of the White Paper of 2010 (see Chapter 31).

References

Department of Health (2000) *NHS Plan: a Plan for Investment, a Plan for Reform CM 4818-1*. London

Department of Health (2003) *Proposals to reform and modernise the NHS Pharmaceutical Services Regulations 1992*. London

Department of Health (2005a) *Consultation on options for the future independent prescribing by extended formulary nurse prescribers; Consultation on options for the future independent prescribing by pharmacists*. London

Department of Health (2005b) Press Release *Dawn of a new era for pharmacy 2005/0151*. London

Department of Health (2010a) *Pharmacy in England: Building on strengths – delivering the future –Regulations under the Health Act 2009: Pharmaceutical Needs Assessments*. London

Department of Health (2010b) *White Paper Equity and Excellence: Liberating the NHS*. Crown London

Royal Pharmaceutical Society of Great Britain (2004) *Fact sheet 7: Prescription collection, home delivery and repeat medication services*.

Websites

Office of Public Sector Information website www.opsi.gov.uk

CHAPTER 30

Private hospitals and care homes

> ## Box 30.1 An unwilling GP
>
> *Rachel was the manager of a care home and a registered nurse. She was on duty one evening and was concerned about one of the residents, Martha, who appeared to be suffering from extreme pain. She phoned the surgery that provided GP services to the residents and was told that a GP would attend the next morning. She decided to use the analgesics of another resident for Martha. Martha became extremely ill and her relatives are now questioning Rachel's actions.*

Care Standards Act 2000

The Care Standards Act 2000 (as amended by the Health and Social Care Act 2008) replaced the Registered Homes Act 1984 and established a new independent regulatory body for social care, and private and voluntary healthcare services in England known as the National Care Standards Commission (NCSC). (In Wales, the National Assembly for Wales set up a department or agency to be the regulatory body in Wales.) These regulatory bodies were also responsible for the regulation of nursing agencies. Subsequently the NCSC was replaced by two statutory bodies in respect of the regulation of the private sector: the Commission for Health Audit and Inspection (known as the Healthcare Commission) took responsibility for the registration and inspection of private hospitals and the Commission for Social Care Inspection (CSCI) dealt with care homes. These two bodies were replaced by the Care Quality Commission (CQC) in April 2009, under the Health and Social Care Act 2008.

Care Quality Commission

The CQC is now the registration body and inspectorate for NHS and independent hospitals, and adult social care providers. From October 2010, all adult social care and independent healthcare providers must be registered, with some exceptions (some providers of non-surgical laser and intense pulsed light services; domiciliary care agencies and nursing agencies that purely provide staff to other registered providers that do not arrange placements for people with personal care needs.) From April 2011 the CQC registers primary care services that directly provide dentistry (NHS and private) and independent ambulance services. From April 2012, primary medical care services (including GP practices and out-of-hours services) must be registered. The CQC website provides information in relation to registration, compliance with its essential standards together with a directory of hospitals and care homes (www.cqc.org.uk). Its website also contains the reports of individual inspections. Rules setting out the details of registration and the duties of the CQC are contained in the Regulations (Care Quality Commission (Registration) Regulations 2009/3112. The CQC published guidance about compliance in the Summary of Regulations, outcomes and judgement framework (CQC 2010a).

Definitions of independent hospital

Under the Care Standards Act 2000 section 2:

(2) A hospital which is not a health service hospital is an independent hospital.

(3) 'Hospital' (except in the expression health service hospital) means

   a. an establishment

   i. the main purpose of which is to provide medical or psychiatric treatment for illness or mental disorder or palliative care; or

   ii. in which (whether or not other services are also provided) any of the listed services are provided;

   b. any other establishment in which treatment or nursing (or both) are provided for persons liable to be detained under the Mental Health Act 1983.

(4) 'Independent clinic' means an establishment of a prescribed kind (not being a hospital) in which services are provided by medical practitioners (whether

or nor any services are also provided for the purposes of the establishment elsewhere). But an establishment in which, or for the purposes of which, services are provided by medical practitioners in pursuance of the NHS Act 1977 is not an independent clinic.

(5) 'Independent medical agency'...

(6) ...

(7) In this section 'listed services' means:

> *a. Medical treatment under anaesthesia or sedation*
>
> *b. Dental treatment under general anaesthesia*
>
> *c. Obstetric services and in connection with childbirth, medical services*
>
> *d. Termination of pregnancies*
>
> *e. Cosmetic surgery*
>
> *f. Treatment using prescribed techniques or prescribed technology.*

These independent hospitals are regulated by the CQC under the Care Standards Act 2000 (as amended).

Part II of the Care Standards Act 2000 sets out provisions in relation to registration, right of appeals, and provisions for the regulation of establishments and standards and creates offences in respect of the regulations. The CQC has set standards for all the homes which it registers. Local authority homes have to comply with the same standards as those set for independent homes.

Independent hospitals

Private hospitals come under the jurisdiction of the CQC which has set standards. Regulations have been issued under the Care Standards Act 2000 (The Private and Voluntary Health Care (England) Regulations 2001 SI 2001 No 3968) and updated in 2009. In addition, the Department of Health (DH) has published national minimum standards for independent healthcare (DH 2002). The legislation followed a government report on the regulation of private and voluntary healthcare (DH 1999). Standards set by the DH in relation to medicines and pharmaceutical services include the following:

- **Standard H8.1:** The medical director or senior registered nurse of a hospice is responsible for safe medicines systems, unless there is a pharmacy department supplying medicines with the same body corporate as the hospice, when the senior pharmacist will be responsible.

- **Standard H8.2:** The hospice has a ward/clinical pharmacy service and pharmacist medicines information service. The envisaged outcome is that responsibility of obtaining, prescribing, storing, use, handling, recording and disposal of medicines is clear.

- **Standard H9:** This relates to the ordering, storage, use and disposal of medicines with the intended outcome that medicines, dressing and gases are handled in a safe and secure manner.

Care homes

A care home is defined under the Care Standards Act 2000 as:

> *an establishment providing accommodation, together with nursing or personal care for people who are or have been ill, persons who have or have had a mental disorder, persons who are disabled or infirm, persons who are or have been dependent on alcohol or drugs.*

However, an establishment is not a care home if it is a hospital, an independent clinic or a children's home (Section 3(3)).

The old distinction in the Registered Homes Act 1984 between nursing and residential care homes was thus abolished. The former nursing and residential homes, now called care homes, come under the jurisdiction of the CQC which acts as both a registration body and also an inspectorate.

Regulations have been published under the Care Standards Act 2000 covering care homes, and updated by the CQC.

The Royal Pharmaceutical Society of Great Britain (RPSGB) published guidance on the administration and control of medicines in care homes and children's services in June 2003 (RPSGB 2003a). This covers the following topics:

- Current legislation
- Policies and procedures
- Record keeping
- Medicines supply
- Storage of medicine
- Administration of medicines
- Disposal of medicines
- Medicinal gases
- Controlled drugs
- Medicine information and pharmaceutical advice in care homes

- Training of care staff
- Regulation of care homes.

   The guidance can be obtained from the RPSGB website (www.rpsgb.org.uk).

Management of medicines

Under the Regulation 13 of the 2010 Regulations (Health and Social Care Act 2008 Regulated Activities Regulations 2010 No 781):

The registered person must protect service users against the risks associated with the unsafe use and management of medicines, by means of the making of appropriate arrangements for the obtaining, recording, handling, using, safe keeping, dispensing, safe administration and disposal of medicines used for the purposes of the regulated activity.

Outcome 9 of the CQC's *Essential Standards of Quality and Safety* (CQC 2010b) provides guidance on this regulation and what the CQC would expect to see in its inspections and audit. It looks at the following outcomes:

1. What should people who use services experience?

People who use services:
- Will have their medicines at the times they need them, and in a safe way.
- Wherever possible will have information about the medicine being prescribed made available to them or others acting on their behalf.

This is because providers who comply with the regulations will:
- Handle medicines safely, securely and appropriately.
- Ensure that medicines are prescribed and given by people safely.
- Follow published guidance about how to use medicines safely.

2. Providing personalised care through the effective use of medicines

9A People who use services receive care, treatment and support that:
- Ensures the medicines given are appropriate and person-centred by taking account of their:
  - Age
  - Choices
  - Lifestyle
  - Cultural and religious beliefs

- Allergies and intolerances
- Existing medical conditions and prescriptions
- Adverse drug reactions
- Recommended prescribing regimes.
- Ensures the person's prescription for medicines, for which the service is responsible, is up to date and is reviewed and changed as their needs or condition changes.
- Includes monitoring the effect of their medicines and action when necessary if their condition changes, including side effects and adverse reactions.
- Includes supporting and reminding them to self-administer their medicines independently where they are able and wish to do so by minimising the risk of incorrect administration.
- Follows clear procedures in practice, which are monitored and reviewed, which explain how up-to-date medicines information and clinical reference sources for staff are made available.

Manage risk through effective procedures about medicines handling

9B Where people who use services receive care, treatment and support that involves medicines, the provider has:
- Clear procedures followed in practice, monitored and reviewed for medicines handling that include obtaining, safe storage, prescribing, dispensing, preparation, administration, monitoring and disposal. Wherever they are required these procedures include:
  - How medicines which are prescribed 'as required' (PRN) are handled and used.
  - Ensuring that staff handling medicines have the competency and skill needed.
  - The arrangements for giving medicines covertly where this is needed in accordance with the Mental Capacity Act 2005.
  - The arrangements for requesting a second opinion in relation to medicines for people detained under the Mental Health Act 1983.
  - The arrangements for recording when it is not possible for a person to be able to self- administer their medicines.
  - The recording of when medicines are given to the person.
  - The arrangements for reporting adverse events, adverse drug reactions, incidents, errors and near misses. These should encourage local and,

where applicable, national reporting, learning and promoting an open and fair culture of safety.

– The arrangements to implement and act upon the recommendations of all relevant medicine-related patient safety communications issued via alert systems within the required timescales.

– An up-to-date list of medicines taken by the person being produced when they begin to use the service.

– The management of discharge medicine to allow for continuity of care until a new arrangement is made.

– The arrangements for medicines management following death.

- Clear procedures, that are followed in practice, monitored and reviewed, for controlled drugs, unless they are taken by the person themselves in their own home, including:

  – Investigations about adverse events, incidents, errors and near misses.

  – Sharing concerns about mishandling.

- Systems in place to reflect on the findings of their service reviews and as it does so, learns from adverse events, incidents, errors and near misses relating to medicines that have occurred within the service and elsewhere, so that the risk of them being repeated is reduced to a minimum.

- Systems in place to ensure they comply with the requirements of the Medicines Act 1968 and the Misuse of Drugs Act 1971, and their associated regulations, the Safer Management of Controlled Drugs Regulations 2006, relevant health technical memoranda and professional guidance from the RPSGB and other relevant professional bodies and agencies.

9C People who use services benefit from a service that:

- Takes into account relevant guidance set out in the Care Quality Commission's Schedule of Applicable Publications (see appendix B).

Promote rights and choices

9D People who use services benefit from a service that:

- Ensures that wherever possible, information is available for people about the medicines they are taking, including the risks.

- Ensures information is available for people about medicines advisable for them to take for their health and wellbeing and also to prevent ill health.

- Ensures there is access for staff to up-to-date legislation and guidance related to medicines handling.
- Ensures best interest meetings are held with people who know and understand the person using the services when covert administration of medicines is being considered, to decide whether this is in the person's best interest.

9E People who use services detained under the Mental Health Act 1983:
- Receive medicines that are duly authorised and administered in line with the Mental Health Act 1983 Code of Practice.

9F People who use services receive care, treatment and support that:
- Follows clear procedures in practice, which are monitored and reviewed and that explain how staff may be permitted to administer homely remedies.

9G Where people who use services receive support with their medicines, the provider has:
- Additional clear procedures followed in practice, monitored and reviewed for medicines handling that include obtaining, administration, monitoring and disposal. Wherever they are required these procedures include:
  – How clinical trials are carried out in line with relevant laws, current guidelines and ethics committee approval.
  – Sharing concerns about medicines handling.
- Established arrangements for obtaining pharmaceutical information by a person who understands the care, treatment or support that is provided by the service.

9H People who use services receive care, treatment and support that:
- Ensures medicines required for resuscitation or other medical emergencies are accessible in tamper evident packaging that allows them to be administered as quickly as possible.

9I People who use services receive care, treatment and support from staff who:
- Ensure they make a record of any medication taken or reminded by the person using the service where this is part of the plan of care.
- Follow clear procedures, that are monitored and reviewed, that explain:
  – Their role with regards to helping people take their medicines.

– What staff should do if the person using services is unable, or refuses, to take their medicines.

9J People who use services receive care, treatment and support from staff who:

- Ensure that patient safety alerts, rapid response reports and patient safety recommendations disseminated by the National Patient Safety Agency (NPSA) and which require action are acted upon within required timescales.

Action taken by CQC

From its inception in April 2009 the CQC made clear its intention to raise standards within the adult social care sector. Thirty-four care homes and eight agencies providing care in people's homes have closed within 12 months of its establishment. The CQC was concerned at such factors as: verbal and psychological abuse of residents, medicines not being managed safely, leaving people at risk of not receiving vital medication, lack of medical and nursing care, staff not legally able to work in the country, poor sanitary conditions and lack of staff training.

Poor medicines management has been a constant factor in prosecutions brought by the CQC. For example, the CQC brought a prosecution against a Yorkshire-based mental health hospital operator in March 2010. The operator of the Yorkshire-based mental health hospital, Linden House, was ordered to pay £17,015 in fines and costs relating to breaches of the Care Standards Act 2000. Guilty pleas were entered by the defendant in respect of five charges relating to the administration of medication. These included offences relating to:

- A patient who was administered medication without the clinician having written up the rationale for prescribing that medication;
- A failure to maintain appropriate stock checks, disposal of medication which had expired, or to record the destruction or disposal of medications;
- A failure to maintain adequate arrangements for the storage of medicines required to be refrigerated. Temperatures exceeded those prescribed by drug manufacturers, the company failed to react appropriately to recordings of temperatures outside the safe range, in some cases simply re-setting the thermometer, and without taking measures to ensure that drugs maintained at incorrect temperatures remained effective to administer. Staff training concerning the storage of safe medication was not completed for all staff with delegated responsibility.

Management of medications was amongst the criticisms by the CQC of a Bristol Nursing Home which was compelled to suspend admissions after inspectors identified concerns in December 2010 that there was not enough information for staff about some medicines being given to people. Inspectors found discrepancies in a small number of medicines that were checked, suggesting that some people had not been given their medicines correctly.

In another case where there had been a long history of concerns the CQC cancelled the registration of the provider and manager in March 2010. In August 2007, Rosehaven, Wirral had been required to make improvements to the storage and administration of medicines as well as meet many other concerns, but in October 2009 these concerns had still not been met. The Care Standards Tribunal ruled that the CQC was right to cancel the registration of the provider and manager of the home and reject their appeal against the closure.

In another prosecution brought by the CQC for breaches in regulations in February 2010 the owner of a care home in County Durham who breached regulations on the handling of medicines and proper care planning for its residents was fined £3,200 by magistrates in Darlington. The CQC brought the prosecution against Orchard Care Homes, the provider of the St George's Hall and Lodge care home at Middleton St George. On Thursday 4 February at Darlington Magistrates' Court, the company pleaded guilty to two charges: failing to comply with care homes regulations requiring them to make arrangements for the recording, handling, safekeeping, safe administration and disposal of medicines, and failing to ensure care plans properly reflected how residents' needs were to be met.

Bulk prescribing in care homes

Bulk prescribing is only legal in England and Wales for medicines and dressings (including bandages) that are not Prescription Only Medicines (POM). Doctors who are responsible for the NHS treatment of 10 or more service users in a care home are able to issue a bulk prescription for the treatment of two or more service users at the home. The RPSGB states that it is the responsibility of the home to know for whom the doctor has prescribed the item and emphasises that:

Bulk prescribing is not a way of obtaining stock items of non-prescribed medicines (homely remedies).

Bulk prescribing does not have the full support of all professionals.

When it does occur it is a local agreement between the home and the GP..

Bulk prescribing as described here is not legal in Scotland.

Application of law to the situation in Box 30.1

Clearly Rachel is at fault. It is a fundamental principle that the medicines prescribed for one resident must not be used for another. The guidance from the RPSGB makes it clear that:

prescribed medicines must only be administered to the person for whom they have been prescribed, labelled and supplied. It therefore follows that prescribed medicines obtained in this manner may not at any time be used for other services users as though they were 'stock' held by the care home.

(RSPGB 2003b)

If she was unhappy about Martha having to wait till the next morning to see a doctor, she should have phoned the surgery to ascertain the arrangements for night visiting or arranging for the patient to visit an out of hours centre. As a consequence of her actions, she could face disciplinary action by her employers and she may be reported to the NMC, who would arrange for an investigation to take place to determine whether fitness to practise proceedings should be held. She would also be reported to the CQC which might query her competence to remain as the person in charge and seek her replacement.

Conclusions

The CQC took over the responsibilities of the Healthcare Commission and the Commission for Social Care Inspection in April 2009 and immediately had an impact upon the standards of care homes and independent hospitals. As the remit of the CQC expands across almost the whole field of health and social care, the effects of it standard setting and monitoring will be felt and it is likely that medicines management in the care sector, which has in the past had a poor record, should improve.

Key points

■ The Care Standards Act 2000, the Health and Social Care Act 2008 and subsequent regulations cover the regulation of Private Hospitals and Care Homes.

■ The CQC is the regulatory bodies for both the public and private sector of health and social care.

■ The CQC has commenced prosecutions where standards, including those in relation to the management of medicines, have not been met.
■ Bulk prescribing in care homes can only be used for items which are not prescription only medicines.

References

Care Quality Commission (2010a) *Summary of Regulations, outcomes and judgement framework*.

Care Quality Commission (2010b) *Essential Standards of Quality and Safety.*

Department of Health (1999) *Regulating Private and Voluntary Healthcare: a Consultation Document.* London, HMSO; Welsh Office (1999) Regulation and Inspection of Social and Healthcare Services in Wales – A Commission for Care Standards in Wales. Cardiff, Welsh Office; Welsh Office (1999) Regulating Private and Voluntary Healthcare in Wales. Cardiff; Welsh Office; Department of Health (2000) Regulating Private and Voluntary Healthcare: The Way Forward. HMSO. London

Department of Health (2001) *Regulating Private and Voluntary Healthcare: Developing The Way Forward.* HMSO London

Department of Health (2002) *Independent Health Care National Minimum Standards Regulations.* The Stationery Office. London

Royal Pharmaceutical Society of Great Britain (2003a) *The Administration and Control of Medicines in Care Homes and Children's Services.*

Royal Pharmaceutical Society of Great Britain (2003b) *The Administration and Control of Medicines in Care Homes and Children's Services.*

Websites

Care Quality Commission website www.cqc.org.uk
Royal Pharmaceutical Society of Great Britain website www.rpsgb.org.uk

CHAPTER 31

The Future

In its White Paper in 2010, the Department of Health envisages major changes taking place in the NHS including the supply of medicines. The White Paper states that:

We will pay drug companies according to the value of new medicines, to promote innovation, ensure better access for patients to effective drugs and improve value for money. As an interim measure, we are creating a new Cancer Drug Fund, which will operate from April 2011; this fund will support patients to get the drugs their doctors recommend.

(DH 2010)

This value-based approach to the payment of drugs companies is to be initiated by 2013-4. Value-based pricing is defined as:

a mechanism for ensuring patients can get access to the medicines they need by linking the prices the NHS pays drug providers to the value of the treatment.

In relation to the pharmacy contract the White Paper states that:

The community pharmacy contract, through payment for performance, will incentivise and support high quality and efficient services, including better value in the use of medicines through better informed and more involved patients. Pharmacists, working with doctors and other health professionals, have an important and expanding role in optimising the use of medicines and in supporting better health. Pharmacy services will benefit from greater transparency in NHS pricing and payment for services.

At the time of writing the Health and Social Care Bill 2011, which contains provision for the changes contained in the White Paper, is being debated in Parliament and can be downloaded from the Parliamentary website (www. parliament.uk).

In addition the devolvement of commissioning to General Practitioners and the abolition of Primary Care Trusts (PCT) and Strategic Health authorities in England will lead to radical changes in roles. The White Paper sees this development in the following terms:

Commissioning by GP consortia will mean that the redesign of patient pathways and local services is always clinically-led and based on more effective dialogue and partnership with hospital specialists. It will bring together responsibility for clinical decisions and for the financial consequences of these decisions. This will reinforce the crucial role that GPs already play in committing NHS resources through their daily clinical decisions – not only in terms of referrals and prescribing, but also how well they manage long-term conditions, and the accessibility of their services. It will increase efficiency, by enabling GPs to strip out activities that do not have appreciable benefits for patients' health or healthcare.

These are far reaching changes and it remains to be seen how easily the Coaltion Government is able to get them through Parliament and enacted. It is also unclear whether the implementation of the changes secures the expected results.

At the time of writing the Government as declared a legislative pause to the debate on the Health and Social Care Bill in order that there can be more consultation across the country on its provisions. The final legislation is likely to be radically different from the initial Bill.

Review by MHRA

In 2010 the Medicines and Healthcare Products Regulatory Agency (MHRA) began a review of medicines legislation and consulted on how exemptions to the Medicines Act 1968 relating to the sale, supply and administration of prescription only medicines should be determined. At the time of writing this review is still on-going.

There is no doubt that significant developments are to take place in both the organisation of the NHS and the relationship between the pharmaceutical industry and the NHS. It is hoped that this book by setting out the basic principles of law which apply will continue to provide a basic understanding which can be used as the foundation for these developments.

References

Department of Health (2010) *Equity and Excellence: Liberating the NHS*. Crown London

Websites

Parliamentary website www.parliament.uk.

Further reading

Appelbe, G. E. and Wingfield, J. (eds) (2009) Dale and Appelbe's *Pharmacy: Law and Ethics*, 9th edn. The Pharmaceutical Press.

Beddard R. (1992) *Human Rights and Europe*, 3rd edn. Cambridge: Grotius Publications.

Brazier M and Cave Emma. (2011) *Medicine, Patients and the Law*. 5th edition Harmondsworth: Penguin.

British Medical Association (2001) *Consent, Rights and Choices in Health Care for Children and Young People*. London: BMJ Books.

Clerk, J.F., (2006) *Clerk and Lindsell on Torts*, 19th edn, Sweet & Maxwell,

Deakin, S., Johnston, A. and Markensinis, B. (2007) *Markensinis and Deakin's Tort Law*, 6th edn. Oxford: Clarendon Press.

Dimond, B. C. (1996) *Legal Aspects of Child Health Care*. London: Mosby.

Dimond, B. C. (1997) *Legal Aspects of Care in the Community*. London: Macmillan Press.

Dimond, B. C. (1998) *Legal Aspects of Complementary Therapy Practice*. Edinburgh: Churchill Livingstone.

Dimond, B. C. (2010) *Legal Aspects of Physiotherapy*. 2nd edn Oxford: Blackwell Science.

Dimond, B. C. (2009) *Legal Aspects of Patient Confidentiality*. 2nd edn London: Quay Publications/Mark Allen Press.

Dimond, B. C. (2009) *Legal Aspects of Pain Management*. 2nd ednLondon: Quay Publications/Mark Allen Press.

Dimond, B. C. (2008) *Legal Aspects of Consent*. 2nd edn London: Quay Publications/ Mark Allen Press.

Dimond, B. C. (2009) *Legal Aspects of Occupational Therapy,* 3rd. Oxford: Blackwell Scientific Publications.

Dimond, B. C. (2011) *Legal Aspects of Nursing,* 6th edn. Hemel Hempstead: Pearson Education

Dimond, B. C. (2011) *Legal Aspects of Health and Safety*. 2nd edn London: Quay Publications/Mark Allen Press.

Dugdale, A. (ed.) (2000) *Clerk and Lindsell on Torts*, 18th edn. London: Sweet and Maxwell.

Grubb A, Laing J and McHale JV (2010) *Principles of Medical Law* 3rd edition OUP

Harris, D.J., Cases and Materials on the European Convention on Human Rights, 2nd rev. edn, Butterworth, 2005

Henderson, C. and Macdonald, S. (eds) (2011) *Mayes' Midwifery,* 14th edn. London: Baillière Tindall.

321

Hendrick, J. (2006) *Law and Ethics in Nursing and Healthcare*. 2nd edition London: Stanley Thomas.

Heywood, J. I. (ed.) (1999) *The UKCC Code of Conduct: a critical guide*. London: Nursing Times Books.

Hoggett, B. (2005) *Mental Health Law*. 5th edition London: Sweet and Maxwell.

Howarth, D. R. and O'Sullivan, J. A. (2008) *Hepple, Howarth and MatthewsTort: Cases and Materials,* 6th edn. London: Butterworths.

Hunt, G and Wainwright, P (eds) (1994) *Expanding the Role of the Nurse*. Oxford: Blackwell Scientific Publications.

Hurwitz, B. (1998) *Clinical Guidelines and the Law*. Abingdon: Radcliffe Medical Press.

Jay, R. and Hamilton, A (2007) *Data Protection Law and Practice*. 3rd edition London: Sweet and Maxwell.

Jones, M. A. (2007) *Textbook on Torts,* 9th edn. Oxford: Oxford University Press.

Jones, M. A. and Morris, A. E. (2005) B*lackstone's Statutes on Medical Law*, 4th edn. Oxford: Oxford University Press.

Jones, R. (2010) *Mental Health Act Manual,* 13th edn. London: Sweet and Maxwell.

Keenan, D (2010) *Smith and Keenan's English Law,* 16th edn. London: Pearson Longman.

Kennedy, I. Grubb, A., Laing, J and McHale J (2010) *Principles of Medical Law,* Butterworth London

Kloss, D. (2005) *Occupational Health Law*, 4th edn. Oxford: Blackwell Scientific Publications.

Leach, P. (2005) *Taking a Case to the European Court of Human Right*s. 2nd edition Blackstone Press Ltd.

Maclean, A. (2001) *Briefcase of Medical Law*. London: Cavendish Publishing.

Mason, J.K. McCall Smith, R A., Laurie GT (2010) *Law and Medical Ethics,* 8th edition Butterworths London

McHale, J. and Gallagher, A. (2003) *Nursing and Human Rights*. Oxford: Butterworth-Heinemann.

McHale, J. and Tingle, J. (2007) *Law and Nursing* 3rd edition Butterworth Heineman London

Miers, D. and Page, A. (1990) *Legislation*, 2nd edn. London: Sweet and Maxwell.

Montgomery, J. (2003) *Health Care Law,* 2nd edn. Oxford: Oxford University Press.

Mowbray, A. (2001) C*ases and Materials on the European Convention on Human Rights*. London: Butterworths.

Painter, R.W. and Holmes, A.E.M. (2006), *Cases and Materials on Employment Law*, 6th edn, Oxford University Press,

Selwyn, N. (2006) *Selwyn's Law of Employment*, 14th edn. London: Butterworths.

Sime Stuart (2007) *Practical Approach to Civil Procedure* 10th edition Blackstone press London

Slapper, G. and Kelly, D., (2006) *The English Legal System,* 8th edn, Routledge-Cavendish,

Smith I, Baker A. (2009) *Smith and Wood's Employment Law* 10th edition Oxford University Press

Stauch, M., Wheat, K. and Tingle, J. (2005) *Source book on Medical Law,* 3rd edn. London: Cavendish Publishing.

Stone, J. and Matthews, J. (1996) *Complementary Medicine and the Law,* 2nd edn. Oxford: Oxford University Press.

Storch, J. (2004) *Towards a Moral Horizon, Nursing Ethics for Leadership and Practice.* Toronto: Pearson Education.

Tingle, J. and Foster, C. (2006) *Clinical Guidelines: Law, Policy and Practice.* 2nd London: Cavendish Publishing.

Tolley's (2011) *Health and Safety at Work Handbook* 23rd edition Lexis Nexis

Vincent, C. (ed.) (1995) *Clinical Risk Management.* London: BMJ Books.

Wheeler, J. (2002) *The English Legal System.* Harlow: Pearson Education.

White, R., Carr, P. and Lowe, N. (2002) *A Guide to the Children Act 1989,* 3rd edn. Oxford: Butterworths.

Wilkinson, R. and Caulfield, H. (2000) *The Human Rights Act: a Practical Guide for Nurses.* London: Whurr Publishers.

Index